PENGUIN BOOKS

A CLASS ACT

Andrew Adonis is a columnist on the *Observer* and was formerly Public Policy Editor of the *Financial Times* and a Fellow of Nuffield College, Oxford. His other books include the acclaimed *Failure in British Government* (1994, with David Butler and Tony Travers), *A Conservative Revolution? The Thatcher–Reagan Decade in Perspective* (1993, with Tim Hames), *Making Aristocracy Work: The Peerage and the Political System in Britain* (1993), *Parliament Today* (1993) and *Subsidiarity as History and Policy* (1990, with Andrew Tyrie).

Stephen Pollard is a leader writer and columnist for the *Express* and was formerly Head of Research at the Social Market Foundation, a leading independent think-tank. His other books include *Ready for Treatment: Public Expectations and the Future of Healthcare* (1997), *Global Perspectives in Healthcare* (1995), *Schools, Selections and the Left* (1995), *Jobs and Growth* (ed., 1995), *Towards a More Co-operative Society* (1994), *Any Southern Comfort* (1994, with Giles Radice) and *More Southern Discomfort* (1993, with Giles Radice).

ANDREW ADONIS AND
STEPHEN POLLARD

A Class Act

The Myth of Britain's Classless Society

PENGUIN BOOKS

PENGUIN BOOKS

Published by the Penguin Group
Penguin Books Ltd, 27 Wrights Lane, London w8 5tz, England
Penguin Putnam Inc., 375 Hudson Street, New York, New York 10014, USA
Penguin Books Australia Ltd, Ringwood, Victoria, Australia
Penguin Books Canada Ltd, 10 Alcorn Avenue, Toronto, Ontario, Canada m4v 3b2
Penguin Books (NZ) Ltd, 182–190 Wairau Road, Auckland 10, New Zealand

Penguin Books Ltd, Registered Offices: Harmondsworth, Middlesex, England

First published by Hamish Hamilton 1997
Published in Penguin Books 1998
1 3 5 7 9 10 8 6 4 2

Contents

CONTENTS

Acknowledgements

The endnotes are a partial – very partial – commentary on our obligations to those who have helped us make sense of contemporary class and social segregation. We are hugely indebted to Azim Lalji for his research assistance while an intern at the Social Market Foundation. For reading draft chapters and/or giving advice we are deeply grateful to David Atkins, Nick Bosanquet, Rachel Brooks, David Cannadine, Evan Davis, Katherine Edwards, Frank Field, Julian Le Grand, Michael Hart, Anthony Heath, Will Hutton, David Jordan, Roger Liddle, Charles Marquand, Anne McElvoy, Roger Mortimore, Jo-Anne Nadler, Ken Oliphant, Bernard Pollard, Sally Prentice, Peter Riddell, David Shepherd, Tom Snow, Karl Sternberg, Mark Suzman, Stephen Tindale and Andrew Tyrie. None of them bears any responsibility for what follows; indeed, some sharply disagree with our arguments, although they may find them less objectionable following their criticism.

Books on contemporary themes are abandoned, not finished. But this one would never have got started but for the enthusiasm and encouragement of Mike Shaw, our agent. Ravi Merchandari embraced the concept as one of his last acts at Hamish Hamilton. For guiding it through to completion we are immensely grateful to Kate Jones, Andrew McAllister and Bela Cunha.

Roderick Nye and his colleagues at the Social Market Foundation, Stephen's employer, gave invaluable assistance and understanding throughout the preparation of the book – not least in letting him beaver away at it to the exclusion of (almost) all else.

ACKNOWLEDGEMENTS

And Andrew places Kathryn in a class of her own for her unstinting support in yet another enterprise which turned out to be rather more ambitious than originally envisaged.

A. A. and S. P.
London, May 1997

Introduction to the Penguin Edition

After the first edition went to press, Diana, Princess of Wales was killed in a road accident in Paris. A book like this on what divides the British would be surreal if it ignored the most unifying national event for a generation.

A few reviewers suggested that Diana's death and the extraordinary outpouring of public grief it engendered, left the book outdated at birth. None said quite *why* it did so. Like so much commentary in the febrile aftermath of the tragedy, it was enough simply to remark that Britain was witnessing a seismic social upheaval, and that things would never be quite the same again.

But what 'things'? Writing some months after the event, with the public temperature back to normal and a longer perspective possible, there is little we would want to change in our account of Britain as a largely class-bound society, shaped by élite class institutions which have adapted so as to perpetuate the status of their patrons. On the contrary, the national mourning of Diana powerfully reinforced this basic argument. We would wish to make only one significant revision. Chapter 5, which describes the monarchy in terms of the 'Windsor sclerosis' of Elizabeth II's reign, underestimates the extent to which the Crown has, almost despite itself, already followed other bastions of the British élite – notably the public schools, Oxbridge and the City – in adapting to modern social imperatives. By concentrating too much on the Queen herself, we neglected the wider forces for change within the royal industry: not just the 'new royalty' led and symbolized by Diana, but its new modes of social, political and media interaction, and their success in underpinning the monarchy for the coming generation.

The opposite conclusion was drawn by most commentators, who saw media and public criticism of royal 'Balmorality' as a harbinger of a radical new public mood. Their critiques had plenty to feed on, particularly the notion of Diana as the 'People's Princess', and the funeral address of Diana's brother, seething with resentment at the royal establishment and invoking his sister as 'a symbol of selfless humanity, a standard-bearer for the rights of the truly downtrodden, a truly British girl who transcended nationality, someone with a natural nobility who was classless, who proved in her last year that she needed no royal title to continue to generate her particular brand of magic.'

Surely a moment's reflection is enough to expose the combination of humbug, wishful thinking here. If Diana was the 'People's Princess', it was not because she came from 'the people'. Lady Diana Frances Spencer, daughter of the eighth Earl Spencer and sister of the ninth Earl Spencer, was born into one of England's grandest and oldest noble families. By the end of her life she may have 'needed no royal title'; but shorn of her previous marriage to the Prince of Wales and her life as Princess of Wales she would have been a symbol to virtually no one. The Diana mystique was nothing without her class and title; in any other context, her remarkable capacity to relate to the 'downtrodden' would have generated precious little 'magic'. So too with her status as 'fairy princess' to the nation's young children, who flocked with their parents to St James's Palace to lay their posies and messages of grief before the funeral.

Diana's achievement was to take the old royal trade of glamour and philanthropy and reinvent it for a new generation as 'Queen of Hearts', extending royal patronage to fields, such as AIDS and landmines, where Balmorality had feared to tread. The causes were new, even daring; the media glamour was on a scale unmatched since the early years of the present Queen's reign (and in international terms it was unprecedented). But the role was age old. So was the public adulation of the stunning, outspoken, fragile, 'excluded' Royal, standing up for 'us' against 'them' in a society where 'they' are still widely seen, particularly by the less well-off, as a class apart. Queen Caroline against George IV after the Napoleonic wars, Edward, Prince of Wales against George V after the First World War – we have been here before, particularly at times of great social stress and dislocation. And the funeral itself was yet another solemn royal rite to add to those other great national-royal staging posts of the century, from Queen Victoria's funeral to the marriage of Charles and Diana in 1981.

The most surprising aspect of the Diana mourning was not the repudiation of old symbols and institutions, but the degree of public yearning, amidst the shock of a universal life plucked young, for them to be refurbished for a new age. Tony Blair proclaimed the advent of a 'modern monarchy'. What a 'modern monarchy' comes to mean in the hands of the teenage Prince William, who has been invested with this mission of modernity, will do much to shape Britain in the new millennium – and far more than any Dome in Greenwich.

This book aims to explode the fashionable notion that Britain is becoming a 'classless society' and to describe the class contours of modern Britain, particularly the impact of a 'two nation' education system and the rise of what we call the new Super Class of top professionals and managers, centred on the City, who are as far apart from the 'middle class' of white collar workers as are the latter from the misnamed 'underclass' at the bottom.

Several reviewers regretted that we did not suggest reforms to overcome the class barriers we identified. In fact, a reform agenda is implicit in every chapter. But in this new introduction we have taken the opportunity to address explicitly what we see as the single most critical public policy challenge in Britain today. How can we create a 'one nation' education system out of the status quo, making Britain's schools a force for social unity, not social segregation?

A fruitful approach to this issue – which became apparent to us after we had completed the first edition, with its separate chapters on the Super Class and on the education and health systems – is to ask a subsidiary question. Why is it that Britain's state-run health system has been so much more successful than the state education system at surmounting and diminishing class barriers? The answer to this question – one virtually unasked in media and academic circles, so compartmentalized is discussion of Britain's welfare state – lies, we believe, in the success of the National Health Service in creating an effective cross-class institution which has survived the rise of the Super Class, a feat the state education system has spectacularly failed to achieve.

Class dynamics lie at the heart of the health–education dichotomy. The success of the NHS lies in its achievement, since its inception in 1948, in reconciling the principles of equal access and state provision with the reality of entrenched class divisions, while the failure of the education system lies in its inability, over the same five decades, to reconcile equal access, state provision and the class system over most of the country, particularly the larger cities.

A word first about 'success' and 'failure'. We are not dealing in black and white. The two sectors are equally afflicted by the rationing of public funding for staff and investment. In health, the NHS has emphatically not succeeded in equalizing the health of the nation. Our study of the health system is a graphic account of class inequalities: a child from an unskilled social class is twice as likely to die before the age of fifteen as a child from a professional family, while the life expectancy of a child with parents in the unskilled manual class is more than seven years shorter than for a child with parents from the professional class. By some measures health inequality is now greater than in the 1950s, a function of increased class segregation in housing and the widening gulf between rich and poor. As for education, there has been unambiguous progress since the Butler Act of 1944, the ambitious end-of-war reform which stands alongside Aneurin Bevan's creation of the

NHS in 1948. Compulsory schooling extended from nine to eleven years; a huge increase in the number of children taking and passing public examinations; further and higher education transformed from élite to mass pursuits – these advances have been to the benefit of all classes, however unequally.

Yet judged by the 'one nation' intentions of reformers of all parties – particularly Labour – health and education are leagues apart. Bluntly, the NHS created an effective cross-class system of health care, while the schools system largely failed to do so. R. A. Butler said his Education Act would 'have the effect of welding us into one nation'. No objective analyst would say it succeeded. In Chapter 2 we quote the verdict of A. H. Halsey, a leading educational theorist of the 1960s and 1970s: 'The essential fact of twentieth-century educational history is that egalitarian policies have failed.' Conversely, the 'classless' quality of the NHS, however exaggerated, is a source of unbounded national pride: in the (somewhat regretful) words of Nigel Lawson cited at the start of Chapter 6, 'the National Health Service is the closest thing the English have to a religion, with those who practise in it regarding themselves as a priesthood.'

Britain's health success and educational failure have three dimensions: institutions, professions and the experience of the poorer classes.

The National Health Service is a cross-class institution; the education system is not, over most of the country. Of course, standards of hospital and GP provision vary widely. Private health insurance is extensive, covering around 15 per cent of the population (rising to 20 per cent in London and the south-east), which is twice the proportion usually cited for private education. Yet two facts say it all: virtually the entire population uses the NHS as its main provider of health care, while virtually no one (beyond the elderly in need of intensive or residential care) moves house purely because of the standard of local doctors and hospitals. Private insurance is largely a top-up service for certain elective operations; even then, its main purpose is to queue-jump, not to get a higher standard of care. All Britain's best hospitals are in the NHS. Much private health care takes place in NHS hospitals, courtesy of pay beds and contracts between the two sectors, and most of it is performed by doctors and consultants who also work for the NHS, often in the same hospitals. Medical training is an entirely public sector business.

In two key respects – the working practices of the medical élite, and the division between public and private provision – the NHS represents a grand compromise. Charges are integral to the NHS, even for essential services such as prescriptions, dentistry and spectacles; and they have been virtually since its creation. As for the medical élite, the ease with which top consultants move back and forth between the public and private sectors is excelled only by the extraordinary degree of tolerance with which the practice has been regarded by health managers and their political masters. True, the enthusiasm with which some top consultants double or even treble their £70,000-plus state salaries generates periodic complaints among managers and auditors; but everyone involved knows that a radical reform of the consultant's contract is out of the question if the goodwill – and ultimately the services – of the medical élite are to be retained within the NHS. Family doctors also enjoy a special status which dates back to the foundation of the NHS. They are not state-salaried but self-employed practitioners; and although their income comes almost entirely from public funds, the freedom with which they regulate their work, and their ability to maximize income, particularly since the advent of fundholding, gives them an autonomous professional status which they guard jealously.

From this we can explain one stark but little-noticed fact. Medicine is Britain's only broadly public sector profession which has continued to thrive in recent decades, in terms of its ability to recruit and retain from the socio-academic élite. It is also the only large public sector profession whose élite belongs to the Super Class of top earners which we describe in Chapter 3. Centred on the City and the professions which service it (notably law, accountancy, banking and consultancy), the Super Class is an otherwise almost exclusively private sector élite. These are two sides of the same coin: medicine recruits easily from the socio-academic élite *because* its top graduates have a well-trodden path to the Super Class.

In all these respects, the education system is a world apart. England's schools are so rigidly divided between public and private sectors that the word 'apartheid' is the fasionable way (which we follow) to describe it. The 7 per cent of fee-paying parents – who include virtually all the Super Class and a fair slice of the professional classes below – are not buying a top-up service: they are opting-out of the state sector entirely, purchasing places in the best meritocratic academies in the country. In chapter 2 we cite the 1996 *Financial Times* survey of the A-level performance of England's 1,000 leading schools: all but 22 of the top 200 were in the private sector and across the 1,000 – which included most of the private sector but only the top of the state sector – the A-level performance of private schools was on average a quarter better than their state counterparts. Since then the 1997 *FT* survey has appeared, and the contrast is starker still. The top state school comes in at 71st and the best English comprehensive falls outside the top 200. 'The country's independent schools have taken an unprecedented stranglehold,' the *FT* informed its largely fee-paying readers, discouraging any slight inclination there might have been to sample the state sector. Virtually all the famous 'public schools' – how that tag sums up the catastrophe of contemporary state education – are in the top 100, so successful is the marriage of money and meritocracy in today's education system.

Behind England's educational apartheid lie massive disparities in funding and a rigid separation of public and private sectors, involving not just schools but also the teaching profession and the very notion of paying for top-up services, which is banned within the state education sector, unlike the NHS. Private second-ary school fees, for day pupils, now average well over £6,000 a year, which is more than twice the average state school funding of about £2,400 per pupil. The top public schools cost up to Eton's £14,000 a year – about the level of the average post-tax wage. As for the teaching profession, the conventional wisdom about a 'crisis of morale' is undeniably true for the state sector, where the number and quality of recruits – at primary and secondary level – is a cause of acute anxiety. However, within the private sector pay and morale are far higher and the ability to recruit from the top universities unaffected. Even in the private sector, teachers are leagues apart from the Super Class in terms of salary; but in terms of social milieu and lifestyle – particularly for graduates keen on sports, the 'great outdoors', or a quasi-academic life better paid nowadays than university research – private school teaching still has strong attractions for top graduates, particularly those who attended private schools themselves. Furthermore, within the state system the concentration of able teachers on 'good' schools is pronounced – to some extent a legacy of the grammar schools, reinforced in recent years by the local management of schools, which has made individual schools, not local authorities or the state, the *de facto* employer of teachers.

Which leads to our third dimension: the experience of what used to be called the working class. For all the class inequalities in health, those in education are far worse, because of the failure to raise the 'floor' condition of those at the bottom of the social scale. Of course, many from poor backgrounds do succeed in state schools. But in the most deprived areas, from even the poorest of which the great child-killer diseases of yesteryear have now been largely eradicated by the NHS, levels of school achievement are pitiful. A virtually anti-education culture is widespread. One in five seven-year-olds in London state schools scores zero in reading tests. In secondary schools serving the poorest areas, less than 15 per cent of pupils achieve five or more GCSE grades A to C, and the best schools in such areas achieve average GCSE scores which are just one-third that of schools in more advantaged areas. These are inequalities quite unmatched in the health system.

Class, as the Chief Inspector of Schools has acknowledged, is the heart of the matter, more or less embracing all the factors described above. Even the contrasting regimes for private provision within the two sectors have a critical class dimension. The professional élite has remained thoroughly wedded to the NHS, as both provider and consumer. It has done so because of the 'grand compromise' enabling it to have the best of both worlds: for the consultant élite, NHS training and employment *plus* private practice; for better-off patients, NHS hospitals and treatment *plus* top-up private care. In education, however, you are on one side or other of the great divide between public and private sectors, as teacher, pupil and parent, and topping-up is banned in the public sector (as it is not in the NHS). Within the state education sector, there is an almost equally stark divide between the small élite of state grammar schools and grant-maintained schools on the other hand, most of them with largely middle class clienteles, and local authority municipal comprehensives on the other.

How did it come to be like this? The proponents of English exceptionalism attribute it to deeply rooted historical forces. They are right, up to a point. Britain's public schools are among its most ancient institutions: the strength and character of private education today is incomprehensible without an understanding of the evolution of the public and grammar schools over the past two centuries. The formation of the medical élite also has deep historical roots, but the Victorian age – a critical period for the formation of Britain's modern élite institutions, from the monarchy downwards – never produced a 'hospital system' to match the 'public school system'.

Yet for all their historical roots, today's education and health systems have been fundamentally shaped by governments since the Second World War. It is in the starkly differing approaches to reform since the war that much of the success and failure we have identified is to be explained. Three reformers stand out pre-eminently: R. A. Butler, author of the 1944 Education Act; Aneurin Bevan, creator of the NHS in 1948; and Tony Crosland, the prime – although not sole – agent of the wholesale introduction of comprehensive schools in the 1960s and 1970s. All three saw themselves as progressive reformers; all three also saw themselves as involved in a class struggle, whatever words they used to describe it. In the contrasting reform strategies of the three – Butler the Tory grandee, Bevan the working-class socialist realist, and Crosland the public-school apostle of social democracy – lies much of the explanation for the success of the NHS and the failure of the education system.

Butler, the Tory grandee, made no attempt in his 1944 Education Act to produce an integrated national education system. A 'one nation' reformer by inclination, the battle with the Tory élites required to assert state direction over the public schools was too much for him. Moreover, although he recognized the perpetuation of separate systems as a social blight, his own background temperamentally disabled him from taking the crucial initiatives at the end of the war. In 1943–4, in the aftermath of the Beveridge report, he had the best opportunity of the century to create a unified schools system embracing the former state and private sectors. Not only the public mood, but the dilapidated financial state of the public schools themselves, created an opening. Butler toyed with a radical reform, but he ultimately – as Chapter 2 relates – backed away. The private sector was left entirely out of his 1944 scheme, Butler noting fatalistically that 'the first-class carriage had been shunted on to an immense siding.' Instead, he concentrated on expanding the state secondary sector, in particular opening up the grammar schools to broader cross-class entry through the 11-plus exam.

It was the grammar schools which, two decades later, Crosland set out to destroy in the name of 'equality of opportunity'. Crosland, the minor public school, Oxford don social democrat, motivated by a social self-abasement so characteristic of his generation of upper-crust Labour politicians, was a disastrous reformer. While Butler recognized the class obstacles preventing the creation of a national, meritocratic education system, and could only half overcome them, Crosland convinced himself they could be ignored entirely and a classless education system be simply legislated into existence. Hence his obsession with abolishing the grammar schools (or 'fucking grammar schools', as he called them), and his determination to replace them with comprehensive schools which, non-selective in their intake and 'modern' in their teaching, would produce 'equality of opportunity' at a stroke.

Even in theory this was a fatally flawed policy, since Crosland did nothing about the private sector, to which the professional classes decamped *en masse* rather than submit to comprehensivization. In many cases they literally took their grammar schools with them into the private sector – particularly when Shirley Williams, one of Crosland's Labour successors as Education Secretary (another upper-crust, privately educated social democrat) moved to abolish the direct-grant scheme, under which the state contracted to buy places in leading private grammar schools. To be fair, Crosland realized the importance of the private sector to his reform objectives. But his bitterly anti-élitist reform strategy left no opening to integrate the private schools by consent, while the strength of the social élites patronizing the independent sector – by now entirely recovered from its wartime crisis of morale and income – made it impossible for him to coerce them. Yet the very existence of so large a private sector reduced, if it did not undermine, the chance of realizing the potential of the comprehensive ideal.

Of the three reformers, the red-blooded Aneurin Bevan was by far the most successful at managing conflicting class ambitions. On the one hand, he was sufficiently radical and uncommitted to the social élite to drive through an integration of public and private medicine into one national system. On the other hand, his awareness of, *and his realism about,* the class pressures involved in medicine – among consumers and suppliers – gave him a proper sense of the concessions necessary to bring the élite on board. This is not to decry Bevan the socialist, but to elevate Bevan the realist. Indeed, Bevan over-estimated the socialist potential of his reforms, believing (wrongly) that private practice would soon die out once the NHS was established with the élite on board. But he never made the key Croslandite error of believing that in a free society the élite could be coerced when its vital class interests were threatened.

Consider the medical profession. A salaried medical service had, before and during the war, been the main priority of the Socialist Medical Association, and the 1945 manifesto committed Labour to this goal. Yet for Bevan, it was the hospitals, not the professions who worked in them, which it was essential to nationalize. He saw that there was no chance of creating a reasonably unified NHS without a single institutional structure; yet equally that there was no real prospect of creating a cross-class NHS if the medical profession had to make a straight choice between public and private sectors, forcing much of it into the private sector along with its patients and (in due course) a parallel set of institutions. Consultants were thus allowed to retain the right to private practice and pay beds in NHS hospitals. 'I stuffed their mouths with gold,' as Bevan put it unsentimentally. Bevan's Labour critics, who spent the next thirty years trying (unsuccessfully) to abolish pay beds and private practice within the NHS, claimed he was too much under the influence of the medical grandees. Yet the Welsh socialist was no one's poodle, as his political battles before and after his service as Health Minister amply demonstrated. He appeased the consultants, and to a lesser extent the GPs, because he knew that if they were not given a special status, guaranteeing a measure of professional independence, many would simply not join the NHS, and that then the NHS would rapidly become – if it did not start out as – a second-class service.

Michael Foot, Bevan's acolyte and biographer, and the archetypal 'upper crust' Labour radical of the next generation, writes of Bevan's foundation of the NHS: 'His outstanding success was the way he applied the anaesthetic to supporters on his own side, making them believe in things they had opposed almost all their lives.' Two generations later, the NHS is lauded as the single greatest triumph for socialism in British history. None other than Margaret Thatcher had to defend it to the last, for all its offence against her belief in free markets, self-reliance and the small state. If Britain is to overcome its two-nation education system, it needs an education reformer in Bevan's mould, ambitious to overcome the public–private divide, yet realistic about the means to do so without alienating the social élite beyond its point of endurance.

Preface

This book is about the segregation of modern Britain. For Britain cannot be understood apart from its class system, which separates its people as clinically today as it did half a century ago when George Orwell proclaimed England 'the most class-ridden country under the sun'.

The classes have changed. But the barriers between them are made of the same old clay: money, education, family and occupation (or lack of them). Far from diminishing, class divisions are intensifying as the distance between the top and bottom widens and the classes at both extremes grow in size and identity.

This should be obvious to all. Indeed, we contend, it *is* obvious to almost all in today's Britain – except, crucially, for much of the nation's élite, which for reasons of fear and self-interest is struggling to eliminate class from the realm of respectable debate. It is doing so by two sleights of mind. The first is the use of the term 'underclass' to denote a minority isolated from the mainstream majority. The second is the transformation of this mainstream into a 'classless society', defined by consumerism, mobility and meritocracy, operating on that quintessential British arena: the level playing field.

This is myth and distortion in equal measure. We need to refer back to money, education, family and occupation (and lack of them) to perceive the rigours of Britain's new class hierarchy. The rise of a new lower class has been matched by the rise of a new upper class, while the middle class – segmented as finely now as ever in the past – lives in a state of constant tension with those below and above. Almost every visible, audible and saleable aspect of modern life betrays this class hierarchy, from Harrow to Hackney, sushi to sausages, sharp suit to shell suit, *FT* to *Sun*, Porsche to Escort, Channel Four to Radio One.

We are describing a class system in an open society, not a caste system in a closed one. Social mobility and social change are everywhere apparent, extending to top and bottom. In this sense there is no 'underclass', just as there is no closed upper class (beyond the recesses of the royal family and the hereditary peerage). But it is a cardinal error to confuse mobility and change, still more meritocracy, with an advancing classlessness. The role of change, mobility and meritocracy in the reformation of Britain's class structure is a major theme of this book. Particular attention is paid to the development of the professional and managerial élite, the least understood part of the modern class system. High incomes have begotten super incomes. And super incomes, increasingly found in pairs with the rise of the professional career woman married to the professional career man, beget super families, their children cloned with all the advantages of ambitious parenting, private education, and the manifold purchases of wealth. The result is the Super Class, a new upper class pulling away from the swathe of lower-paid professionals, mainly in the public sector, as surely as the mis-termed 'underclass' is pulling away from the surviving working class.

The tale we tell is of social change deeply rooted in its cultural, economic and political context. From the public schools to the National Health Service, the monarchy to the National Lottery, Britain's national institutions feature prominently, both as reflections and causes of class segregation. The political parties are no exception: despite their transformation in recent decades, the Labour and Conservative parties remain the voice of powerful class interests. The fault-line between them, every bit as serious as the class divisions of old, divides a public sector élite which looks largely to the Left from a private sector élite – the Super

Class – wedded mostly to the Right. Only thus can one make sense of the great political battles of the 1980s and 1990s: Thatcherism, privatization, the emasculation of the old manual trade unions (by both the Tories and, latterly, Labour), and the reconstruction of the Labour party as a social coalition under the firm control of the public sector professionals.

Few are ridiculous enough to claim that the classless society has *arrived*. Like the most powerful social myths, its potency rests on the belief that it is *coming* and that it is irresistible.

All of which has an eerie resonance. For it was, of course, Karl Marx who coined the term 'classless society' and the myth of its inevitability, driven forward by historical forces beyond the control of mere governments and nations. Marx had a 'working' classless society in mind, and believed it still a long way off; his heirs today proclaim a 'middle' classless society, and believe it imminent. Yet the similarities are striking. Among today's Marxists of the bourgeoisie, there is the same assumption that technology and economic progress will destroy class divisions; the same belief in victory for one social group and way of life; the same beguiling mantra of *equality* ('equality of opportunity' being today's catchphrase); and the same derision of progressive politics – the patient work of bridging real existing class tensions and divisions as best one can – as futile and irrelevant. It was false and dangerous as a manifesto for the twentieth century; it is false and dangerous as a prospectus for the twenty-first.

A preparatory word about classes and Britain. Our concern is to explore and expose the reality of entrenched social divisions, not to satisfy purity tests in the definition of classes. We are therefore unashamed in using the term to embrace different and often overlapping identities, from fairly small and objective groups like the 'public sector professional class' to those two amorphous nations of the 'working' and 'middle' classes. Identities are rarely exclusive, least of all class and social identities.

As for Britain, much of what we say – particularly about education – applies mainly to England. Scotland, in particular, has many institutions which are beyond our scope. Yet its social structure is similar to England's, and many of its institutions – from council housing to the NHS – are shared. Indeed, much of what we say echoes well beyond Britain. A new language of class is developing rapidly in the United States, and at a lesser but unmistakable pace within continental Europe, particularly in the context of schools, élites and the growing disparities of wealth and income.

But therein lies another book. Our concern is with Britain and the British. And why, half a century on, it is not just Orwell but Betjeman who still rings true:

> Think of what our Nation stands for,
> Books from Boots' and country lanes,
> Free speech, free passes, class distinction,
> Democracy and proper drains.

PART ONE

Foundations

We are forever being told we have a rigid class structure. That's a load of codswallop. In many cases, there are more opportunities than ever to do just about anything you want.

Prince Edward, April 1996

Our task is to allow more people to become middle class. The Labour party did not come into being to celebrate working-class people having a lack of opportunity and poverty, but to take them out of it.

Tony Blair, *Sunday Times*, 1 September 1996

My job is not to say to people: 'Here you are, here is what you want on a plate.' My job is to provide the ladders and then say – work out your goal and aim for it. That is what I mean by the classless society: opportunity for everyone.

John Major, interviewed in *The Times*, 25 July 1996

1. A CLASS ACT

The segregation of modern Britain

One of the most commonly voiced misconceptions is that 'we are all classless nowadays'. It has been said for at least half a century, though with mounting irritation in those who assert it.

Richard Hoggart, *The Way We Live Now* (1995)

Asked whether the class war was over, Sir Peregrine Worsthorne, the former editor of the *Sunday Telegraph*, famously replied: 'Yes, we won.' But the public are not so sure. Gallup, the *Daily Telegraph*'s favourite pollsters, have been seeking their views on the subject since the early 1960s. In 1995 a remarkable 81 per cent of Gallup's representative sample replied 'yes' to the question: 'There used to be a lot of talk in politics about a "class struggle". Do you think there is a class struggle in this country or not?'

Initially this finding struck us as rather quaint. We were at one with Brian Deer, the enterprising journalist who spotted it amidst Gallup's regular opinion surveys about footwear and women's hygiene: 'The concept of class struggle is now so archaic, so apparently irrelevant and so absent from the media, that to use it, except in sarcasm, is a hint that you are somehow not of this world'.[1] It may have made some sense back in 1961, when nearly two-thirds of employees were manual workers, still chuckling at Peter Sellers as the Bolshie shop steward in *I'm Alright Jack*. But not, surely, in the supposedly classless 1990s.

Yet this was no one-off. Gallup asked the same question eighteen times between 1961 and 1996, and the proportion lining up behind the class warriors rose across the three decades, from around 60 per cent in the 1960s to 70 per cent in the 1980s and 80 per cent in the 1990s. Moreover, this trend turns out to be fairly typical of attitudes to class segregation. By a margin of more than five to one the punters were telling Mori, in a 1991 survey, that 'there will never be a classless society in Britain'. Nearly four in five agreed that the country 'has too many barriers based on social class', while a large majority rejected the notion that 'it is easy for people to move up from one social class to another'.[2] More striking still was a 1995 Gallup poll which found 85 per cent subscribing to the existence of an Underclass[3] – among the highest levels of support ever found for a controversial proposition repudiated by the government of the day.

The polls were just the start. Month by month as this book progressed, so did the saga of Britain's class divisions, distinctions and obsessions. The middle class Simpsons moved into the working-class estate of *Brookside*, while the arriviste Buckets ('no, Bouquet, my dear') struggled on in *Keeping Up Appearances*. Footballers and cricketers played out their worst class stereotypes before a besotted media (the Gazza wedding and subsequent thuggery; Ian Botham suing Imran Khan for ungentlemanly conduct). Class past, as much as Colin Firth in stockings, was the season's television drama hit in Jane Austen's *Pride and Prejudice*. Glasgow's Underclass made a screen debut in *Trainspotting*. The utility 'fat cats' fattened, to national opprobrium, while report after report highlighted the chasm between rich and poor. The National Lottery prospered, to the delight of London opera-goers. 'I do not like the crudity of the words rich and poor,' remarked Lord Gowrie, whose job as chairman of the Arts Council was to transfer Lottery largesse from one to the other under the guise of 'good causes'.[4] And the politicians talked about class incessantly: John Major went on about the 'classless society' yet devoted his Tory conference speech to jibes about Tony Blair's privileged education ('New Labour: Old School Tie'), while Tony Blair proclaimed New Labour's mission as 'to allow more people to become middle class', as though governments distributed rights of passage.[5]

Most illuminating of all was the April morning when John Prescott announced that *he* had become middle class. The deputy leader of the Labour party, a gruff Northerner, son of a railwayman, who failed the eleven-plus, left school at fifteen and started out as a waiter on Cunard cruise liners, was replying to a Radio Four interviewer's jibe that New Labour was a middle-class party. 'Why are you so disparaging about the middle class?' Prescott fired back. 'You're middle class. I'm middle class.' Told he was supposed to be working class, Prescott went on: 'I was once . . . My roots, my background and the way I act is working class, but it would be hypocritical to say I'm anything else than middle class now.' On £43,000 a year, with two homes and a Jag, Prescott's lifestyle was hardly proletarian. But his remarks caused a sensation. From housewives to peers and professors, everyone had a view. Was Prescott *really* middle class? Even the politician's 78-year-old mother was indignant ('He's never referred to being middle class to me; John comes from a solid line of working-class people, he's a working-class man at heart and always will be,' she told a journalist). Yet as to the persistence of a class-bound society, there was near universal agreement. One notable dissenter was Prince Edward, who dismissed class as 'a load of codswallop'. Most people had no doubt where *he* stood in the pecking order.

The same story was told in a stream of publications. Right and Left, empirical and polemical, they all took class for granted and debated the widening of social divisions. *Unequal But Fair? A Study of Class Barriers in Britain* issued from a right-wing think tank. Will Hutton's *The State We're In* topped the best-seller lists. The number-crunching Institute for Fiscal Studies published *Two Nations? The Inheritance of Poverty and Affluence*. A summary of sociological disputations was entitled *Conflicts About Class*, and joined self-explanatory titles such as *Who Gets What?*, *The Winner-Take-All Society* and *How to Save the Underclass*.[6] 'The central problem,' one of the studies concluded, 'is not why classes have been dying but why they have been so persistent.'[7]

There was, it became clear, no great mystery at hand. The public belief in class, even class conflict, was strong and growing because the perception of social segregation was also strong and growing. Attempts by politicians and pundits to promote the 'classless society' have made virtually no popular headway. This made our task simpler than we anticipated. There was no need to justify a book seeking to put class back into the debate about Britain's future. We could get on with explaining why and how class remains so entrenched, while so many politicians and opinion-formers insist, perversely, that Britain is on the road to a classless society.

Making sense of class

Ever since Marx, the word 'class' has been heavily loaded. Yet virtually all modern social analysis – whether by Whitehall, the media, academics or market researchers – divides people by class, sex or age, often by all three. And standing back from the various schemes of class categorization on offer, it is the degree of agreement, not disagreement, which is remarkable.

Occupation and family are generally taken as the starting point. From families and jobs flow the patterns of income, values, advantage and social behaviour which go to make up classes. Disagreements between class analysts are essentially second order: mainly about whether to assess class membership in an 'objective' or a 'subjective' way (that is, by set criteria, or by people's self-perception), and how to allocate specific occupations, or types of employment, to classes. Even here, a fair degree of consensus exists behind the use of two contemporary class gradings, the six-class A, B, C_1, C_2, D, E hierarchy adopted by market researchers in the 1950s, and the Goldthorpe seven-class schema used by many social scientists. Both of them divide occupations into classes along a broad manual/non-manual spectrum (see Table 1). The manual of the Institute of Practitioners in Advertising allocates every occupation a place on the A to E scale, from admirals (As), moderately qualified zoologists (Bs) and acrobats (C_1s), to hedge-builders (C_2s), barrowboys (Ds) and semi-skilled zinc-workers (Ds).[8] Neither structure makes income the sole determinant of class: it is a commonplace that many skilled blue-collar C_2s have more disposable income than lower-middle-class C_1s, while Goldthorpe's 'petty bourgeoisie' of the non-professional self-employed earn less on average than his 'working class'. Yet the separation between manual, non-manual and 'executive' jobs underpins both structures, signifying broad differences in income and lifestyle. Exceptions and flagrant anomalies abound. Vicars earn less than miners, lorry drivers more than primary-school teachers; one critic even lights on 'the London taxi-driver who loves opera, has a PhD in history, and goes hunting at week-ends'.[9] But it may be safely assumed that such complex class characters are rare, even in London taxis.

The A to E classes need no introduction in media, political and marketing circles. Every party leader and consumer goods strategist has a plan for 'targeting the ABs'. The *Financial Times* television critic Christopher Dunkley begins a review thus for his sophisticated AB readership, pandering to its every prejudice: 'When you do find something that is not carefully designed to appeal to the tastes of C1 female viewers between the ages of eighteen and thirty-eight (or whatever) the tendency is for expectations to be raised to an impossibly high level.'[10] Defending his editorship of the *Sunday Times* from criticism that he had taken the paper downmarket, Andrew Neil protested that he had gained readers among 'ABC1s, the most educated and affluent in society and the group advertisers crave for. We were doing especially well among well-educated Bs in full-time employment. Our losses had been among C2DEs, 55+s and the less educated.'[11]

Yet few would describe *themselves* as an A or a B, let alone a C2. Many are unsure of their class or reject the idea that they even belong to one, making subjective class analysis difficult. The Mori poll cited earlier is revealing. While it found large majorities subscribing to the class system and 'too many barriers based on social class', it also recorded a two-to-one 'no' response to the question: 'Do you ever think of yourself as belonging to a particular social class?' Furthermore, when respondents were asked to assign themselves to the middle or working classes regardless, 61 per cent volunteered 'working class' and only 30 per cent 'middle class'. This marks a huge increase in the size of the subjective

Table 1: Analysing class

(a) The market researchers' view of class

	Class	% of heads of household (1991)
A	Upper Middle Class (e.g. professional, higher managerial, senior civil servants)	3
B	Middle Class (e.g. middle managers)	16
C1	Lower Middle Class (e.g. junior managers, routine white-collar or non-manual workers)	26
C2	Skilled Working Class (e.g. skilled manual workers)	26
D	Semi-skilled and Unskilled Working Class (e.g. manual workers)	17
E	Residual (e.g. those dependent on long-term state benefits)	13

Source: *National Readership Survey*, NRS Ltd, July 1992–July 1993.

(b) The Goldthorpe seven-class schema

Class classifications from British General Election Surveys, by respondent

		1964 %	1992 %
I	Higher salariat	7.0	11.6
II	Lower salariat	12.3	16.3
III	Routine clerical	16.5	24.2
IV	Petty bourgeoisie	6.6	7.1
V	Foremen and technicians	7.6	4.8
VI	Skilled manual	17.8	10.9
VII	Unskilled manual	32.4	25.1

Source: Dr A. Heath, Nuffield College, Oxford.

working class from that found by Gallup back in 1949, when it stood at only 43 per cent, despite the collapse in manual employment since. It came about because more than a third of today's ABs describe themselves as working class, as do more than half of the 'lower middle class' C1s. By contrast, the DEs say what was expected of them, only 16 per cent declaring themselves middle class.

To add to the confusion, consider those now ubiquitous terms 'classless society' and 'middle class'. The first might naturally be taken to mean a society without classes, while the second, historically and in wide current usage, carries the *Concise Oxford Dictionary* definition of 'the social group between the upper and working classes, particularly those in professional and managerial occupations'. What, then, are we to make of statements like these:

> In modern Britain, we seem to be left with three class groups, and perhaps a fourth is on the way. Much the largest is the 'classless' middle class, which is engaged in by far the greater part of the work of the country (William Rees-Mogg).[12]

> The present class system is a 'fat cat' upper class, a huge middle class and an underclass. There's no working class any more (John Mortimer).[13]

> The proportion of working class people enjoying a middle class lifestyle is large and rising (BBC television reporter, January 1996).

In the course of three brief comments we have a classless middle class, the abolition of the entire working class, a middle class which includes the greater part of the 'workers', a working class enjoying a middle-class way of life, an underclass (to which virtually no one confesses to opinion pollsters that they belong), and an upper class comprising 'fat cat' corporate managers who fall squarely within the dictionary's middle class. And this comes after a public which claims that class is endemic, while significant minorities either refuse to apply its categories to themselves or embrace the 'wrong' class in the view of the experts. Class, like beauty, might seem to be purely in the eye of the beholder.

Yet standing back from the kaleidoscope, a reasonably coherent picture emerges once a distinction is made between *class labels* and the *class system*.

The old labels 'working' and 'middle' class make less and less sense in the context of radically changing patterns of occupation, income, lifestyle and authority. It is a truism that social mobility abounds and that most of the 'working class' – meaning manual workers – leads what even a generation ago would have been considered a middle-class consumer lifestyle. 'They may still be C2s relative to everybody else,' the columnist Simon Heffer quips about Essex Man, 'but C2s, like almost everybody else, are not what they used to be.'[14] Statistics on everything from videos and home ownership to foreign holidays and school staying-on rates tell the story. Add in the erosion of former distinctions between routine blue-collar and white-collar work, and the collapse of old sources of authority – 'there are hardly any injunction-givers, finger-waggers, these days', in the cultural historian Richard Hoggart's words[15] – and we are witnessing the mainsprings of a 'middle-classless' mentality embracing the two-thirds or so of the population who are fully part of today's consumer marketplace.

Yet this 'middle-classless' mentality co-exists with old-class mentalities and with brute economic forces making for a more, not less, divided society. Cultural distinctions and nuances remain legion. Accents, houses, cars, schools, sports, food, fashion, drink, smoking, supermarkets, soap operas, holiday destinations, even training shoes: virtually everything in life is graded with subtle or unsubtle class tags attached. 'Snobbery is the religion of England,' wrote the historian Frank Harris in 1925.[16] There has been no mass apostasy since. And underpinning these distinctions are fundamental differences in upbringing, education and occupations. It is here that we confront head-on the public perception of a class system, in the sense of deep structural barriers and inequalities reflecting and intensifying social segregation. Hence the 1996

British Social Attitudes survey found two-thirds agreeing that 'there is one law for the rich and one for the poor' and that 'ordinary people do not get their fair share of the nation's wealth', while an overwhelming 87 per cent said the gap between those with high and low incomes was 'too large' (from a choice of 'too large', 'about right' or 'too small').[17] Moreover, like our earlier figures for the belief in a class struggle and class barriers, this belief has become far more pronounced, reaching 87 per cent in 1996 from 72 per cent in 1983.

This is a rational response to income divisions underpinning the class hierarchy, which were stark to start with and widened further during the 1980s, a decade when income inequality grew faster in the UK than in any developed country apart from New Zealand. Table 2 needs little elaboration: in 1979 the bottom tenth of the population received 4.1 per cent of national income; by 1991 this was down to 2.5 per cent, while over the same period the share taken by the top tenth increased from 20 to 26 per cent.[18] Much hot air is expended on movements up and down the income scale; yet however it is measured (see Table 2) there has been a close correlation between being better-off and becoming still better-off; and year-by-year movements in income are mostly short range.[19] At the bottom, unemployment is pervasive, while at the top, by 1992 the richest tenth of wealth holders held nearly half of all individual wealth.[20] A similar story can be told about employment security. It was fashionable during the recession of the early 1990s, when the dread hand of downsizing reached white-collar and professional Britain, to claim that insecurity had crossed the class divide. Yet the 1996 Social Attitudes survey found nearly one in three semi-skilled and unskilled manual workers experiencing unemployment in the previous five years, more than double the proportion among professionals and managers.[21]

These fundamental shifts in employment and income patterns are the driving forces behind the transformation of the top and bottom of the social hierarchy. Top *and* bottom, for the changes at both ends of the spectrum must be seen together – something

Table 2: To those that have . . .

Shares of total income (after housing costs)

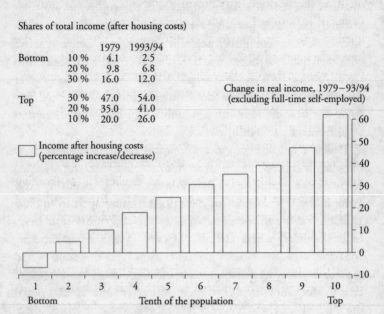

		1979	1993/94
Bottom	10 %	4.1	2.5
	20 %	9.8	6.8
	30 %	16.0	12.0
Top	30 %	47.0	54.0
	20 %	35.0	41.0
	10 %	20.0	26.0

Change in real income, 1979–93/94
(excluding full-time self-employed)

Income after housing costs
(percentage increase/decrease)

Tenth of the population

1 Bottom · · · · 10 Top

Source: DSS

rarely done – in order to understand modern class segregation. The very term *Under*class militates against such an approach, implying the existence of a monolithic *Over*class when in fact a highly differentiated range of manual, non-manual, professional and executive occupations are to be found 'above', leading up to a Super Class of top private professionals and managers who are as far apart from white-collar C1s as they are from the Underclass.

A part, at least, of the so-called Underclass is in fact a new Servant Class: the army of cleaners and menial service workers, paid a pittance, often working only a few hours here and there, cash-in-hand, no questions asked, ministering to the world above in its homes, offices, hospitals and schools. Unenamoured of tax returns, the Servant Class is hard to track, but it gives every appearance of having burgeoned in size in response to unemployment at the bottom, enrichment at the top, and the growing demand for menial support services. Beneath the servants, unemployment and unemployability are the leitmotifs of the lower class, a product of helplessness, hopelessness, poor single-parenthood (meaning almost invariably single-motherhood) and educational failure. It is fashionable in certain quarters of the Right to add genetics to the list, a notion we reject as unfounded. But there is no question that upbringing plays a big and probably growing role in transferring poverty and social inadequacy from one generation to the next. Two late-1990s figures say it all: around a quarter of all children are growing up in families with no working adult, more than twice the proportion in the late 1970s; and a third of school drop-outs – those who leave school with no, or virtually no, qualifications – are unemployed, up from 6 per cent in 1970.[22]

At the top, the expansion of professional and managerial employment to nearly a quarter of the total is the most obvious development. Yet equally significant is the scale of change within the professions, as a 'winner-take-all' culture spreads. The professions never were a unified group: in the post-war decades the 'establishment' was centred on Whitehall and the Bar, management enjoyed an ambiguous status, and there was a long tail, in which school teachers predominated. The tail has got longer still, while a new élite has emerged, which we call the Super Class, dominated by a transformed City of London and by the higher reaches of private sector professions, including corporate management. Perhaps the critical event of this book, the rise of the Super Class is as much a psychological as a social and economic development. Success and merit are its watchwords. The professional élite has ceased to regard itself as a middle class between a manual 'working' class and a leisured, aristocratic 'upper' class: on the contrary, it now sees itself as a meritocratic labouring élite, and is more self-confident about its role and rewards than any élite in modern times. Even a liberal profession like the law, historically an adjunct to the aristocracy, has become suffused with the new labouring ethic. Asked to declare his class for a newspaper symposium on the subject, Sir Bernard Ingham, Margaret Thatcher's gruff former press secretary, replied: 'In so much as I have always had to work for my living, I consider myself working class.'[23] This inverted working-class ethos has become so pronounced that the Conservatives, drawing on focus group research, made the cause of the 'hard-working class' a key theme at their 1996 party conference.

Yet for all the modern change and uncertainty, old classes run deep. When given a straight choice by pollsters, large majorities in each class on the A to E spectrum, excepting only the lower middle class C1s, still claim their traditional 'working' or 'middle' class tag.[24]

Decoding classlessness

What, then, are we to make of the idea of the 'classless society'?

The phrase, recited largely by politicians and pundits on the free-market Right, is a clever ruse to discredit the notion of class divisions without actually denying their existence. For whatever the impression created by their words, the merchants of classlessness do not in fact question the existence of classes and deep social inequality. There was a triumphalist phrase in the late 1980s when some sought to go this stage further, questioning the existence of poverty. The celebrated instance was the 1989 'end of the line for poverty' speech by John Moore, then Social Security Secretary and fleetingly the media's heir apparent to Margaret Thatcher. Rattling off the consumer society statistics – 70 per cent had a colour TV, 85 per cent a washing machine, etc. – Moore derided as 'false and dangerous' the notion of widespread poverty, adding for good measure: 'The poverty lobby would, on their definition, find poverty in paradise.' Nicholas Timmins records the upshot laconically in his biography of the welfare state:

The speech was out of tune with times in which the rich were plainly getting richer while homelessness around the country was rising, the cardboard cities were growing on London's South Bank and the teenagers barred from benefit the previous September in the Youth Training Scheme changes were beginning to appear begging on the London Underground ... Two and a half months later Moore was sacked.[25]

After which poverty was reinstated, and has flourished ever since.

The classless society is therefore not a society without classes, but the age-old goal of a meritocratic society providing means for people to advance by ability regardless of class origins. In John Major's words, it is an 'opportunity society' in which the role of government is to 'provide the ladders' enabling citizens to rise to 'whatever level that their own abilities and good fortune may take them from whatever their starting point'.[26] Classlessness is thus the opposite of what it claims. 'It is not freedom from social caste, a tardy liberation,' claims George Walden, the former Tory minister and diplomat, 'but class consciousness erected into a system more rigorous, intrusive and unforgiving than any that has gone before'.[27] The economist Joseph Schumpeter remarked long ago: 'Class barriers are always, without exception, surmountable and are, in fact, surmounted.'[28] But this does not of itself mean that the barriers are easy to surmount, still less that they are non-existent.

The use of the term 'classless society' has insidious effects. Not only does it beg the existence of the classes it has linguistically abolished: it helps foster the fallacy, now deeply rooted in Britain, that the single test of a healthy society lies in the existence of ladders for those with ambition and ability but low class background. Yet however desirable the existence of élites open to talent, the condition of classes is far more important than the mobility between them. Minorities are on the ladder; majorities stay put – even in periods of rapid occupational change, when opportunities to rise are abundant. Indeed, the capacity of individuals to climb at all depends upon their not being more than a ladder-length from their destination. And there is always downward mobility, within and between generations. No ladders are needed to fall; and apart from the rite-of-passage joys of student poverty, the further the fall, the greater the grievance and despair. For all its drawbacks, the word Underclass captures the essence of the class predicament for many at the bottom: a complete absence of ladders, whether basic skills, role models, education or a culture of work.

At first sight the classless fallacy is a renaming of the social evil identified long ago by Michael Young in *The Rise of the Meritocracy*. 'Do not the masses, for all their lack of capacity, sometimes behave as though they suffered from a sense of indignity?' inquires Young's bemused Meritocrat in 2033.[29] In reality a true meritocracy is far less imminent than its devotees hope or its opponents fear. There is plenty of social mobility in modern Britain, but so there has been in every age: the figures show that mobility today is probably no greater than, say, during the Industrial Revolution.

However, the march of meritocracy is again controversial because of claims that today's class differences largely reflect the genetic inheritance of intelligence and aptitude. The now classic statement is Richard Herrnstein and Charles Murray's US book *The Bell Curve* (1994), which argues that the structure of American society is now closely related to an IQ meritocracy. Their supporting statistics have been challenged,[30] and Murray's reactionary political agenda is well known. None the less, the theme has been taken up in Britain by Peter Saunders, a critic of John Goldthorpe's empirical school which has relentlessly marshalled education and occupation statistics to question the notion of accelerating social mobility.[31] In a 'pure meritocracy', Saunders argues, 'bright people will tend to rise to higher positions, and because bright people will tend to produce bright children, there will be a tendency for the children of the middle classes to outperform the children of the working class'.[32]

Saunders is studiously ambiguous about how close Britain is

to becoming a pure meritocracy: his tract is entitled *Unequal But Fair?*, implying that today's class barriers are acceptably meritocratic while leaving a tantalizing question mark in the balance to avoid quite saying so. But let us follow his evidence. It consists of analysis of the UK's National Child Development Study, a unique research project tracking the health, education and development of the 17,414 people born nationwide in a week in March 1958, more than 11,000 of whom could still be located – aged thirty-three – when interviews were last carried out in 1991. Analysing, first, the scores of the children in a general ability test taken at the age of eleven, he shows that these reflected the social background of their parents to a marked extent, with children of managerial and professional parents scoring far higher averages than the others. Combining this finding with other indicators of youthful motivation (such as an attitude assessment of the children at the age of sixteen), he finds, secondly, a strong correlation between scores on these measures and success in the job market, gauged by occupational class attained at the age of thirty-three in 1991. Taking Michael Young's definition of 'merit' as 'intelligence and effort together', this leads Saunders to claim that Britain's class system is 'more meritocratic than has commonly been assumed'.[33] For instance, he finds that those who by the age of thirty-three were in the census department's top two social classes (professionals, managers, administrators and employers) achieved an average test score at the age of eleven of 51.6, against only 36.3 for those ending up in the bottom two classes (semi-skilled and unskilled manual workers).

The problem, of course, is his first finding about the deep class differences at the age of eleven. Here Saunders' analysis shows an average score in the general ability test of 50.6 for the children with parents in the top two social classes, against 40.2 for those from the bottom social classes. And this almost certainly underestimates the scale of the difference, since for no good reason Saunders entirely excludes from his analysis those who were unemployed or working only part-time when they came to be interviewed in 1991, a disproportionate number of whom would have scored at the bottom.

Were these differences evidence of genetic meritocracy in action, as Saunders half suggests, then we could debate whether life chances are indeed unequal but fair. But this is to make three assumptions, the first highly implausible, the second profoundly pessimistic, and the third counter to common sense. The implausible assumption concerns the inheritance of intelligence. It may very likely be that intelligence is inherited, although this has still to be proved; but even if true, it is implausible to the point of incredible to believe that a notably lopsided class concentration of intelligence, let alone of ambition, has been genetically engineered over the two or three generations since intelligence came to play a largely (though still far from wholly) separate role from inherited class in the market for jobs and sexual partners.

Moreover, even if it had done so, it is profoundly pessimistic to suppose that the less naturally intelligent are incapable of high achievement. In his judicious assessment of *How to Save the Underclass*, the economist Robin Marris cites US research on the success of intensive education programmes in raising the IQ of low-IQ children by huge amounts, sufficient to reduce their probability of dropping out of school by as much as a factor of five.[34] This would not surprise anyone familiar with school performance in the UK. Visit a middling English private school, one where many of the pupils owe their places more to parental money, upbringing and expectations than to innate IQ, and you find almost all the pupils doing well enough in GCSEs to study for A-levels, with the great majority going on to university courses of some kind.[35] It was pressure from such schools and parents which helped persuade the Major government to rename polytechnics as 'universities' in 1992, so raising the prestige of the higher education institutions patronized by many less able students from professional parental backgrounds.[36]

This leads to the third weakness of Saunders' analysis: it defies any common sense view of the schools around us. Only the blind can be oblivious to deep class divisions between schools in their recruitment and learning environments. These divisions are entrenched by the primary level: virtually every metropolitan centre in Britain is divided between 'middle class' and 'working class' primary schools, and all parents know which are which. Indeed, the divergence is probably greater today than it was in 1969, when the children born in 1958 came to be tested for 'general ability'. Today's professionals begin their quest for the best start for their children long before primary school. The annual *Good Nursery Guide* says it all, with its description of 300 top institutions for toddlers, including those like the Pooh Corner Montessori School in Kensington, unabashed about equipping its three-year-olds with 'the best possible chance to beat the hot competition for places in London's élite private schools'.[37] In Britain's class meritocracy, all children are equal but some are more equal than others.

Education, education, education

Education, the meritocratic ideal and chronic inequality underpin class divisions in modern Britain. The three are closely interwoven. School segregation is the critical driving force: largely a reflection of birth (professional parents colonize the best schools, the inner-city poor the worst), it mints class divisions anew each generation. This is quite compatible with the fact that meritocracy reigns within the top schools, with those of low birth who make it through their gates having advantages equal, or nearly equal, to their classmates. Britain's Asian community, whose parents put education above all other aspirations for their children, are climbing the class ladder fast in consequence. But meritocracy in modern Britain is mostly the creed of the élite, not the mass; and it is practised most faithfully in the old public and grammar schools serving a predominantly professional and managerial clientele, however leavened by a few children from families forgoing holidays and second cars to buy a 'decent education' (as they put it), helped perhaps by a government assisted place.

England's education system is the product of three distinct

reform projects of the past century (the story is somewhat different in Scotland). The first project was the expansion of secondary education beyond the old public (i.e. private and fee-paying) schools, moving away from the official late-Victorian view that 'the different classes of society require different teaching'.[38] Edwardian reformers began this process, which culminated in R. A. Butler's 1944 Education Act raising the school-leaving age to fifteen, abolishing fees for state-aided pupils in secondary schools and guaranteeing access to grammar schools for all those able to get through the entrance exam (soon dubbed the 'eleven-plus'). The second reform project, designed on a bipartisan basis in the 1950s and 1960s by 'progressive' Tory and Labour politicians led by Tony Crosland and Sir Edward Boyle, had 'equality of opportunity' as its catchphrase. Its instruments were the reorganization of state schools into non-selective comprehensives (proceeding fast after 1965), the raising of the school-leaving age to sixteen in 1972, and the drive to equip all school-leavers with exam certificates. The third project was the expansion of higher (post-eighteen) education, notably in the 1960s with the creation of the polytechnics and 'redbrick' universities, and in the late 1980s and 1990s with a huge increase in the number of student places, particularly at polytechnics. At each stage reformers have had two objectives in view: an increase in educational provision to meet economic demands; and, partly through this expansion and partly through restructuring, the extension of opportunities down the social scale. As R. A. Butler said of his 1944 Education Act, it would 'have the effect of welding us all into one nation ... instead of two nations as Disraeli talked about'.[39]

The three projects expanded the education system well enough. Before the 1944 Act only one in seven of thirteen- to eighteen-year-olds attended a state-funded secondary school; as recently as 1987 only one in seven of eighteen-year-olds went on to higher education, a ratio slashed to one in three in less than a decade thereafter. But expansion has manifestly not produced 'equality of opportunity'. Table 3, drawn from research by Oxford University analysts led by Anthony Heath and A. H. Halsey, shows that each of the three reform waves increased the *absolute* number of school/college participants or achievers from the 'working' and 'intermediate' classes, yet did little to narrow the *relative* differences between them and the 'salaried' (professional and managerial) classes. Furthermore, when sweeping reforms – such as compulsory secondary schooling and raising the school-leaving age – succeeded in entirely eliminating one set of differentials, a new set perpetuated class segregation at a higher level. Mere attendance at secondary school gave way to the quest for better formal qualifications, pursued at progressively higher levels. Thus three-fifths of all children born to salaried-class parents between 1956 and 1965 went on to university, polytechnic or college, while barely one-sixth of those with manual-class parents did so.

Anthony Heath goes so far as to claim that the twentieth-century reform doing most to promote equality of opportunity was – wait for it – the 1907 Free Place Regulations, which opened secondary education to most of the working classes for the first time and greatly expanded school openings for the lower middle classes, making it possible for some of the less affluent displaying 'intelligence and effort' to compete as meritocrats.[40] It was the 1907 reform and its extension after the First World War which produced the dynamic 'grammar school boy' generation – the class led by Harold Wilson, Roy Jenkins, Denis Healey and Edward Heath – which so largely shaped Britain between the 1940s and the 1970s. Ironically, among its prime legacies was the destruction of the grammar school system.

We are looking at a great moving-up show in which class divisions, based on education, remain stark despite a transformation in the educational experience of the population across the century. For a broader picture of what this means, we must return to the National Child Development Survey and its 17,000 children born in 1958. When they were surveyed at the age of thirty-three, more than half of those who had made it to the top quarter of income earners were found to have had fathers who were also in

Table 3: Education and class:
the three twentieth-century waves – more provision, similar class
difference

Wave one (1910–50): The rise of academic secondary schools

Father's class	*Percentage of those born within each ten-year period attending selective secondary schools (males)*		
	1910–19	*1930–39*	*1940–49*
I (higher salaried)	69	86	74
II (lower salaried)	57	77	62
III (routine non-manual)	34	51	47
IV (petty bourgeoisie)	35	49	41
V (foremen)	22	38	33
VI (skilled working)	19	30	21
VII (semi/unskilled working)	15	27	23

Wave two (1950–80): The rise of secondary school qualifications

Father's class	*Percentage of those born within each ten-year period obtaining an O-level pass*	
	1940–49	*1960–69*
I (higher salaried)	63	83
II (lower salaried)	72	83
III (routine non-manual)	67	84
IV (petty bourgeoisie)	40	61
V (foremen)	39	70
VI (skilled working)	30	55
VII (semi/unskilled working)	26	46

the top quarter, while nearly half of those with parents who were unemployed or in the bottom fifth of the income distribution were in one or other of those categories themselves.[41] Sons of managerial or professional fathers were three times more likely to end up in similar occupations than the sons of semi-skilled or

Wave three (since 1960): The rise of post-school education

Years of birth and Social class	No post-school education	Percentages in each category		
		University	Polytechnic	College
Born 1936–45				
Salaried class	64.0	14.0	2.5	19.5
Intermediate class	83.9	4.8	1.7	9.8
Manual class	94.1	1.3	0.6	4.0
Born 1946–55				
Salaried class	52.8	16.5	6.1	24.6
Intermediate class	74.9	5.9	3.9	15.4
Manual class	89.6	1.7	1.6	7.1
Born 1956–65				
Salaried class	44.3	17.7	10.3	27.7
Intermediate class	67.4	6.6	6.5	19.2
Manual class	83.1	2.0	2.8	12.0

Sources: A. Heath and P. Clifford, in Ch. 16 of D. J. Lee and B. S. Turner, *Conflicts About Class* (1996); M. Egerton and A. H. Halsey in *Oxford Review of Education*, 19 (2) (1993).

unskilled manual fathers. Unemployment, too, was passed down: those sons who at sixteen had unemployed fathers were more than twice as likely as the others to have been out of work for a year or more by the time they were thirty-three. 'Many will find this data evidence of quite an encouraging degree of mobility,' comments David Willetts, the Tory MP and intellectual guru[42] – revealing more, perhaps, about modern élite mentalities than modern social mobility.

The view from the top of the educational tree is breathtaking. In the *FT*'s 1996 survey of A-level performance in England's 1,000 leading schools, all but twenty-two of the top 200 schools – educating around 150,000 children between them – were in the private sector.[43] The *FT*'s 1,000 top schools comprised most of the independent school sector but only a fraction of the state sector; yet even within this selective group, including most of the remaining state grammar schools, the A-level performance of private schools was on average a quarter better than their state counterparts. Set this alongside the fact that two-thirds of private school pupils have parents in the AB professional and managerial classes, and the character of today's class meritocracy is clear.[44]

And clearer still when we move on to the universities. Half of all the entrants to Oxford and Cambridge universities in 1995 came from private schools, although the independent sector accounted for only 7 per cent of the total school population. Given the pattern of Oxbridge recruitment even from state schools, which is tilted heavily towards the 161 remaining state grammar schools and comprehensives in affluent neighbourhoods, it is a fair supposition that at least two-thirds of each year's total Oxbridge intake are ABs. So self-selecting are Oxbridge entrants that the universities have barely two applicants for each place, the lowest ratio for all universities. Oxbridge claims, with an apparently straight face, to be thoroughly meritocratic. As Michael Beloff QC, president of Trinity College, Oxford, euphemistically puts it, there are 'disparate standards of education in British secondary schools'; none the less, 'it is not our policy to try to redress that imbalance by positive discrimination to the detriment of standards; still less to engage in social engineering'.[45] Yet social engineering has already taken place – in the schools. As for the engineers, suffice it to note that the proportion of Oxford graduates going into state school teaching declined by nearly two-thirds between 1971 and 1996, while the number taking posts in the independent sector at least remained static and may have risen. In the typical top public school, at least a third of the staff are Oxbridge – including among recent recruits.[46] Equally telling is the fact that the independent school share of university entrants declines with status of university, from half for Oxbridge to about a quarter for the 'old' universities (i.e. those bearing that title before the sector was diluted by the polytechnics in 1992) and a fifth or less for the former polytechnics.[47]

As for the bottom of the scale, in 1994 inner London Islington's state secondary schools, from which the borough's ABs have largely decamped, secured five or more good GCSE passes for barely one in four of their 1,300 sixteen-year-old pupils. In the same year they entered a total of 79 pupils for two or more A-levels, which was fewer than the number of pupils Eton alone sent to Oxbridge – virtually all of them boasting three or more A grades at A-level. To complete the picture, a third of Etonians in 1996 were sons of Etonians. 'This is down from about half a generation ago,' says an Eton master, adding without a trace of irony: 'It has been very traumatic but we are a meritocracy these days.'[48]

Education, meritocracy and inequality: all three themes come together in the rise of the Super Class, Britain's new professional and managerial élite described in Chapter 3. In occupational terms the Super Class is the product of a City of London transformed since the 1960s into 'the Clapham Junction of international finance'.[49] Equally important are the City's satellites: the closely interlinked cadres of lawyers, accountants and corporate executives. What makes the Super Class a reasonably distinctive class is its size, exclusivity, and increasingly separate lifestyle and self-consciousness. Meritocracy is its governing myth: the Super Class thinks of itself, in Christopher Lasch's description of its American counterpart (whose imprint on the City is deep and deepening), as a 'self-made élite owing its privileges exclusively to its own efforts'.[50] This accounts for its cohesion and uniformity, since it is largely 'self-made' in Britain's top schools and universities. It also accounts for its steely equanimity in the face of growing national inequality, since in its own eyes it is the core of the 'hard-working class' we encountered earlier. The self-righteousness with which the Super Class and its apologists defend the cause of greater social inequality is without precedent since the Victorian landed and business classes confronted Britain's working classes in the nineteenth century.

Education and meritocracy lead inescapably to the issue of gender. Speak to a vice-chancellor in the eighties and nineties and an instant denial would have greeted the suggestion that he – they were virtually all men – was not working hard to expand social opportunities. But typically he would not have mentioned the unfashionable word 'class', except perhaps indirectly with a sigh at the continued dominance of the public schools.[51] Instead he would have talked about women, and what was being done to open the student and lecturing community to greater female participation. This might have meant admitting women for the first time, perhaps after a ferocious internal battle; more often it was a matter of ensuring that their presence was more than tokenistic.

Promoting opportunities for women was, of course, long overdue. And promoted they were: between 1950 and 1990 the proportion of women among full-time university entrants rose from about 30 to 45 per cent, and by 1995 it had reached almost exactly half of the annual intake.[52] Yet in class terms – and here we enter sensitive but crucial territory – the effect has been to *intensify* class divisions, for three reasons. First, the pressure for institutional reform came largely from women from professional and managerial families, who were also the main beneficiaries from greater sexual equality. Secondly, as sex discrimination became *the* 'equal opportunities' concern of the élite, readily measurable and visibly offensive when not tackled, the more nebulous and less apparent dimension of class vanished from sight.

Then, thirdly, there is the natural tendency of men and women to marry their social peers. Known to sociologists by the ugly phrase 'assortive mating', this is a practice with powerful class-intensifying properties as women have taken on careers and acquired independent incomes. In the marriage and class arena, two plus two equals significantly more than four. Professional couples not only have two large incomes: the process of stirring aspiration and achievement in their children, so much more powerful when instilled by the mother, is dramatically enhanced. By contrast, families with only unskilled and/or unemployed adults – accounting for about a third of all children in 1997 – have neither money nor aspiration to confer from either side.

Mickey Kaus remarks of this phenomenon in the US in his book *The End of Equality* (1992): 'What if the $60,000 lawyer marries another $60,000 lawyer, and the $20,000 clerk marries a $20,000 clerk? Then the difference between their incomes suddenly becomes the difference between $120,000 and $40,000', and 'although the trend is still masked in the income statistics by the low average wages of women, it's obvious to practically everyone, even the experts, that something like this is in fact happening'. It is obvious in Britain too. Take lawyers as an example.[53] Women now account for well over half of all new entrants to the solicitors' profession. Between 1985 and 1995 the number of practising solicitors rose by 42 per cent to 66,000: women accounted for most of this growth, and their share of the profession doubled to 30 per cent over the decade. Moreover, women are breaking through the so-called 'glass ceiling' to reach the top in large numbers: by 1995, 15 per cent of all partners in solicitors' firms were female.

As for expectations among the next generation of women professionals, the weekly parents' newsletter of one of London's leading girls' private schools in December 1996 says it all. After notices about a parent–teacher forum on 'the work ethic' came a tailpiece by the headmistress:

> One rather disgruntled parent wanted to know why we were suggesting that his daughter should become a carpet fitter!! On the face of it, this did seem strangely out of step with our avowed policy of raising girls' aspirations. It transpired that the girl had been using one of the computer careers advice programmes. But, like other girls who have been encouraged to take up window dressing or typing, she had erroneously skipped that part of the programme which asked for her academic level of achievement![54]

Dwarves, giants and hot-air balloons

'We mould our institutions and they mould us,' Winston Churchill declared at the opening of the new chamber of the House of Commons, replacing the one destroyed by the Luftwaffe. To understand Britain's segregated society it is not enough to recite statistics and reports: an understanding of national institutions and their contemporary social role is vital. In this book we dissect the institutions which matter most: the public schools, Oxbridge, the professions, the City of London, Parliament, the political parties, the Crown, the Lords, the BBC and the NHS, to take just the foremost. We shall also look at the National Lottery, the most important national institution created by the British state since the NHS in 1948. Institution by institution we ask: Who runs it and for whose benefit? How has its history shaped its contemporary character? How is it serving to mould the society of which it is part? And, though we are mainly concerned with public institutions, we also frequently touch on that critical private institution, the family.

It is commonly believed that 'Britain changed more in the fifty years from 1945 to 1995 than in any other fifty-year period.'[55] This is the conceit of modernity, each generation conceiving of itself as less marked by the past than ever before. In truth, modern Britain is as much the product of social continuity as it is of social change, and continuity has been channelled through powerful institutions.

There is no such thing as the unchanging institution: even those, like the monarchy, whose meaning vanishes without their past, have changed radically over time. And the way institutions condition change, and interrelate, is significant in shaping society at large. Without, for instance, the rise of the international financial markets there would be no Super Class; yet nor would it have evolved without the City of London, the professions, the public schools and universities, and the Conservative party, which in the 1980s forged the legal and ideological framework essential for its growth. The Underclass is a similarly complex creation. A product of the collapse of manual employment on the one hand, it has been equally shaped by the inheritance of poverty (of aspiration as much as of income) and by institutions – notably schools and social housing – which reinforce it.

Much of Britain's institutional fabric predates not just the Second World War but the death of Queen Victoria, and even this century's most radical reforming governments can claim only a modest role in reforming it. The NHS is the one major institutional legacy of Attlee's post-war Labour government. The National Lottery may turn out to be the sole big institutional survivor of the Thatcher–Major years. Across the board the tale is of renovation and adaptation as élites holding sway over institutions have sought to protect their positions while co-opting, or being obliged to co-opt, from below.

In a few cases, institutional reform has been pioneered by governments intent on promoting the interests of the less advantaged. The creation of the NHS in 1948 is the classic case, a decisive political act to socialize health care and thereby reduce class inequalities. It did much on both fronts, but far less than generally supposed – largely because politicians and professionals, ever reluctant to talk about class, glibly sustain the myth of a classless NHS which bears little relation to the true position. Aneurin Bevan built the NHS on the foundations of a highly stratified medical profession; and it has remained so since. Thus, for instance, the medical élite of consultants, an integral part of the Super Class, sustains its social standing by doubling or trebling its NHS income from private practice, to which it devotes much of the time and public resources at its disposal under arrangements tacitly endorsed by governments of all parties. As for the health of the nation, it remains sharply differentiated by class: the life expectancy of a child of unskilled manual parents is more than seven years shorter than that of a child from a professional family.

Other reforms inspired by class-eroding goals have had even less success. The textbook failure is the introduction of comprehensive schooling in the sixties and seventies. Generalizations are fraught: in many provincial areas comprehensives helped to promote social integration and improved performance at all levels. But most of England's population is city-bound (a quarter live in London, Manchester and Birmingham and the West Midlands alone), and across metropolitan England, far from spreading classless schools, the comprehensive drive gave a powerful impetus to further segregation. Selection by mortgage replaced selection by the eleven-plus for the best comprehensives; an élite of state grammar schools joined the fee-paying private sector rather than submit to reorganization; and the persistence of chronic failure within the bottom third or more of the school system continued. Year by year, England's schools mould children of low achievers in their parents' image, one in ten school-leavers entering the job market with no paper qualifications at all, most of them barely literate and functionally innumerate. Whereas a generation ago most of this group could count on unskilled work, they are now more likely to find themselves unemployed and virtually unemployable except in the lowest-paid ancillary jobs.

So much for institutional reforms designed to narrow class divisions. Much institutional modernization has had a radically different purpose: to reflect and exploit existing class differences, and thereby in effect (if not stated intention) to entrench them. The evolution of the BBC and the foundation of the National Lottery come into this category. The marketization of broadcasting, starting with the launch of independent television in 1955 and culminating in the cable and satellite revolution of the 1990s, transformed the BBC's ambition to elevate and educate into a mission to top the ratings by giving different classes of viewers what they wanted, within certain bounds. Apart from news, where tight regulation still applies, less attempt is now made by broadcasters to diminish class barriers than at any time in the history of radio and television. Indeed, any such goal is branded patronizing and repugnant in today's vocabulary of fake anti-élitism.

The story of the National Lottery is a particularly compelling commentary on class dynamics in modern Britain. Conceived nearly two decades before it was finally set up by the Major government in 1992, the lottery was the brainchild of the arts and heritage lobbies and their grandee patrons. Their strategy was unashamed and brilliantly successful: to boost their state subsidies in an era of public spending constraint by tying them to the one obvious untapped source of popular taxation, a national lottery. Supported by an alliance of aristocratic grandees and Super Class luminaries, the idea was sold to John Major. Concessions had to be made on the way, notably the inclusion of charities alongside arts and heritage as so-called 'good causes' to share in the largesse. 'Paris was worth a mass and the mass was bringing in the charities,' as David Mellor, the minister-cum-opera-buff responsible for drawing up the lottery legislation, put it with characteristic ebullience.[56] Mass gambling concentrated among the working class – children included – became a 'harmless flutter, all in a good cause', another facet of the 'classless society' (anything but, on examination) with which we are now familiar. Meanwhile the BBC, true to its newfound mission, turned the weekly draw into a popular Saturday-night festival.

It is only a short step from the National Lottery to institutional reforms consciously designed to reinforce class divisions. In the early post-war decades governments were wary of this course, although they did not eschew it entirely. A notable instance was the efforts of Conservative governments to safeguard the House of Lords, which led to Harold Macmillan's 1958 Life Peerages Act and a remarkable aristocratic renaissance in the following decades. However, the most important class-institutional renovation of recent decades has been largely a private sector affair – the reconstruction of Britain's private school system. In the space of barely three decades, the private schools transformed themselves from a disparate and vulnerable collection of institutions, the best known of which were more about inculcating the habits of 'old class' than meritocracy, into a fairly unified structure of 400 private meritocratic academies. Some have been more successful than others, and a certain cachet still attaches to the Etons and Westminsters; but apart from a short tail of institutions which, for instance, cater for less able children, they all see themselves as engaged in the same enterprise: to equip young ABs, together with a minority of children there by dint of parental effort and/or state assistance, with the means to succeed in the meritocratic society. In this they have done more than simply co-opt new money alongside old. The entire basis of privilege has changed. Money and upbringing are no longer enough: effort, education and exams – the 'three Es' of modern meritocracy – are the new order, and the prime job of private schools is to convert money into meritocratic success.

Which brings us to the dwarf, the giant and the hot-air balloon. According to Peter Saunders in *Unequal But Fair?*, the experience of these two aerial adventurers is a metaphor for the benign transformation of modern society. As the dwarf and the giant take off in the balloon, they benefit almost equally from the change of air and view, even though the dwarf never quite reaches the giant's height. 'It is their joint ascent which is in reality far more crucial in determining the quality of the view which they can each now achieve,' argues Saunders. Translating the metaphor, he presents a working class and a middle class which have 'shared equally in a marked improvement in their chances of achieving a high position, and it is this which has arguably had the major impact on our lives' over recent generations.[57]

But the dwarf and the giant feature in another modern morality tale. The Dutch economist Jan Pen imagines a God who stretches or squashes people's heights according to their incomes. Average income meaning average height, the result is 'a parade of dwarfs and a few giants', the giants being 'colossal figures: people like tower flats measured in miles . . . their heads disappear into the clouds and probably they themselves do not know how rich they are'.[58] In Jan Pen's balloon the dwarf and the giant do not share remotely the same view as they rise, since the height difference between them is so great to start with.

This is the more meaningful metaphor for Britain today. For all the change and social mobility of recent decades, including the rise of a unified consumer and popular culture, the separation of classes remains one of the key facts about modern Britain. And segregation has become more, not less, marked in the last generation as a large and distinct lower class has separated from the old working class, while a smaller but equally distinct and immensely powerful Super Class has taken off at the top. As for the middling majority, the perception of being sandwiched between the Underclass and the Super Class is strong and growing, animating the manifold distinctions, fears and ambitions which have always dominated middle-class life.

Classless fantasies – whether of the Marxist or the neo-liberal variety – are the bane of social progress, and nowhere more so than in Britain: impossible as a goal, they are ludicrous and deeply damaging as a view of society today. The only constructive way forward is to recognize Britain's deep class divisions for what they are: a product not just of the human impulses to dominate, differentiate, advance and specialize, but of those impulses fortified by powerful élites and institutions, the most class-segregated education system in the western world, and hereditary privilege extending from the old aristocracy to the new Super Class and beyond.

There are no quick fixes, no blueprints; and if there are plenty of radical ideological experiments waiting to be tried, the experience of the twentieth century may, perhaps, teach the twenty-first to be a little cautious and sceptical. But a governing philosophy rooted in the British 'one nation' tradition of incremental social improvement should be addressing the two most acute class problems of the day: the growing divorce of the Super Class from society at large, and the condition of what we call the 'failing third' at the bottom. As it does so, Britain may in time become a less class-divided and unequal society.

2. EDUCATION

Degrees of class

The failure of boys, and in particular white working-class boys, is one of the most disturbing problems we face within the whole education system.

Chris Woodhead, Her Majesty's Chief Inspector of Schools, 1996

I'm afraid that Darren, Dean, Damian, Liam and Nathan can't do it, never will do it, and frankly would not give a damn if they don't do it at all.

Nigel Turner, teacher at William Crane Comprehensive School, Nottingham (where 8 per cent of children achieve five GCSE passes at grades A to C), at the National Association of Schoolmasters Conference, April 1997

Can economic renewal be sustained when Britain's schools are vehicles for the transmission of an atavistic class culture? How can Britain become one nation so long as it has a two-nation schooling system? How can we pretend to any kind of modernity so long as we are schooled into belonging to tribes and castes?

John Gray, *Times Literary Supplement*, 9 May 1997

A week after John Major took office in 1990, an astute *Sunday Telegraph* reporter spent a day at the Prime Minister's *alma mater*, Rutlish School in Brixton. He wanted to find out what the school's brightest sixth-formers thought about the 'classless society'.

> The boys ... were from middle-class families, sons of teachers, a dentist, a civil engineer. They planned to read languages and music (at university). They wanted to work in the media, or in music, or to do a job that allowed them to travel.
>
> These were the sort of sophisticated, metropolitan sixteen- and seventeen-year-olds who are often said to find class

differences irrelevant, even to deny that such a thing exists. Interestingly, the more they talked, the more clearly they defined their own class consciousness and, while rejecting such divisions, the more clearly they decided nothing would change.

'We do feel we are middle class,' said Michael Ahmed, sixteen, who plans to study music, and who works for a DIY chain on Sundays.

'Enlightened middle class,' said Andrew Spencer, seven-teen, applying to read languages. 'Going to a comprehensive [Rutlish went comprehensive in 1969], we are not shielded from working-class people. It's not an élitist system with wealth or intellect dividing us.'

'I try to blend in at work. I try to hide my middle classness. I am embarrassed about it,' said Michael.

'If John Major wants a classless society then he'll have to abolish the public school sector,' said Paul Carey, seventeen. 'We can't have equal opportunities with two different sectors. If that's what he wants, then toes will have to be trodden on.' Liam Kennedy, seventeen, agreed, Michael and Andrew shrank from such radicalism: 'You can't just abolish the public school system. You have to build a better state system to attract people in, then there won't be a need for the private system,' said Andrew. 'There is prejudice in the system. People are still biased towards people who've been educated in the public school system,' said Liam.

All said they instantly recognised the origins of the public school boys they met: 'You feel different from them. It's not equal. They start off on a different level,' said Michael. 'It's not necessarily intelligence, it's more attitude. I still see them on an equal basis – perhaps that's because I play rugby,' said Andrew. 'You do tend to have prejudices: public school boys tend to feel superior,' said Liam.

They knew boys from primary school who were now at public schools because the state system was not working properly. How many in the Cabinet had been to public school? Who among them sent their children to state schools?

So what would create the classless society of opportunity envisaged by the Prime Minister? 'A complete overhaul of the education system,' said Paul. Michael nodded. 'To attract back people from the public school sector,' said Andrew. 'As long as it exists it will attract the élite,' finished Liam.[1]

We can begin by answering the Rutlish boys' questions. All but four of the members of the 1990 Conservative Cabinet were educated at private schools. Virtually all of those with children educated them privately. As for the Labour party, Tony Blair is a public schoolboy (Fettes College, Scotland's Eton) with an Oxford degree, whose appeal to Middle England is based upon his being neither a Scot nor working class. To underline the point, he sends his eldest son to a highly academic Catholic school – eight miles from his old inner London home – which, although in the state sector, has opted out of local authority control and practises selection by parental interview.

Education is the engine of social mobility, and Britain's – particularly England's – education system does not remotely provide equality of opportunity. A 1996 study on social mobility by the Institute for Fiscal Studies put it bluntly: 'Bright children do seem to have a better chance of escaping low incomes ... There is a clear correlation between high mobility up the income distribution and a high level of educational attainment. Non-movers are almost five times as likely to have no qualifications as big movers; at the other end of the scale, big movers are more than seven times as likely to have A-levels or better than non-movers are.'[2]

This chapter tells the story of English education since the 1950s. Like its subject, it is rigidly segmented. The first section describes the Premier Division: the private school sector, catering mainly for the nation's professional and managerial classes. We then move on to the Second Class state sector, which educates 'the other 93 per cent' of the school-age population. In the third section we examine higher education, where an equally rigid hierarchy holds sway, although within a formally unified university structure. England, not the UK as a whole, is our focus, because it is in England that the class-intensifying properties of the education system are starkest.

English apartheid

Since democracy reached South Africa, the term 'apartheid' has been looking for other regimes to damn. It has found one in England: the national school system.[3] English educational apartheid has two faces: a separation of *classes*, and a separation of *systems*. On both fronts the word apartheid is a gross exaggeration, since in neither case is the separation total or founded in law. It should be seen rather as emotive shorthand – schools being the one subject besides sport which generates emotion among the English – for a school system which, more than any other in the western world, is founded on a division between state and private. The wealthy have an educational head start the world over, but in England the division is singularly entrenched. America has its private schools and expensive Ivy League universities; Japan has its armies of private tutors; across Europe, parents' status and support are a boon to their offspring. What marks England out is the degree to which its schools segregate the socially advantaged from the rest. In most systems, money makes a fundamental difference to opportunities only at university level, by when the basis for success has been established (or not). In England, by contrast, money matters when it counts most: at school, from five to eighteen. For the English, nearly free universities are largely a state subsidy and reward for those who have paid their way to get there. This has little to do with academic élitism or selection: the top French *lycées* and German *Gymnasien* are unashamedly élitist, yet they are integral to a state school system whose fate is of vital concern to the French and German chattering classes and policy-makers. In England, by contrast, few members of the élite have a close personal interest in the success of the state school system.

At the top of the English school pyramid come the private, fee-paying, schools. Then come grant-maintained (or opted-out) schools, funded directly by central government and free of Local Education Authority (LEA) control. Third are the 'voluntary' schools, owned by religious institutions but funded by either the LEA or central government. These may or may not select pupils according to their religion. Fourth comes the most common type of school: LEA-controlled comprehensive schools, with no selection (other than by gender in a small number). These four categories comprise the overwhelming majority of schools, but there are another six types of schools left: the 161 remaining grammar schools; a small number of 'specialist' schools, partly funded by central government or LEAs and partly by outside sources (such as City Technology Colleges and Paul McCartney's 'fame' school in Liverpool, which draw in business funding); 'special' schools, funded by LEAs, which select on the basis of disability; 'units' where disruptive children are educated; home-based and hospital tuition funded by LEAs (for invalids and the sick); and finally home education supervised, funded and often carried out by parents.

We saw in the first chapter how entrenched the independent school sector has become in the meritocratic exam leagues. Everyone knows this: surveys repeatedly show that a majority of parents who cannot afford to pay private school fees would jump at the chance to send their children to a private school. A typical poll found that only 40 per cent would stick to the state sector if they had the money to go private.[4]

Yet it was only relatively recently that private schools started to fashion themselves as exam hothouses. In their traditional role as bastions of privilege, cricket and rugger were the core curriculum. It was *who* you knew that counted, not *what*. Private schools were only for 'people like us': grammar schools looked after the able rest. Today they claim to be just like any other service provider – available to anyone who can pay the fee. Certainly, aside from the Etons and Winchesters, few private schools go out of their way to exhibit their social exclusivity. Although a survey in 1993 by Mori found that most private school parents had a gross annual income of more than £40,000 (they have, after all, to be able to pay the fees), it also showed that a majority of parents had not themselves attended private schools, a far cry from a generation earlier. Rather, the new upper professional and managerial class, however its members were educated themselves, has decamped en masse to the private sector.

The census does not ask about the education of children, so exact class correlations are not possible. But two figures are deeply suggestive: the 1991 census identified 740,000 school-aged children from professional, managerial and skilled non-manual households in the UK as a whole, which can be set alongside the 610,000 children attending private schools.[5] Not all of the first group can afford school fees, and some of the latter are from abroad, or on assisted places subsidized by the government. But it is clear enough that most parents who can fairly easily afford to leave the state school system do so.

In some cases they have literally taken their schools with them, as the leading direct-grant schools (which were self-governing but state funded in return for taking scholarship pupils from state primary schools) left the state sector in the 1970s rather than abandon selection. In the post-war decades direct-grant schools such as Dulwich College provided a far more effective bridge between the state and private sectors than the more recent assisted places scheme. The direct-grant scheme succeeded, without any fanfare, in opening up many of the best independent schools to ability rather than wealth. It is a sad irony that in destroying the direct-grant schools on the altar of equal opportunity, the 1974–9 Labour government succeeded only in denying opportunity to many poor children and increasing the number of fee-paying parents. From then on, for any parent concerned to secure a rigorously academic education for his child, there was generally little choice but to go private. While the total school roll fell during the eighties, the number of children in private schooling rose. In 1978 5.8 per cent of children were privately educated; in 1997 the figure stands at over 7 per cent, despite hard times for many private schools and their parents in the recession of the early nineties.

Change usually seems predestined after the event, and so it is with the contemporary dominance of the public schools. But there was nothing inevitable about this transformation, a product of institutional renovation, class dynamics and government policy, all three intertwined over more than a century of educational evolution. Adaptation is the leitmotif: private schools, once regarded as a monolith of ancient privilege, have in reality proved highly adaptable élite institutions.

The purpose of the traditional Victorian public school was to produce 'good chaps': dependable, solid men with the requisite 'character' for their class, whether inherited or adoptive. As Old Squire Brown put it in Thomas Hughes' *Tom Brown's Schooldays*: 'I don't care a straw for Greek particles, or the digamma, no more does his mother. What is he sent to school for? Well, partly because he wanted so to go. If he'll only turn out a brave, helpful, truth-telling Englishman, and a gentleman, and a Christian, that's all I want.' The first great expansion in private schooling, in the second half of the nineteenth century, was driven by a new middle class that wanted to spend its money on an education conferring the requisite class manners and entrée on its children. Knowledge of manners, not maths, was the demand of the era, and public schools were there to provide it.

But demands were changing. In the 1860s the Clarendon Commission, set up to investigate Eton, Winchester, Harrow, Westminster, St Paul's, Charterhouse, Merchant Taylor's, Rugby and Shrewsbury, railed against an academic education which was 'a failure even if tested by those better specimens, not exceeding one-third of the whole, who go up to the Universities'.[6] The commission's syllabus reforms – languages, maths, science, history and art or music – became the foundation both for new schools established to cater for the expanding professional class, and for the traditional private schools whose offspring were now required to pass competitive examinations to gain entry into the army and the civil service. Thus adapted, the public schools were good for the first decades of the present century, well able to hold their own against the slow, piecemeal rise of the state secondary school sector. For George Orwell,

> the year is 1910 – or 1940, but it is all the same. You are at Greyfriars, a rosy-cheeked boy of fourteen in posh, tailor-made clothes, sitting down to tea in your study in the Remove passage after an exciting game of football . . . The king is on his throne and the pound is worth a pound . . . Everything is safe, solid and unquestionable. Everything will be the same for ever and ever.[7]

But then came the social levelling of the Second World War, and a crisis of confidence extending beyond the old aristocracy to embrace the solid professional class. Rumblings of dissent had been evident since the First World War, not least in the radical writings of Robert Graves and Graham Greene. The defeat of the British Expeditionary Force in France even led T. C. Worsley, a master at Wellington, to declare: 'If the public schools are national assets because of their leadership training qualities, what are we to think of those qualities when we survey the mess into which their leadership has brought us?'[8] The demise of the public schools was widely prophesied, even before the 1945 election swept an avowedly socialist government to power. It was Churchill himself who, in 1940, had told the boys of his old school, Harrow, that 'After the war the (social) advantages of the public schools must be extended on a far broader basis.'[9] The mood of the times went hand-in-hand with brute economics. 'It was feared,' wrote Michael Young, author of Labour's 1945 manifesto, 'that impoverishment of the middle classes would remove their capacity to pay fees, and some of the strongest supporters of the public schools looked to the state to prevent catastrophe. They were not only ready to accept a proportion of poor pupils, they pleaded with the state to pay for their places.'[10]

The fears proved groundless. Nicholas Timmins, in his biography of the welfare state, views R. A. Butler's wartime failure to reform the public schools in his 1944 Education Act as 'a great lost opportunity. The combination of financial crisis in the public schools themselves and widespread criticism of their role and performance in the early 1940s provided the only time in the twentieth century when the political will and political votes to integrate them into the national education system just might have been assembled'.[11] Butler took the first tentative step, establishing an official inquiry into the subject which, like the Beveridge committee on national insurance, was given a brief to produce a grand plan if it so chose. But Lord Fleming, its dour and unimaginative chairman, was no Beveridge: he deliberated for two years, issued his report a matter of days after the passage of the 1944 Act, and produced a damp squib of a scheme for uniting the state and private sectors. As Butler put it, 'the first class carriage had been shunted on to an immense siding'.[12] It might easily have been hauled back on to the main line by the post-war Labour government, with its huge majority and reformist mission, but Clement Attlee, Haileybury and proud of it, attached no urgency to the issue. In the public schools, as in the army, Whitehall, the House of Lords and the monarchy, the old élite behaved with enough circumspection to keep reform at bay, while sustaining its collective confidence sufficiently to want to keep its old institutions intact. The moment for transformation from above had passed, and by the early 1950s had passed irrevocably. As Michael Young observed: 'The middle class proved as tough as ever; they survived high taxation and high prices and went on sending their children to the same old venerable schools. In the middle 1950s, of people with more than £1,000 p.a. – a miserable enough sum by modern standards – nineteen out of every twenty sent their children to private schools.'[13]

The egalitarian educational reforms of the 1960s, notably the replacement of grammar schools by comprehensives, precipitated the next decisive phase of adaptation: the conversion of the public schools into fully fledged meritocratic academies. The speed of the process needs emphasizing. In the late 1960s the state grammar schools and quasi-state direct-grant schools were intact, and together easily outclassed the independent sector in terms of academic output. The proportion of public-school-educated undergraduates at Oxford was, for instance, on a steady downward path after the Second World War. In 1946 65 per cent of male arts students were from independent schools. By 1967 the proportion had fallen to 58 per cent. The pattern was even clearer with women, the share falling from 57 per cent of arts undergraduates in 1946 to 39 per cent in 1967.[14] Yet the next decade saw both these meritocratic pillars of the state school system collapse. In 1971 35 per cent of all state schools were comprehensive; in 1981 the figure was 90 per cent, by when virtually all the former direct-grant schools had become fully part of the private sector. Moreover, it was amid this upheaval in the 1970s that higher education became *de rigueur* for aspiring professionals, even in such generally academically undemanding lines as accountancy, stockbroking and estate management, where a generation before a degree was unnecessary if not positively egregious. The demands of the dispossessed metropolitan middle classes and the rich-must-have-degree were at one, to be met by public schools targeting their resources on 'academic value added', appropriating at least a modicum of the old grammar school ethos in the process. The transfer of leading city grammar schools into the private sector, fleeing the same egalitarian tide, gave a powerful impetus to reform. To take a typical case, when Bristol's top grammar school went private rather than comprehensive in the mid-1970s, Clifton College, the city's leading 'public' school, found itself charging fees twice as high while achieving far less impressive exam results. Clifton's buildings were grander, its rugby fiercer and it was a boarding-rather than a day-school: but parents wanted exam grades too, even for their less able offspring. Clifton adapted accordingly – 'painfully in many respects, but with no sense of there being an alternative', in the words of one senior master.[15] Upgrading both its results and its facilities, admitting girls in the sixth form and some day pupils alongside the boarders, by the late 1980s it was marketing itself on a package of exam results, sports, boarding and facilities (including a newly built theatre), not to mention its surviving cachet.

If the combination of changing parental requirements, crisis in the state sector and the defection of the direct-grant schools was the transformative tonic of the 1960s and 1970s, the publication of league tables gave a similar boost to the private sector in the 1990s. Most of the old public schools were selective and exam-oriented enough to reach the top few hundred schools nationwide in the first league tables appearing in 1991 and 1992. By then Eton boasted twenty members of staff with PhDs, more than many Oxbridge colleges. Competition was mostly between private schools, not between the state and private sectors. But the publication of rankings, during a severe recession hitting demand, increased the pressure on individual schools to sharpen their performance further still. Clifton, for instance, was still far below Bristol Grammar in the 1991 league tables, a pattern repeated in many other cities. The minds of governors and head teachers were concentrated wonderfully. In 1996 the headmaster of Cheltenham College was sacked because the school was not high enough in the league tables – a defining moment.

A few facts will put the status quo into perspective. The 1995 league tables show pupils at the top ten private schools securing an averaged A-level score of two As and one B. The next fifty average three Bs, while the independent secondary sector as a whole – some 500 schools – produced an average of one B and two Cs. Eighty per cent of fifteen-year-olds at private schools achieved five or more grade A–C passes at GCSE, against a national average of 43 per cent; and 80 per cent of private school pupils gained three or more A-level passes, against 58 per cent of candidates as a whole (and the latter figure is, of course, boosted by the inclusion of private school results). Finally, almost 90 per cent of private pupils go on to higher education, comprising 25 per cent of all university entrants.[16] Private schools in the 1990s boast theatres, orchestras, language facilities and science labs superior to those of many universities. Their teachers are on average better paid, qualified and motivated than their state counterparts, and significantly so in the top private schools. The private sector markets itself professionally as a service business offering successful child development as its product. It is, of course, a two-way contract. Commitment and motivation among parents and pupils are prerequisites: but unless they were forthcoming from at least one, and in most cases both, of the parties, little Johnny or Lucy would not be in a private school to start with, paying fees averaging (in 1996) £6,150 per annum for day-schools, and £10,500 for boarding.[17]

This picture can be extended to primary schools. National test results in English, for instance, show that a fifth of private school pupils aged eleven are four years ahead of what is expected for their age. Almost one in four fee-paying pupils was awarded the top grade in national spelling and handwriting tests for eleven-year-olds.[18] The contrast with many state schools could not be starker. Four out of five eleven-year-olds in Islington, for example, cannot pass even a basic reading test. 'We are,' as one Islington teacher puts it, 'condemning these children to the dustbin of society.'[19]

An important aspect of the meritocratic reformation of the private sector has been the change within girls' schools. Although a small number boast a long tradition of training for universities, most of them were previously little more than finishing schools for 'ladies'. As recently as 1985 far fewer female than male pupils achieved three A-level passes (41 per cent as opposed to 54 per cent of all those entered). By 1990 the gap had narrowed to 69 per cent and 72 per cent respectively. In 1995 more girls than boys entered private day-schools and each year sees a steady increase in the number of boys' schools going co-educational.[20]

In the 1950s and 60s the children of prosperous Jewish immigrants began to be a common sight at many of the lesser public schools (the major schools were usually financially secure enough to be able to reject what they saw as ill-fitting Jews; the minor schools could not afford to be choosy), fostered by the traditional Jewish emphasis on education as a means of self-advancement. By the 1980s it was an unusual private school that did not have a substantial Jewish presence. Asians, on the other hand, were scarcely to be seen. But the adaptation of the independent schools has not stopped, and their current phase of change is focused on meeting the educational demands of England's more socially ambitious black and Asian communities. The late 1980s and the 1990s have seen a tremendous increase in the number of Asian pupils, in particular. As one private school teacher put it: 'When I began teaching in 1981, you could literally count the number of black faces in the school on the fingers of one hand. Today it is so normal to have black pupils that you don't notice the colour of their skin.'[21] Patel is now the commonest name on the register at Dulwich College in south-east London.

For all the emphasis on meritocracy, the public school tradition remains strong – if understated. Few parents would want it otherwise: it is a large part of the product for which they are paying. As Michael Mavor, headmaster of Gordonstoun (the Prince of Wales' *alma mater*), wrote to *The Times* in 1989: 'What heads, deputy heads and those who run boarding schools spend most time doing is trying to instil in teenage boys and girls a real sense of decency, straightforwardness, common sense and loyalty.'[22] There is no great sentimentality about the job. David Newsome, a former headmaster of Wellington, declared in some exasperation: 'When I observe the shallow materialism of some of the homes from which our boys come, and the glib expectation that a school such as mine will provide the culture, sensitivity and spirituality that are so flagrantly inconspicuous in the domestic *mise-en-scène*, I feel a twinge of despair.'[23] But should the despair triumph, there can always be a change of head: long headmasterly reigns have become a thing of the past in today's high-pressured schools.

It is often said, dismissively, that 'only' 7 per cent of school-age children are at private schools, as though their parents are somehow atypical, marginal, unusually selfish, or all three. But think about this. 'Only' 7 per cent means some 610,000 pupils and more than one million parents. The pupils represent a large part of the academic cream of their generation; the parents constitute a majority of those with children among the higher professional and managerial class, and include virtually all of the Super Class parents we shall meet in the next chapter. Accordingly, on almost any measure of élite position one wishes to take, the private schools sweep all before them: seven out of nine foremost generals, thirty-three out of thirty-nine of the most senior judges; and so it goes on. The Roll of Honour at Sandhurst, the training college for Britain's military élite for more than a century, is a public school directory. Of the 180 new officers who passed out in August 1995, more than 120 were privately educated. A quarter came from just fifteen institutions: Eton and Radley headed the list with six officers apiece; Ampleforth and Wellington College had nine between them; Rugby, Tonbridge, Cheltenham and St Edward's, Oxford, boasted three each; Harrow, Winchester, Marlborough, Haileybury, Charterhouse, Sherborne and Brighton College managed two each.

And in case it is objected that the law and the army remain atypical bastions of the pre-meritocratic élite, consider the civil service, second to none in its efforts to recruit the brightest and best from a broad social spectrum. At the end of 1995 half of the eighteen permanent secretaries were educated at private schools. As for the future, of the ninety-four Grade Three officials then aged under fifty, just over half (fifty) attended state schools. Half and half: that seems relatively good. However, among the fifty who were state educated, the great majority went to grammar schools whose character has changed out of recognition since they attended them. Twenty-six grammar schools feature on the list, with Manchester Grammar School alone accounting for four of the fifty (as many as Eton). Of these twenty-six grammar schools, seven have since gone private, including Manchester Grammar. Only one remains as a state grammar school, while the other eighteen have either gone comprehensive or disappeared altogether. There is little comfort to be had even among the state school alumni.

As for the political élite, the Conservative party is firmly in the grip of private schools. Of the twenty-three Cabinet ministers at the end of the Major government in 1997, eighteen were privately educated (and seventeen attended Oxbridge). A product of neither, John Major headed a tiny minority in his own government, which is perhaps why he was able to discourse on the 'classless society' with a straight face. And a rapprochement with the private schools is one of the hallmarks of New Labour. When David Blunkett appeared early in 1995 to suggest that Labour might tax school fees, the idea was publicly disowned by Tony Blair. The Blairs' eldest son, Euan, attends the London Oratory school – a selective, grant-maintained school. Harriet Harman sends one son to the same school as Euan Blair and the other on a fourteen-mile journey to St Olave's grammar school – about as close to the private sector as one can get without paying fees.

What about the Conservatives' assisted places scheme, trumpeted throughout the 1980s as the means to make the private schools classless? Introduced in 1981, by 1996 the scheme applied to 294 schools, which received £115 million a year between them. Few of those who have gained decry the experience. As one parent, who was a persistent truant and left school with four O-levels, put it in an interview:

> It was a friend of mine from a very different walk of life who taught me about the importance of education. He had a very high regard for James Allen's Girls School, and told us about the assisted places scheme. Our twins sat the entrance exam,

they got in, we took it from there. I've another daughter, a year older, who is at a local (state) school. Her teachers say she is doing well, but the work she and the twins do is worlds apart; it's very disappointing. I feel grateful for the opportunity we've had. Every child deserves that sort of education. I hope the twins will go on to university. I know what makes the world go round now and frankly I'm ashamed of myself: ashamed of my accent, ashamed of the area we live in. I don't want my girls to experience that.[24]

None the less, there is good reason to think that the scheme has largely been a subsidy for the middle classes who have fallen prey to hard times or creative accountants. A 1995 Mori poll revealed awareness of the scheme to stand at 70 per cent for social classes A and B, while among those it was designed to help – the C2s, Ds and Es – it was a mere 30 per cent. Between 1981 and 1996 it helped just 70,000 children.

Marginal though its impact was, its abolition will make the social composition of private schools still more uniform. Martin Stephen, high master of Manchester Grammar School, one of England's leading former direct-grant schools, private since the mid-1970s, spoke for many fellow heads when he observed that his school, with its reputation and results, could replace its 300 assisted place pupils with no difficulty, but that the school would merely become still more divorced from its roots and wider society if it did so. 'For me, the importance of the scheme is that it contributes to a culture where the entry requirement is intelligence not parental income,' he said, eliding the fact that the majority of his pupils, judging by their achievements, appeared to combine intelligence and parental income in fairly equal measure.[25] But then, as we noted in the introductory chapter, money, motivation and the ability to pass exams are far more closely related than many meritocrats would have us believe.

Sometimes simple statistics can speak volumes:

Table 4: Figures for state and private schools

	State	Private
Number of UK schools	31,000	2,540
Number of pupils	8,883,000	610,000
Cost per secondary pupil	£2,250	£3,600–£8,700 (day)
Pupil:teacher ratios	18:4	9:8
A-level results		
% of all A grades, 1994	59	41
GCSE physics		
% of all candidates, 1995	41	59
GCSE physics		
% of all A grades, 1995	32	68
A-level classics		
% of all candidates	10	90
Entry to higher education (%)	27	88
Oxbridge:		
% of all entrants, 1994	54	46

Source: George Walden, *We Should Know Better*, 1996, p. 43.

State system, second class

'The class system has never recovered from Rab Butler's Education Act of 1944, and its condition is now terminal,' says Dr Eric Anderson, then headmaster of Eton and now rector of Lincoln College, Oxford.[26] This is about as clear a misreading of the situation as it is possible to imagine. One in five seven-year-olds in London state schools scores zero in reading tests. In state schools serving the most disadvantaged areas, less than 15 per cent of pupils achieve five or more GCSE grades A–C. The best schools in such areas achieve average GCSE scores per pupil which are just one-third of that of schools in more advantaged areas.[27] On average, children of parents in social groups D and E obtain only a third as many GCSE grades A–C as do state-educated children from higher social groups.[28] The plain fact is that the divide between state and private schools is today stronger than at any other time since 1945. The divide between the classes is not narrowing, as the educational reformers of the 1950s and 60s assured us it would following the introduction of comprehensive schools, but widening, as those at the top perform steadily better in their private and selective state schools, while the mass of 'white working-class males' – to take the group defined by Chris Woodhead, the Chief Inspector of Schools – continue to languish in an almost anti-education culture in underperforming comprehensive schools. The comprehensive revolution has not removed the link between education and class but strengthened it. The revolution which afflicted state schooling from the 1960s is one of the most profound and incendiary factors influencing the state of British society. It was not merely a technical educational change, but changed the nature of the country.

Our argument – that money buys a good education and the opportunities that follow, and that the absence of money denies them – is objected to on the grounds that not all state schools are bad, and not all private schools good. This is quite true. But as George Walden points out, 'In our culture of evasion we cling to the exceptions for dear life, and treat them not as proving the rule, but as casting doubt on it. The statement that the grass is green could be equally well contested on the grounds that we have all seen yellow or brown patches.'[29] The statistics we have already cited show the truth of the maxim. According to the *Independent on Sunday*'s survey of the link between house prices and high-performing state schools in December 1996, the truth is clearer still:

> The premiums in some towns for a top-school catchment area house are so high that families are paying up to 30 per cent more than the price for a similar property in an adjoining, but non-catchment neighbourhood . . . In St Albans, Hertfordshire, local estate agents have spotted the . . . effect on prices . . . Parents are particularly keen to get their daughters into St Albans Girls School, which was the fourth most successful comprehensive school in the ratings of schools.[30]

And a survey by the estate agents Knight Frank and Rutley in 1995 also found that the presence of a good state school has a marked effect on house prices – and revealed a significant increase in the numbers of people moving to be near the best remaining state grammar schools, such as in Guildford, Tunbridge Wells and Beaconsfield, a process which reinforces this trend.

Furthermore, the contrast between the physical condition of state and private schools is marked. Consider Broadoak Secondary School in Weston-super-Mare – founded in the 1930s – a typical state school. In 1992 engineers condemned the building, warning that the core would last only until 1998. The school was bombed in the Blitz, and the 'temporary' corrugated iron roofs put up in 1942 are still there. The boilers, a long-time cause of concern, broke down in April 1995 – but work to repair them only began seven months later. The basic necessary repairs to the school have been estimated by contractors at £10 million.[31] This is no isolated case: the National Audit Office reported in 1988 a £2 billion backlog of school maintenance across the country.[32]

In 1965 the Labour-controlled House of Commons resolved that moving to a comprehensive system would 'preserve all that is valuable in grammar school education for those children who now receive it and make it available to more children'. Few would maintain that this has in fact been the case. Roy Hattersley – a last-ditch defender of the comprehensive revolution – has written of one school that

> the low esteem of some London comprehensive schools has . . . complicated causes. Islington Green illustrates most of them. The liabilities begin with the first impression that the school creates. Islington Green Comprehensive School looks awful . . . The main building is six storeys of glass and concrete . . . Two lift towers – windowless and weather-stained – dominate one side of the façade. The lifts within them are used only by staff and handicapped students. Islington Council cannot afford the cost of constant repair and re-

novation . . . There are no playing fields at Islington Green.[33]

There is, of course, always a danger of argument by anecdote, and there is no denying that the situation is radically different in small-town provincial England. But most of England's population lives in large conurbations, and it is where most people live that the state schools are worst. A survey in 1996 by the moderate teachers' union, the Association of Teachers and Lecturers, found that 88 per cent of its member teachers said that schools in their area were overcrowded, 92 per cent had temporary classrooms, and 36 per cent still had outside toilets.[34] Britain devotes 3.9 per cent of public capital expenditure to school buildings and infrastructure, compared with an EU average of almost 8 per cent. Capital spending on schools is today half what it was twenty years ago. For much of the 1980s it was a third of 1974–5 spending; in 1974–5 £1.82 billion was spent, in 1984–5 the figure was £604 million (in real terms).[35] As Chris Woodhead put it in his 1996 report: 'At least one primary school in seven and one secondary school in five suffers from some shortfall in accommodation such as cramped classroom spaces, poor or non-existent facilities for art, design and technology or science and cramped playgrounds' (the very categories which private schools sell themselves on). He continued: 'Teachers who work in poor buildings experience problems which at best frustrate and at worst defeat their attempts to do a proper job.'[36]

But there is, as Tony and Cherie Blair spotted, one 'get out of jail free card' (as Anne McElvoy of the *Spectator* puts it) for parents who want to ensure a decent state education for their children: the remaining 161 grammar schools, and the top Church secondary schools, as well as the comprehensive former grammar schools that have managed to cling on to their old ethos and standards. To take the Catholic schools, McElvoy has described

the new sect (that) has emerged within the Catholic Church, namely the 'Educatholics', whose devotion is closely linked to their understandable anxieties about British education

... who considered themselves 'lapsed' until they reached child-bearing age ... The truly keen drag themselves to the thinly attended 8 a.m. Mass ... 'More chance of being noticed by the Reverend,' explains an Islington acquaintance ... The practice is rife in N1 [Islington] because the state schools are so dire there.

Catholic schools enjoy the benefit of selection (all prospective parents and children attend an interview, formally to check out their Catholic credentials), whilst in theory describing themselves as 'all ability' – an interesting play on words since even the most selective school 'mixes' ability. As McElvoy writes, 'You can justifiably continue to prescribe the local comprehensive with its Ecstasy problem and random violence, for non-Catholics, on the grounds that it "needs more middle-class intake to make it better", while your own children learn Latin and sing in the Messiah.'[37]

So bad is the situation that the Chief Inspector of Schools feels compelled to write that

the failure of boys, and in particular white working-class boys, is one of the most disturbing problems we face within the whole education system. Research shows that white working-class boys are the least likely to participate in full-time education after the age of sixteen, and that white boys are the most likely to be completely unqualified on leaving compulsory education ... The fact is that our most disadvantaged children, especially boys, remain disadvantaged at the end of their schooling.[38]

The very children most dependent upon state education are thus the children most failed by the system.

What went wrong? Grammar schools, formally opened to all who were bright enough by Butler's Act, enabled a proportion of working-class children to mix with their similarly able middle-class peers. That is why the 1944 Education Act, which enshrined the idea of a grammar school place for the intellectually able rather than the socially well connected, was the culmination of the arguments of socialists such as Sidney Webb and R. H. Tawney. The challenge for the next generation was to widen access to grammar schools, while extending their ethos and emphasis on qualifications and standards to the secondary modern sector, emulating the achievement of Germany and Holland in particular, with their vocational schools. The comprehensive revolution, tragically, destroyed much of the excellent without improving the rest. Comprehensive schools have largely replaced selection by ability with selection by class and house price. Middle-class children now go to middle-class comprehensives, whose catchment areas comprise middle-class neighbourhoods, while working-class children are mostly left to fester in the inner-city comprehensive their parents cannot afford to move away from.

Far from bringing the classes together, England's schools – private and state – are now a force for rigorous segregation.

The Ivy Class League

Universities are fashioned by the schools that supply them. It should come as no surprise, then, that England's foremost universities are dominated by the country's private schools and a tiny subset of its most successful – mainly selective – state schools.

Until the Second World War it was taken for granted that Oxford and Cambridge were as much bastions of class privilege as the public schools from which they recruited. Of those men entering Oxford in 1938, 55.2 per cent came from private boarding-schools and 12.6 per cent from direct-grant schools – a total of 74.6 per cent from the private sector, and only 19.2 per cent from the state sector.[39] The passing of the 1944 Education Act, with its meritocratic lien, and the rise of the 'grammar school boy', changed this. For if Oxford and Cambridge were to maintain their academic pre-eminence, they had no alternative but to increase dramatically the proportion of places awarded to state school children – and so drastically reduce the share of places awarded to private schools. Oxbridge rapidly expanded its provision of scholarships and exhibitions to secure academic talent from the state grammar schools. By the 1960s, with the creation, thanks to the Robbins Report, of the redbrick universities such as Essex, Keele and Sussex, Oxbridge colleges were faced with an entirely new phenomenon – the belief that university education was a right for all, based on talent, and not a privilege for the few, based on breeding. Thus, by 1965 the state sector – excluding direct-grant schools – supplied 40.2 per cent of men and 42.7 per cent of women going up to Oxford – although, compared with the university sector as a whole, there was still a long way to go: in 1963 state schools accounted for 64 per cent of men and 72 per cent of women who secured places in all British universities.[40]

Modern mythology has it that the number of privately educated children at Oxbridge is on a steadily declining path. And indeed it *was* – in the heyday of the state grammar schools in the 1960s. By 1969 only 38 per cent of places at Oxford were awarded to privately educated children – a sharp reduction for the private schools even on their 1965 proportion. And yet in the 1990s, thanks to the destruction of the grammar schools and the consequent decamping to the private sector of many of the most able children, the figure now hovers around the 50 per cent mark. Beneath these bare figures, of course, lies the reality that, even within the state sector, the only realistic opportunity of getting to Oxbridge is to be educated in an élite school. In 1993 ten private schools accounted for 6 per cent (233 students) of Cambridge freshers. The top state schools – Royal Grammar School, High Wycombe, and Colchester County High School – sent 8.4 per cent and 11.3 per cent respectively of their final year pupils to Cambridge. Westminster, the top private school, sent forty-four pupils – a third of its leavers.[41] Eton regularly sends between seventy and eighty to Oxbridge, out of an upper sixth of about 250, and recently sent 102.

There is an element of self-selection here. Many of the freshers who apply to one of the 119 other universities, whether traditional, such as Durham and London, or redbrick, or one of the former polytechnics, have academic qualifications to match those who get into Oxbridge. But such is the exclusivity of Oxbridge – by reputation, whatever the reality – that they simply do not regard themselves or, more tellingly, are not regarded by their school, as 'Oxbridge material'. Oxford is for them, Essex is for us. This explains the apparent paradox that while several other universities have six or more applicants for each place, only two or three compete for an Oxbridge place. This is just one of the many ways in which the psychological class segregation which characterizes British class and society at large starts in the education system. Edward Shils wrote in 1955: 'If a young man, talking to an educated stranger, refers to his university studies, he is asked "Oxford or Cambridge?" And if he says Aberystwyth or Nottingham, there is disappointment on the one side and embarrassment on the other.'[42] Not much has changed since. As A. H. Halsey puts it in the official history of Oxford University: 'Whether in the pages of eternity twentieth-century Oxford was a "good thing", is an open question; the cultural fact of its superior image is a closed one.'[43] Oxbridge is Brideshead; Oxbridge students live in beautiful quads, with scouts to do their washing, and move from glittering dining clubs to the Union to debate matters of state. Essex students live in grotty halls of residence and work behind the bar in the student union building to make up for the cuts in student grants.

Chris Measures, the 1994 Cambridge Students Union communications officer responsible for the Target Achievement Programme, designed to overcome these class barriers, pointed out in *Varsity*, the Cambridge student newspaper, that the 'tradition of Oxbridge applications is a big advantage to schools . . . they know the procedure and what to expect'.[44] A Westminster pupil quoted in the same piece continued by pointing out the rigorous and specific coaching received by Oxbridge applicants. Eton has an annual planning meeting, where tactics for each year's Oxbridge assault – seeing that applications are spread across the colleges;

directing a candidate with a particular contact to the right college, etc. – are planned with military precision.

Astonishingly, given the tale so far, the public schools suffer from a victim complex when it comes to university admissions. The former headmaster of Eton, Eric Anderson, voices a typical public school concern that 'some factors now militate against Etonians. When it comes to filling the last few places each year, a number of those (college heads) who wrote to me admitted that, other things being equal, their colleges might well choose candidates from state rather than independent schools.'[45] Dr Anderson's own transition from Eton to the headship of Lincoln College, Oxford is a fitting commentary on the reality behind this mild psychosis. In truth, a 'stern meritocracy' emerged from the 1970s, to quote the official history of Oxford.[46] Where the proportion of undergraduates admitted with high A-levels (AAA, AAB, AAC or ABB) was stable for the university sector as a whole at around 22 per cent, in Oxford it was 58.6 per cent and rose to 73.5 per cent by 1980.[47] In 1969 20 per cent of those admitted had achieved three As at A-level, and 53 per cent had AAC/ABB or better. In 1989 the figures had risen to 55 per cent and 90 per cent respectively – and over 95 per cent of conditional offers were for a minimum of AAC/ABB. The 'amiable, well-connected public school dunce, keen on rugger and beagling but usually too drunk for either, likely to pass without effort (or qualifications) into the upper-middle ranks of government or business, to the ultimate detriment of British power, prosperity and social justice, but sure to turn up to Gaudies' (to quote one keen observer) has effectively disappeared from Oxford, wherever else he has remained. Indeed, although the 'right sort of background' does still count for something, it is difficult to imagine quite so blatant and unashamed a piece of string pulling as Ian McIntyre recounts in his biography of Lord Reith. Reith's son was, as the phrase has it, 'not academically gifted'. But Reith was concerned to ensure that he went up to Oxford for all the usual reasons. Trading on his own position, he contacted the provost of Worcester College. 'He will take C. S.,' noted Reith, 'to oblige me. He has turned down about a thousand fellows but said his conscience was quite clear because of what I had done for the country.'[48]

Why such a strong emphasis on Oxford and Cambridge? For the same reasons that we stressed the centrality of the 'only 7 per cent' who attend private schools: they form the core of England's élite. A random survey of 250 men and women in the 1996 *Who's Who* shows 114 to be from Oxbridge (including William Hague). Five hundred and ten out of 1,186 members of the House of Lords in 1991 were Oxbridge. Two-thirds of the eighteen civil service permanent secretaries attended Oxbridge. Eighteen out of twenty-three members of the Major Cabinet were Oxbridge. Oxford has provided nine prime ministers this century (including Tony Blair), Cambridge three, out of nineteen in total. In every walk of Britain's national life, Oxbridge dominates. A country of fifty-seven million people is governed by 2 per cent of her graduate total.

In itself there is no reason to be worried by this. No society can exist without élites, and élites chosen with an eye to meritocratic factors are better than the opposite. It is no more than a sign of Oxbridge's effectiveness that its products become many of the nation's success stories. But the point is not what happens to those who leave, but who enters – and it is here that the figures should worry us. No society can call itself open, let alone classless, if entry to its great universities is de facto restricted to a tiny proportion of its citizens.

This restricted entry has been compounded by another of the liberal establishment's well-meaning gestures – the extension of university status to the former polytechnics. Although for a short while students seemed to think that a name change would have a real effect on outside perceptions, and applications rose even more steeply to these former polytechnics than to the rest of the university sector, the honeymoon has ended. A new Ivy League is now well established, with Oxbridge at the top, London and the other old foundations next, then the redbrick universities, followed by former polytechnics at the bottom. No one is fooled, for instance, by Leicester Poly becoming De Montfort University – except the applicants, well aware of its status but unable to find De Montfort on the map. As Martin Stephen, high master of Manchester Grammar School, puts it: 'The government has created a very different university map . . . which has hugely increased the popularity of the Ivy League top fifteen at the expense of those lower down the pecking order' – an interesting recurrence of the 1960s 'redbrick effect' when the post-Robbins universities experienced a surge in applications, only to fall swiftly behind their traditional rivals in a few years.[49]

'Egalitarian policies have failed'

So what are we to make of England's educational evolution in recent decades? Class segregation is the dominating fact.

The reformation of the private schools is one critical dimension; the introduction of the comprehensive school in the 1960s, the other. The comprehensive revolution had two goals: one educational, the other social. Many of the most influential educational theorists in the 1950s and 1960s genuinely believed that mixed-ability teaching and comprehensive schooling 'gives all children a fresh start in the secondary school . . . The expectations which teachers have of the majority of their pupils are better – and their pupils, sensing and responding to this higher regard, in turn achieve more,' as one of the leading advocates put it at the time.[50]

There was a more profound objective underlying the reform. 'In spite of the virtual abolition of poverty, in spite of the rise there has been in the rewards of labour, in spite of the fact that . . . the great bulk of the nation now regards itself as middle class, Britain is still a jealous and divided nation,' argued *The Times* in 1961.[51] Education, which was seen by the advocates of comprehensive schools 'as a serious alternative to nationalization in promoting a more just and efficient society' (as Tony Crosland, the education secretary who would not rest until he had 'destroyed every fucking grammar school', put it), was thus to be a vital plank in moving towards a classless society.[52]

The tragic irony is that for all the good intentions, the destruction of the grammar schools – in the name of equality of opportunity – only had the effect of reinforcing class divisions. Those who can afford to flee the system desert it for the private sector; those who have the money to escape to a leafy middle-class catchment area leave the inner cities; and those who can't are left to pick up what is left over for them. As A. H. Halsey, a leading egalitarian theorist of the 1960s, put it starkly: 'The essential fact of twentieth-century educational history is that egalitarian policies have failed.'[53]

This solidifying of class divisions goes beyond the structure of the state system. Supposedly classless theories of progressive teaching, exemplified by the Plowden Report in the 1960s, have had a similarly detrimental effect. 'The progressive classroom,' writes Adrian Wooldridge,

> was a laboratory of the classless society – an idyllic place in which co-operation flourished and competition was un-known. Nothing angers progressive teachers quite so much as testing, which, they argue, measures little more than social background and so simply perpetuates and justifies social inequalities. Children who are labelled as failures at primary school are likely to go on to fulfil their own low expectations. The yobs on the football terraces were venting their anger at those nasty spelling tests.[54]

The state school classroom has in some instances become an unfamiliar environment to those who work on the basis of fact and reason. As a recent guide for trainee teachers published by the London Institute of Education – home of many of the country's most influential educationalists – asserted: schools are guilty of too often 'legitimizing one popular view of mathematics' – arithmetic, algebra and geometry – and so devaluing 'the students' informal mathematical experience and skills . . . which are equally, if not more, valuable to the individual'. Maths is oppressive; it should be replaced by 'ethnomathematics', since 'the view that "official" mathematics dominates "ethnomathematics" is consistent with that of Western cultural/educational imperialism in mathematics education'.[55] Our everyday experiences are what maths is really about, not the pedagogic instructions of a teacher. As the headmaster in Lambeth who appointed an expert in Nigerian cooking, with no experience of maths, to teach maths in his school put it: 'It is real life maths with Ibo cookery – transferable maths.'[56]

Such horror stories demonstrate the damage done by the divorce of the professional classes from the state system. When a similar contagion threatened to envelop the French state system, politicians of all parties were mobilized to prevent any damage because they all had a stake in the system. And it was a left-wing politician, the socialist Jean-Pierre Chevènement (dubbed France's Tony Benn), who as Minister of Education led the fight against these 'progressive' notions through his policy of *élitisme républicain*. Similarly, in Germany even left-wing state governments halted the spread of comprehensives in favour of improving the existing tripartite system of grammar, technical and higher schools. For the 'paradox of Plowdenism', as Wooldridge calls it, is that it strengthens the class divisions it is supposed to tear down. Poor children simply cannot adjust to the unstructured, loose environment of such schools – unlike their middle-class peers whose confidence typically sees them through alien experiences, and whose parents compensate for the failure of teachers and schools to do their job.

And it also matters that entry to Oxbridge is dominated by the private schools. Not because Oxbridge is, as some would have it, some sinister freemasonry, but because no society can call itself open and meritocratic – certainly not classless – if entry to its élites is largely restricted to a lucky few. When Her Majesty's Chief Inspector of Schools identifies more than a quarter of those secondary schools classified as 'outstanding' as grammar schools (which account for only 0.7 per cent of the total), can society really continue to accept an education policy which refuses to acknowledge that state education is, by design, failing to offer anything approaching equal opportunities to children?

PART TWO

Elites

What I want to know is: what is actually wrong with an élite, for God's sake?

Prince Charles

3. THE SUPER CLASS

Britain's winner-take-all élite

> The general course of recent history no longer favors the levelling
> of social distinctions but runs more and more in the direction of a
> two-class society in which the favored few monopolise the advant-
> ages of money, education and power.
>
> Christopher Lasch, *The Revolt of the Elites*

The thirty years since the mid-1960s have seen the rise of the Super
Class – a new élite of top professionals and managers, at once
meritocratic yet exclusive, very highly paid yet powerfully convinced
of the justice of its rewards, and increasingly divorced from the rest
of society by wealth, education, values, residence and lifestyle. It is
a seminal development in modern Britain, as critical as the rise of
the gentry before the English Civil War and the rise of organized
labour a century ago, and rivalled in contemporary significance
only by the disintegration of the manual working class.

New was built on old. The Super Class draws on pre-existing
professions and institutions; and this being Britain, their ancient
façades are beguiling – whether in Clubland, Oxbridge, the Inns
of Court, or the City of London with its medieval Corporation
and Lord Mayor. But the Super Class is a recognizably new
phenomenon. Its size and character are shaped by extraordinarily
rapid growth in one industry, financial services: an industry concentrated in the City, truly international, largely foreign-owned and
heavily US-influenced in ethos, regime and remuneration. The
Super Class has transformed career patterns and expectations
among the social élite produced by Britain's – particularly England's – top schools and universities. In the course of a single
generation, at this élite level, the status of the public sector has
collapsed in favour of a narrow range of private sector professions.

And within those professions, inequality between top and middle has widened on a dramatic scale.

Furthermore, the rise of the Super Class was as unexpected as it remains underappreciated. The growth of professional and managerial employment used to be seen as the best hope for a less class-ridden society. As late as 1980 sociologists talked confidently of the increasing 'room at the top' of the occupational pyramid as a development which could steadily reduce inequalities of life chances.[1] The 'room at the top' has indeed expanded; and for millions who have moved up, as teachers where their fathers were miners, with degrees where even a few years ago they would have left school at fifteen with practically nothing, there are no regrets. Yet a transition to classlessness it is not. Not only is the gulf between graduates and most of the rest as great as ever (graduates have *careers*, the rest *jobs*), but the centrifugal forces within the professional classes strengthen year by year. Partly this is a function of size and diversity. Yet there has also been a transformation at the very top, as an élite, mostly in legal, corporate and finance-related occupations, has detached itself from the rest of educated and qualified Britain, even in its own professions. This is the Super Class.

Social change is rarely neat. Old and new élites co-exist and overlap; and so it is with the Super Class, a predominantly private sector élite which co-exists with old public sector Establishment centres in Whitehall and the universities, and with Britain's old aristocratic élite. The aristocracy has been substantially absorbed into the Super Class: old money found its way into the City a century ago and into business earlier still, and old families no longer care for the tradition of public service.[2] Far less smooth have been relations between the Super Class and Britain's public sector élite, itself a fairly recent – essentially post-war – formation in its present size and character. In his influential book *The Rise of Professional Society*, the social historian Harold Perkin argues that incompatible interests, brought to a head by uncontainable conflict over public spending and taxation, have turned public and private professionals into 'two warring factions'. While public professionals depend upon high government outlays and a strong welfare state ethos, private professionals rebel against high taxation and political interference with their ability to milk their fiefdoms. Perkin concludes expansively: 'As the struggle between lord and peasant was the master conflict in feudal society, and the struggle between capitalist and wage-earner the master conflict in industrial society, so the struggle between the public and private sector professions is the master conflict of professional society.'[3]

Perkin's analysis offers a fitting challenge to explore the evolution of Britain's professional classes. Although the public–private division is important, we argue that his 'master conflict' is essentially a transitory phase in the construction of the Super Class. This is not because of any grand compromise between the public and private sectors, but because the past two decades have seen a fundamental realignment of the social élite produced by Britain's top schools and universities behind the City and its associated professions. There is no master conflict because there are few master combatants. Rather, social conflict is taking on far broader dimensions, as those outside the Super Class, particularly lesser professionals, in the public and private sectors, resent its growing rewards and exclusivity.

Like every economic élite in history, the Super Class is steering more and more income towards itself, and claiming this to be for the public good.[4] The result, in the US, has been dubbed the 'winner-take-all society'.[5] And nothing exemplifies its rise in Britain better than the two *causes célèbres* of the mid-1990s with which we start: the Cedric Brown and Nick Leeson affairs.

Gasman to rogue trader
First came Cedric Brown – the most unlikely hate figure of recent times, a bluff northerner who rose from gas fitter to chief executive of British Gas after a blameless career.

British Gas, one of the Thatcher government's biggest privatizations, was sold off to City institutions and an army of private investors ('Sids') in 1986. Among the most pressing issues for board members of the newly privatized company was how to ratchet up their pay from 'public' to 'private' rates. It was the same in all the privatized utilities and many of the strategies adopted were controversial, from the steps taking the chairman of British Telecom's salary from £84,198 in 1984 to £663,000 in 1994, to the array of generous share option and executive incentive schemes adopted by the 'fat cat' directors of the newly privatized water and electricity companies in the mid-1990s. These controversies, however, were as nothing compared to the furore which greeted the revelation in November 1994 that Cedric Brown's pay had been increased by 75 per cent, taking it to £475,000 a year. Overnight it was Cedric the Pig with his snout in the trough – culminating in a live pig bearing the gas chief's name swilling from a huge bucket, before the television cameras, outside British Gas's annual general meeting the following summer.

On holiday when the story broke, Cedric spoke to the media at his Buckinghamshire home. This was his first error. The cameras and sketch writers got going on the £250,000 'neo-Georgian mansion' (never 'house') in leafy Beaconsfield, with its mock gold taps and latest registration Merc in the drive. His second mistake was to regurgitate the stock corporate platitudes. 'Company salaries should be enough to attract, motivate and retain top managers,' he recited, looking distinctly shifty. 'I have nothing to do with setting my pay. It is decided by the non-executive directors.'[6] Compounding these errors, he backtracked a day later, following a row in the House of Commons in which Tony Blair accused John Major of standing idly by while 'millions of people feel disgusted and outraged at this excess and greed'. Cedric now said he was thinking of giving some of his pay back.[7] Such heresy was soon stamped on within British Gas. Richard Giordano, the company's £450,000-a-year part-time American chairman, recruited shortly before from British Oxygen (where he had been Britain's highest-paid executive), told the press that his chief executive would keep every penny, which was 'well below the cash compensation earned by most executives holding comparable jobs in British industry' and necessary to bring him into line with the 'median of a large sample of UK plcs'.[8]

Then it emerged that British Gas was seeking to cut pay and increase working hours for its showroom staff, on wages averaging £13,000 a year. Norman Blacker, the director in charge of the company's retailing division, had just received a £60,000 pay rise taking his annual salary to £250,000. In a letter to showroom staff Blacker had told them their pay was 'unrealistically high' and needed to be brought into line 'with market levels'. 'Fat cat Norman Blacker,' one paper reported, 'insists it is his 2,600 employees who are holding back profits.'[9] It went on to analyse Blacker's share options. In the previous year he held shares worth £143,000, made £113,000 profit selling share options and was 'sitting on another 156,000 options which could have made him £123,000 profit at yesterday's prices'.

Even the Tory and business press left Cedric to swing, their journalists, well paid by public sector standards, nevertheless as resentful as Joe Public at City and boardroom super salaries. Barry Riley, the respected *Financial Times* commentator, penned a Christmas column on 'Santa's package for rich executives', with Santa roving around the utilities telling their executives how to mint it:

At British Gas headquarters the chairman, a charming American, came quickly to the point. 'Frankly, it's a bit embarrassing,' he said. 'My pay is £450,000 although I work only part time as a non-executive. But our full-time chief executive, Mr Brown, is paid only £270,000. It looks out of line. What do you advise?'

'Well,' said Father Christmas, 'you could reduce your own pay. But after all, it is nearly Christmas. What's more, I have a database of top executive pay all around the world – except in poor countries, of course – which proves that Mr Brown is blooming well substantially undercompensated.'

'Now, £500,000 might look a bit much, so let's split the difference. Therefore I recommend you pay him, er, £475,000.'[10]

British Gas's Sids were also mobilizing. An articulate group of small shareholders led by Professor Joseph Lamb, a Fife-based academic (public sector, of course), organized protests for the company's AGM. It called for the company's articles of association to be changed so that pay rises for directors could not, in percentage terms, be more generous than the average for all British Gas employees.[11]

The political storm raged for months. Tony Blair condemned Cedric Brown's pay as an offence against the 'British sense of justice' and demanded that the Major government 'take a grip on these privatized utilities' with their doctrine of 'greed at the top and insecurity for the rest'. John Major, anxious to minimize the fuss without intervening to restrain private sector practices so strongly supported on the Tory benches behind him, weakly complained that Blair was seeking to 'capitalize on a grievance felt by some'.[12]

Yet the private corporate élite was as passionate in its own defence as Blair had been in attack. Sir Iain Vallance, the chairman of British Telecom, claimed in a forthright *FT* article at the height of the fracas that a fundamental principle of 'distributive justice' was at stake.[13] Britain's leading private sector companies 'underpin our economy', he claimed. A 'just reward' for a top executive should depend on four criteria: the demands of the job, its comparability with 'other similar jobs', performance, and the acceptability of the salary 'to the other stakeholders with a legitimate interest'. The trouble with these arguments was that they could just as easily have justified doubling the pay of, say, doctors and secondary school head teachers – a reaction Vallance himself provoked when, shortly afterwards, he unwisely told a Commons committee examining boardroom pay that his job was so strenuous he might find it 'relaxing' to swap with a junior hospital doctor.

The blunt reality came at the end of his *FT* article, where Vallance arbitrarily limited his 'stakeholders with a legitimate interest' to shareholders; and even they, he claimed, had an interest only in the proper functioning of board remuneration committees – committees composed of fellow corporate directors with a vested interest in boosting the general level of executive pay.

The controversy rumbled on for a year, until Cedric took early retirement. None the less, the British Gas pay regime remained unchanged, and the rest of the utilities continued down the same path as if nothing had happened. The flotation of the National Grid as a separate company in 1995 saw its directors make millions, despite a media outcry. Across the utilities, at least fifty millionaires were created by privatization, and in each company the next few tiers of managers below board level shared in the largesse on a smaller but still lavish scale. By 1996 virtually every privatized company – irrespective of sector or competition – had salary and executive share incentive schemes akin to those of the long-standing corporate giants.

Nowhere, however, had pay risen so fast or high as in the City since the Big Bang of 1986, which brings us to our second *cause célèbre*, exploding just as Cedric was reaching the back-burner: the collapse of Barings Bank in February 1995, precipitated by the £869 million of losses in illegal futures and options trading run up by rogue trader Nick Leeson. Few – even among the directors of Barings, it seemed – knew much about the complex financial instruments being traded. Easily understood, however, was the scale of City salaries and the extraordinary bonus culture revealed by the Barings débâcle.

The bonus culture was exposed at once, for Barings collapsed on the very day on which bonuses were due to be paid to the bank's staff for their performance in 1994. The sums at stake were staggering, and this in a relatively small merchant bank. No fewer than fifty-eight Barings employees had been due to receive bonuses of between £250,000 and £499,000 each. Another five were to get between £500,000 and £749,000, while the bank's top four executives, led by chairman Peter Baring, were in line for more than £750,000 apiece.[14] More than £100 million had been earmarked for bonuses alone, equal to 55 per cent of Barings' profits for the year – all on top of Super Class salaries.

Within days of the collapse, the Dutch merchant bank ING came forward to buy Barings as a going concern for £1, taking on Leeson's losses as part of the deal. The bonuses should have been slashed, based as they were on notional profits of £205 million for 1994 when the true figure, subtracting Leeson's phantom earnings, was far lower. But as part of the purchase deal ING agreed to honour the bonuses in full – paying some £95 million in all, excluding only those directly implicated in the bank's collapse. (Even one of the executives dismissed, and criticized in a Bank of England inquiry, later sued for her £500,000 bonus, claiming that her bonus was guaranteed whatever the company's performance.[15]) ING was no woolly philanthropist: Barings bond holders, including many small savers, were offered paltry compensation for their losses. The bonuses were paid, bluntly, to ensure a smooth transition and to prevent a haemorrhage of the bank's best staff.

The bonus episode was testament to the City's mega-pay culture, which dated back to the Big Bang deregulation of 1986 and the influx of US firms, their Wall Street practices in tow. Leeson's defence against criminal charges relied heavily on the bonus imperative. 'The biggest crime I am guilty of,' he declared from his prison cell while awaiting trial, 'is trying to protect people and ensure that the bonuses they expected were paid, and it is this that led to the escalation of the problem.'[16] The expectations started at the top. In 1985, on the eve of Big Bang, Barings' then chairman, Sir John Baring, was paid £293,920; by 1993 his successor, Peter Baring, was receiving around £1.3 million, more than £1 million of it in bonus.[17] As a chronicler of the Barings collapse puts it, bonuses had by now become 'sacrosanct'; 'money had become the main, perhaps the sole, standard of judgement about a person's value'; and the new breed of bankers and traders 'were more like mercenaries, hiring out their labour to the highest bidder'.[18]

Overnight Nick Leeson became the exemplar of this new breed. But the contrast at Barings could hardly have been starker. On one side was the bank's star trader: son of a Watford plasterer, brought up on a council estate, who joined the City as an eighteen-year-old school-leaver and had to be bailed out of a Singapore court for exposing his buttocks to a woman passing the quayside pub he frequented with the lads after work. On the other side, Peter Baring: Eton, Magdalene College, Cambridge, chairman of Glyndebourne Opera, who succeeded his cousin Sir John Baring (later Lord Ashburton) at the helm of the family bank in 1989. 'Peter's grasp of details was sometimes tenuous,' said one colleague, 'and even when he was finance director he occasionally got lost among the figures.' The gentleman banker destroyed by the crudest of the yuppies, subverting old class with new money – the 'shagloads of it' Leeson told his Watford friends he intended to make before leaving for Singapore.[19]

What do the Cedric Brown and Barings affairs tell us about the evolution of the professional and managerial élite? In the first place, that it is not a rigid social caste, even at the heights of income and position. A tongue-tied engineer with a northern accent and an untutored taste in 'how to spend it' (he bought a *new* house), Cedric did not remotely look the part of the high-flying corporate executive. The barrow boy Leesons, flourishing on the Wild West of City trading and dealing rooms, are today's crudest *nouveaux riches*, seeking and often reaping huge rewards from new and highly uncertain trades by dint of raw energy and nous. Yet, secondly, this situation defines them as a highly exceptional group. Most City executives would barely rate Leeson a professional, but a highly paid white-collar operative (Peter Baring insisted on calling him a 'clerk'). Within the City the barrow boys are hardly to be found in the upper reaches of banks and consultancies, let alone in City solicitors' or accountancy firms, where the university – particularly private school and Oxbridge – educated reign supreme.

The Peter Baring gentleman banker presiding over the family firm is rarer still. Symbolically, Leeson brought down Barings as Peter Baring was on the verge of retirement; his successor was to have come from outside the family. The old boys' network still counts for much in the professions, but most of its members are now there by meritocratic achievement at the old schools and universities, not courtesy of friends and family. It is a marriage of money and meritocracy, not money and nepotism, which underpins today's Super Class.

However, if Cedric and Leeson were unrepresentative as types, their notoriety was firmly rooted in the media and public perception of them as icons of a new class. There were the brute facts about City pay, bonuses and culture, graphically exposed by Leeson and the Barings collapse. There was also the public–private dimension, Cedric focusing attention on the cause of the difference in the treatment of top professionals in the two sectors, which was simply a question of who paid and sanctioned their salaries. The classic corporate argument for jackpot pay – the need to attract and retain talented managers to lead highly competitive businesses – was manifest nonsense in Cedric's case, since he was *in situ* running a domestic monopoly. British Gas implicitly conceded as much in Richard Giordano's defence of the salary hike as necessary to bring Cedric in line with 'the median of large British plcs' – in other words, simply because his job had moved into the private sector. This was a common tale: between 1979 and 1995 privatization transferred more than fifty businesses, generating about a tenth of total GDP, from the public to the private sector.[20] No one suggested that onerous managerial posts in the public sector should carry super salaries, even when directly comparable with private sector counterparts. Shortly after the Cedric Brown affair, a utility chief executive with a job at least as demanding – Bill Cockburn at the nationalized Post Office – quadrupled his salary without media fanfare. He did so by moving to the helm of W. H. Smith, a company with a fraction of the Post Office's turnover.

This encroaches directly on Perkin's notion of a 'master conflict' between public and private sector professionals. Much of the resentment against both Cedric and Leeson was undoubtedly driven by deep public professional grievances about relative pay and status. The political ramifications are significant since, as explained in the next chapter, the division between public and private professionals is the fault-line between the contemporary Labour and Conservative parties. Public–private professional conflict, however presently subdued, has the potential to explode in ugly fashion. However, from the stance of the professional and managerial élite itself, a different picture emerges. Here we are looking at a class highly adaptive to the changing professional world, if not *within* then certainly *between* generations. The old public sector élite has not stayed and fought; it has fled to the moneypots with barely a glance backwards, realigning itself decisively with the top private sector professions and largely deserting the public sector. This is to generalize, of course. But not unduly so, as we shall now see.

The transformation of the professional élite

Until the mid-1960s Britain's professional hierarchy had little to do with public or private sectors, everything to do with tradition, rewards and exclusivity. In the first division came the law, medicine, military officers, the senior civil service and academe – professions with hallowed pasts, tightly restricted entry, customs inimical to outsiders and an indisposition to change. Hierarchies were strict and formal. Barristers ranked above solicitors, consultants above GPs, Oxbridge dons above redbrick lecturers, the Guards and cavalry above lesser regiments and all army officers above naval and RAF underlings, the diplomatic service above the home civil service, the Treasury above the rest of Whitehall, and Whitehall above local government. In some professions these hierarchies cut across the public–private frontier, notably in teaching, where Mr Chips in his grammar or public school was a league above teachers in the lesser independent and state secondary schools.

Education mattered, but as much for where you went as what

you achieved. Sandhurst was the preserve of the leading public schools, only a tiny number of officers bothering with degrees. In the other prestigious professions Oxbridge reigned supreme, except in medicine where it shared status with London's teaching hospitals. The best Oxbridge graduates spread themselves across the Bar, Whitehall, the diplomatic service, the media and the universities. A second Oxbridge tier went into public and grammar school teaching, solicitors' firms and non-Whitehall administrative careers. Thereafter, noted two critical observers in 1964,

> the choice of a formal career for the Oxbridge graduate turns out to be a good deal more limited than is generally supposed. Many skilled professions are closed to him. He is unwilling to submerge his gentlemanliness – his most prized asset – in the grubbier regions of the business world. He cannot be a Tinker or Tailor, a Soldier or a Sailor.[21]

Family firms, commerce, engineering and industry generally attracted a share of the less able.[22] Until the 1980s management barely counted as a profession (not until 1996 did Oxford propose to locate a US-style business school at the centre of the university). In status, business was closely allied to accountancy, the one chartered profession drawing largely on non-graduates. At the bottom of the professional heap came the swathes of lesser secondary and primary school teachers, mostly non-graduates with teaching certificates.

The allocation of rewards reflected this hierarchy. Successful lawyers, accountants, stockbrokers and directors did better financially than their mandarin and academic counterparts. But excluding the giants of the Bar and a few City partners and company chairmen, they were not hugely better-off, once the state sector's generous pensions and other perks were taken into account. The concentration of honours on the public sector helped bridge even this gap. Judges, permanent secretaries, military chiefs, and senior local government officers and vice-chancellors got almost automatic knighthoods, making 'ladies' of their wives. CBs, CBEs and OBEs were distributed to public servants in profusion. The diplomatic service had its own separate order of St Michael and St George – ascending, in the half-serious quip, to CMG (Call Me God), KCMG (Kindly Call Me God) and GCMG (God Calls Me God). The private sector fared poorly in the honours stakes, beyond captains of industry and local notables gaining recognition through service in local government and the Conservative party.

Average professional pay (as opposed to rewards for the top cohorts) matched this pattern. A 1956 survey put medical consultants at the top of the professional tree, earning £3,353 a year on average.[23] Next were solicitors (£2,205). National Health Service GPs (£2,102) were marginally ahead of barristers (£2,075), whose average pay was depressed by the large number of low earners (in the infancy of legal aid). Then came accountants (£1,814) and 'graduates in industry' (£1,660). University lecturers notched up £1,541 – a healthy 85 per cent of an accountant's average and ahead of engineers (£1,497). Teachers fared poorly, but here again there was little difference between public and private sectors at the secondary level. This picture did not change much over the next twenty years. A 1977 study found that the earnings of solicitors in private practice were roughly on a par with middle managers and administrative grade civil servants, with legal salaries rising more slowly than both prices and average male earnings in the high-inflation, union-dominated 1970s.[24]

Viewed from the mid-1960s, professional segmentation was rigid. At the bottom, hundreds of thousands of school teachers, accounts and City clerks, middling civil servants and local government officers, and their like, had no degree: other qualifications and a (low) salary conferred middle-class status, but gave them little else in common with the higher reaches of their own professions. At the top were three distinct if overlapping élites. First, the *old school tie, no degree* group, providing the army officer class and much of the City above the level of clerks. Secondly, the *grammar/public school, no degree but qualified* group, spread broadly across banking, accountancy, business and service professions. Thirdly, the *grammar/public school, graduate* group, the senior of the three in status and proximity to power. A cohesive professional élite centred on the law, politics, media, medicine, Whitehall, the universities and the Church of England, and moulded largely by Oxbridge, this third group was the Establishment. It bestrode the higher reaches of the public and private sectors, an amalgam of sons of the upper class (highly defensive in mentality), of the small pre-war professional élite (dedicated to public service in the imperial tradition) and of the meritocratic grammar school graduates nurtured by the post-war welfare state. Its attitude to an expanded role for government in welfare and industry ranged from the tolerant to the wildly enthusiastic. For these were White-hall's prime agents: even the serious businessmen among them looked as much to the public sector, with its expanding base of nationalized industries, as to the private sector.

This essential structure survived until the 1970s, withstanding, even drawing strength from, discontinuities such as Labour governments, the end of empire, and the arrival of the redbricks and polytechnics. It has been transformed in the two decades since.

In the process few institutions have been eradicated: they rarely are in Britain. Everything from Oxbridge High Tables to grand ambassadorial residences, regimental messes and the Inns of Court remain in full working order. So do even the most apparently vulnerable professions. Consider the Church of England. Clergy pay has withered to the level of social workers'; practising Anglicans are outnumbered by Catholics; the worshipping public is a tiny fraction of the population. But the top universities still teach theology (Oxford fills sixty places a year in the subject, more than for either economics and management or engineering and computing). Numbers training for the ministry have fallen sharply since the 1960s, but even in 1996 a quarter of all ordinands were graduates of five top universities (Oxbridge, London, Manchester and Durham), training for the ministry in theological colleges arranged in a hierarchy headed by those at Oxford and Cambridge. Bishops are drawn largely from this élite and twenty-six of them still have seats in the House of Lords, guaranteeing status and prominence. Yet declining social status has left its mark: once a bastion of old Toryism, today's clerical élite has a public service, anti-Conservative mentality, calling on spiritually minded graduates – in the words of David Sheppard, the Bishop of Liverpool – to 'turn away from financially profitable jobs and serve people in other ways'.[25]

Beneath the old vestments, professional Britain has been transformed. It is most obvious in the sphere of qualifications. Teaching and all the chartered professions now require degrees. Beyond the trading floors, few now go into professional jobs in the City without them. Even Sandhurst has become a graduate preserve: in 1995 more than 80 per cent of its intake were graduates (or destined to be), up from 42 per cent a decade previously. The effect has been to dissolve the first two of the old professional groups (*old school tie, no degree* and *grammar/public school, no degree but qualified*) into what, at first sight, appears to be a single graduate élite. Universities have expanded to the point where almost every eighteen-year-old with reasonable A-levels can expect a place, and every profession, without exception, now boasts of its openness to all comers with suitable degrees, especially women and members of ethnic minorities. Old class practices have not entirely dissolved, but they are muted even in their former bastions. Eton's tally at Sandhurst has slipped steadily since the 1960s; and if the military academy stands accused of forcing behaviour 'towards a more middle class template',[26] this is no different from the other old professions. At any rate, it has ceased to be an *upper* class template.

At the same time, the professional class has burgeoned. In parts of the public sector this is a continuation of trends going back to the Second World War. Recent increases have been dramatic even so, taking the number of university lecturers (for instance) from 2,000 at the turn of the century to about 30,000 in 1970 and 60,000 by 1995, and the number of doctors and dentists from around

25,000 in 1911 to 108,000 in 1984 and 126,000 in 1994. In the private sector, growth on this scale is more recent, but has taken off in recent decades. The number of practising solicitors fell between the First World War and 1950. In the following fifteen years it grew slowly (from 17,000 to 21,000, the same number as in 1911); since 1965 it has more than trebled (to 66,000). The number of practising barristers rose from 1,900 in 1960 to nearly 8,000 in 1996. It is a similar picture in accountancy. England's established professions – including management – now employ some 1.6 million (see Table 5), perhaps twice the number in 1955; and virtually all new entrants are graduates. United in their degrees and professional ethos, and set against the broad twentieth-century expansion of the salaried middle class, which has risen from roughly a quarter to nearly half of the workforce since the First World War, it is tempting to see them in the vanguard of a progressively less classbound society. The continued predomin-ance of the public sector professionals reinforces this impression: although in 1996 the state employed barely 15 per cent of the hired workforce, it comprised nearly half of all professionals because of the huge size of the teaching profession.

Such a view is misplaced. When in 1980 John Goldthorpe and his colleagues in the Oxford social mobility project foresaw increasing 'room at the top' providing the occasion 'for inequalities of life chances to be reduced', their crucial proviso was that growing professionalization would take place 'without the members of any class having to become less advantaged than before in absolute terms'. Their assumption, conventional for the time, was that the 'room at the top' would increase while income differentials narrowed within and between occupational groups, continuing a trend dating back to the 1880s. But this trend was already going into sharp reverse. The 1980s and 1990s saw the income gap between professionals and the rest grow across the board. And within the professional mansion, the increasing *room* at the top was accompanied by a dramatic raising of the *roof* at the top. The result is the Super Class – a private sector élite considerably

Table 5: Professional groups by size (1995–96)

Large overlapping groups are categorized once only (e.g. teachers are not included within the local authority total), but there is some double counting (e.g. engineers who are senior local government officers and business executives). (Figures rounded to the nearest thousand.)

Public sector		Private sector	
Teachers	436,000	Teachers	56,000
University professionals	60,000		
Solicitors	5,000	Solicitors	58,000
Judges (full-time salaried)	1,000	Barristers	9,000
Accountants	15,000	Accountants	170,000
Engineers	45,000	Engineers	190,000
GPs	33,000		
Senior health administrators	15,000		
Hospital and other doctors	68,000	*(public and private sector)*	
Dentists	23,000	*(public and private sector)*	
		Vets	11,000
Senior civil servants	16,000	Managers in industry	50,000
		Business consultants	20,000
		City finance executives (not in other categories)	200,000
Military officers	37,000	Journalists	40,000
Senior local government officers	25,000	Architects	32,000
Total*:	**745,000**		**871,000**
Voluntary/charitable/religious sectors			
Religious leaders	25,000		
Charity executives	6,000		

*Notionally dividing hospital doctors 2:1 public:private and dentists equally between the sectors.

Sources: Government departments, trade unions and professional associations; some figures are estimates.

more advantaged in absolute and relative terms than previously, promoting a new dimension of inequality within professional Britain.

It is not the case that 'private' professionals have seen their pay rocket across the board while their 'public' counterparts have uniformly languished. The government's annual occupational earnings survey for 1995 puts most professional salaries within brackets similar to those of 1956 noted earlier.[27] Medical practitioners, solicitors, senior police officers, underwriters, brokers and most non-financial managers earned between £31,000 and £39,000 a year on average. Beneath them, in the £24,000 to £30,000 a year range, come university and secondary school professionals, chartered accountants, architects, engineers and technologists. University lecturers did better on average (£30,000) than either chartered accountants (£26,000) or architects (£25,000). The 1995 average pay league is headed by one 'public' group (senior central government administrators, on £47,000) and one 'private' group (company financial managers, on £44,000). The prestigious professions have long tails: according to the Law Society, a quarter of solicitors – mostly in small practices – earn less than the average for secondary school teachers.

However, in contrast to 1956 this pattern changes out of all recognition when we move from *average* to *top* professional salaries. Large groups of private professionals ascend heights their counterparts (in either sector) can only dream about. Table 6 is a snapshot of salaries for 1995–96 in the public and private professions with the highest pay ceilings. To avoid gross distortion and enable realistic cross-profession comparisons to be made, we have taken the average salary of the top tier of appreciable size within each profession (i.e. commercial QCs as a whole, not just the stars at the Bar; all partners in the leading solicitors' and accountancy firms, not just senior partners; brigadiers and above in the army, and their equivalents in the navy and RAF, not just generals, and so on). The table is based on published sources where available, and private interviews otherwise.

Table 6: Salaries of top professionals

Sample salaries from the top cohort of a reasonable size within each profession, as defined in each case (i.e. £76,000 is the 1996 salary of a circuit judge, although high court and senior appeal court judges earned up to £150,000).

Public		**Private**	
Judges	£76,000	Solicitors (partner, large City firm)	£200,000
		Barristers (commercial QC)	£350,000
Military officers (brigadier)	£58,000		
Local government officers (senior chief exec.)	£75,000		
School teaching (head of 1,200 pupil secondary school)	£49,000	Accountants (partner, Big Six)	£190,000
University professors (top professorial cadre)	£46,000		
NHS administrators (mid-size NHS trust chief exec.)	£67,000		
Consultant	£65,000 public + £70,000 private		
Dentist	£100,000 (*public and private*)		
Civil servant (grade 3)	£75,000	Industry (director, FT-100 plc)	£270,000
		City (managing director or equivalent, broking and investment banking)	£400,000

Sources: Government departments; annual reports; Monks Partnership reports on boardroom pay; private interviews.

Table 6 shows the public and private sector professional élites to be leagues apart. Encompassing some 8,500 top earners in the private sector and 4,000 in the public sector, the table suggests an order of remuneration and differentials applying to many times that number in the tiers below. Excluding the private income of medical consultants, all of the top public sector professional groups come in at between £49,000 and £76,000 a year. By contrast, the worst remunerated of the top private sector groups in the table notched up an average of £190,000 (partners in the 'Big Six' accountancy firms) – two and a half times as much as the public sector ceiling (for top civil servants and local authority chief executives). As to the next private sector tier, suffice it to note that in 1996 some 140,000 income-tax payers earned more than £100,000 a year[28] – many of them in early or mid career, working their way up into the Super Class.

This is not to say that the higher reaches of all private sector professions are in the £180,000-plus league: some, like (non-BBC) journalism, engineering and architecture have pay rates for senior staff closer to the public sector ceiling. But then the top cohorts of some mainstream public sector professions – such as university lecturing – receive well below the £75,000 of central and local government administrators. The broad picture is unmistakable. Analysing comparative data, the government's pay review body for NHS doctors and dentists concluded bluntly in 1996 that 'doctors and dentists have lost out against higher earners in the economy since 1985, a result of the widening of earnings differentials in the private sector'.[29]

By far the largest groups in the table – in either sector – are solicitors, accountants and City executives. Since most of the solicitors and accountants in question are partners in City firms dealing with corporate clients, they should be seen as part of a single, cohesive City cohort. This City élite – the heart of the Super Class – comprises upwards of three-quarters of the 8,500 top private sector earners covered by Table 6. Top barristers and company executives are more loosely attached to the City, but attached none the less: most of them are London-based, and their business either depends upon, or interacts with, the City at every turn. Of the top-earning groups, only medical consultants – of whom some 500 are at the £150,000-plus level – have no connection with the City, although even they are disproportionately London-based. As to groups not included in the table, a handful of pop stars, media personalities and sportsmen are in the same league, but few among them reached the Super Class as a result of family and career preparation and expectation in the same way as the City élite.

Let us briefly survey the Super Class by sector.

A rare public glimpse of the remuneration regime for top accountants was given in the 1996 annual report and accounts of KPMG and Ernst & Young, two of the 'Big Six' accountancy firms. The first such documents ever published, they revealed earnings for KPMG's 586 partners ranging from £123,000 a year for the most junior to £740,000 for the senior partner. 'We have to pay the partners at this level otherwise we are not going to have any,' said the senior partner, Colin Sharman, arguing he was losing 'very good people' to merchant banks and elsewhere.[30] At Ernst & Young, average earnings for the 397 partners were precisely £200,000 while the firm's 6,150 non-partner staff made an average of £31,000. As for senior City solicitors, the average for partners of leading law firms – some 2,500 solicitors in all – was around £200,000 in 1996, but again with a far higher ceiling.[31] When in May 1996 a US law firm advertised for three London partners at up to £700,000 a year, a legal recruitment consultant commented: 'The big hitters on the Wall Street firms are now getting about £1 million. Here the top partners are likely to be nearer £500,000, though some may earn more.'[32] Big salaries can come early: the youngest partners in accountants' and solicitors' firms are in their early thirties. In 1996 banks were reportedly poaching eighteen-month qualified capital markets lawyers, on £30,000 a year, for £82,000 apiece.[33]

The Bar, the boardroom and the City are the veritable top of the roof. QCs at the commercial Bar – about a third of England's 900 leading advocates – are said by insiders to earn around £350,000 a year on average, and few QCs (even in criminal practice) would make less than £130,000. A 1996 survey found even a barrister's clerk – an office manager for a set of chambers, with no legal or higher qualifications – earning £350,000, with the average salary for senior clerks in London's 300 chambers being £100,000.[34] In the law as in the City, the mere trading of mega money is enough to coin it.

Moving to business, the average remuneration for chief executives of the largest hundred companies listed on the London stock exchange was £501,000 in 1995, while the other 500 or so full-time board members of these companies received around £270,000 apiece – both figures exclusive of share options and long-term incentive plans (L-tips), one or other (often both) of which now embrace almost all senior executives of UK plcs, significantly boosting average earnings.[35] A study of annual reports of the 1,600 companies listed on the London stock exchange in 1995 found some 2,400 executives being paid more than £130,000 a year, exclusive of share options and L-tips.[36]

As for the City, recall our earlier foray into Barings, a small merchant bank where sixty-seven employees were awarded annual bonuses of £250,000 or more on top of their salaries. Taking merchant banks, brokers, strategy and management consultancies, and trading houses, the number of executives earning more than £150,000 a year in 1995 is put by insiders at around 10,000. According to one recruitment consultant, speaking from his own records, the average salary for a head of fund management in 1995 was £129,100 with an additional 28 per cent annual bonus plus car. The typical recruit would be in his/her early thirties. The stars of the profession fare far better, as the saga of Nicola Horlick, the 35-year-old fund manager at Morgan Grenfell sacked from her £1.15 million a year (with bonus) post in early 1997 after allegedly negotiating to take her team to a rival bank, revealed to a bemused public.[37]

The rise of the Super Class as a large and distinct group is inextricably bound up with the growth of the City as an international trading and financial services market since the 1960s. But there have been other significant influences, notably the reform of local taxation and the slashing of top tax rates on incomes rising fast in real terms. The 1988 budget, reducing the top tax rate of income tax from 60 to 40 per cent, cut the Super Class's effective marginal tax rate by a third, while the change from the rating system to a regressively banded council tax had the same effect on local property taxes. The Super Class would have been better-off still had the poll tax survived, which was the Thatcher government's first local tax reform; but the worst riots in recent British history, and mass civil disobedience, put paid to that somewhat too crude attempt to redistribute the tax burden from the better-off.[38]

Then there was the eradication of the large nationalized industrial sector, which had previously served as an indirect check on boardroom pay at large. In 1981 a Whitehall permanent secretary earned 45 per cent of the average executive chairman's salary for one of Britain's top one hundred listed companies, and 10 per cent more than the managing director of nationalized Cable & Wireless, the former imperial telecoms division of the Post Office (far smaller than British Telecom). By 1995 the permanent secretary was down to barely 19 per cent of his top one hundred company chairman counterpart, and earned a paltry 12 per cent of the salary of the chairman of privatized Cable & Wireless (at the time Lord Young, a former Tory minister, who received a severance payment of £1.5 million when forced to resign during the course of that year).[39]

Moreover, privatization took off just as the industrial side of the economy was declining rapidly vis-à-vis the financial side, which had always been more distinct from the public sector in its mentality and remuneration. This magnified the impact of cultural changes sweeping across the City in the 1980s, notably the importation of US firms and practices. In particular, it turned the higher reaches of the old professions of law and accountancy largely into adjuncts of the City. Clifford Chance, the UK's largest solicitors' firm, dealing mostly in City commercial and property work, doubled its number of fee-earners between 1985 and 1995, by when it had more than 1,500.

For all the media attention paid to individual 'fat cats' and City celebrities, the size and wealth of the Super Class has been surprisingly well disguised. Limited public disclosure of City salaries, and poor awareness of the impact of tax changes and the Big Bang, are partial explanations. Also important has been the cult of leading-edge private sector management practices within the state sector. By the early 1990s every senior public sector professional could recite the mantra of the 'new public management', with its stress on the bottom line, re-engineering and the motivation of managers by financial incentives.[40] Even school head teachers and family doctors were managing budgets and being encouraged to believe they were running their own businesses. The early 1990s saw most of Whitehall's 500,000 white-collar civil servants hived off into agencies managed by chief executives working to performance targets and performance-related pay. An 'internal market' was created within the NHS, complete with 'purchasers' and 'providers' of health care and annual contracts between the two.

Yet for all the similarity of jargon and function, rewards for top public sector managers and professionals are far removed from those of their private sector counterparts. It is not just a question of pay: non-monetary perks have also been sharply pruned. Downsizing, driven by the imperative to contain public spending, has killed the public sector's 'job for life' mentality even at the top: a third of senior Whitehall officials were purged in 1995 and 1996 under senior management reviews. Furthermore, honours have been redistributed to the private sector – the very tokens of esteem which, previously, were integral to the public service compensation for *not* being in the private sector. Not a single local authority chief executive was awarded either a knighthood or a CBE under the Thatcher or Major governments, although one or other honour had previously been the accepted perk for chief officials of the largest councils.

The Super Class, like the medieval clergy and the Victorian factory owners, has come not just to defend but to *believe in* the justice of its new wealth and status. Buttressed by a revamped official ideology (which even New Labour dares not question) lauding financial rewards as the hallmark of success and economic growth, and rejecting post-war notions of social cohesion, by the late 1980s the professional and managerial élite was unapologetic about the explosion of income differentials and prepared to concede few if any social disadvantages to the process. Underpinning this new self-righteousness is the Super Class's conception of itself as a meritocracy: an élite which has risen through dint of personal effort and achievement, deserving 'every penny' of their salaries and bonuses. In the words of Peter Cole, managing partner of Eversheds, Britain's second largest law firm, 'It is vital to create the environment where people can earn what they think they are worth' – a concept of 'worth' alien to a state sector where, as the government told the pay review bodies for professional staff in 1996, constraining salary growth 'has a key part to play in maintaining healthy public finances and delivering efficiencies and other savings across the public sector.'[41]

The hegemony of the City and the professionalization of corporate management have been critical to this reformation in mentality. Having achieved status equality with the old liberal professions, the parvenu managers and City executives are annexing the rewards to match. In his defence of Cedric Brown in the *FT*, Sir Iain Vallance of BT (who started his career as a trainee in the nationalized Post Office) laid bare this new mentality:

> As a society we have adopted an odd set of priorities over remuneration. We put a high price on escapism (pop groups, footballers, film stars, lottery winners). Entrepreneurs and the well-heeled professions go largely beyond rebuke. But we quibble about the often much smaller sums that go to the bosses of the major companies which underpin our economy.[42]

Moreover, the Super Class is in no doubt that it *earns* its way. Behind the mega salaries lie dawns, days, evenings and often nights in the office – for those on the way up, at any rate (those who have got there can relax more). The very scale of rewards, and the peaks awaiting the promoted, give private professional employers claims over their employees' time, energy and private life their public counterparts dare not claim – junior hospital doctors excepted, and even their hours were reduced after a skilful media campaign by the doctors' union. Job insecurity, although greatly exaggerated by professionals, is a further self-justification for maximizing pay and perks as fast as possible; for as their official spokesmen recite daily, what the market giveth, the market taketh away. The early 1990s recession, temporarily halting the upward march of bonuses and salaries, strengthened this perception. As John Nicholson, chairman of a leading business psychology consultancy, put it in 1995:

> Ten years ago, the professional classes took great satisfaction when the miners and the printers were forced to adapt to the realities of the marketplace. But now it's bankers and stockbrokers and solicitors and civil servants who are feeling the knife. And it's creating a tremendous amount of apprehension.[43]

When the recession ended, they took appropriate action.

Changing places

Were this the end of the story, Perkin's 'master conflict' between public and private sector élites might still be looming. For all the privatizations since 1979, in doctors, teachers, academics, military officers, BBC journalists and civil servants the public sector still comprises many of the most qualified, ambitious and vocal groups in society, well equipped to resist a progressive assault on their relative social standing. However, two trends only lightly touched upon so far have mitigated the conflict and greatly strengthened the security of the Super Class. The first is the inter-generational

Table 7: Careers of Oxford graduates, 1971 and 1994

	1971	1994
Public sector		
Teacher training (a)	226	91
Central government	54	35
Local government	37	5
Armed services	20	15
Medical/health authorities	80*	123
Total public sector	417	269
Private sector		
Commerce (mostly City firms)	114	446
Chartered accountancy	62	157
Solicitor's training	82	227
Bar training	50*	63
Industry (b)	201	118
Private education	30*	30*
Publishing/journalism (c)	24	73
Leisure and entertainment	24	43
Total private sector	587	1,157
Private sector % of total	**59**	**81**
Total graduating (d)	2,332	2,743

Notes: First degree graduates only

*estimate

(a) subtracting those taking a PGCE but then teaching in the private sector (estimated at ten a year)

(b) includes those entering nationalized industries (public sector)

(c) includes those entering the BBC (public sector)

(d) total number of first degree graduates for whom career information known (i.e. more than 90 per cent of the graduating total in each year)

Source: Oxford University Careers Service.

shift of Britain's social élite – the products of its leading schools and universities – towards the Super Class professions. The second is the subtle process of merger between the higher reaches of the public and private sector professions. This is serving both to sustain quality and minimize grievances among the core groups still required to perform senior public sector functions.

Table 7, revealing the sea-change in the career destinations of Oxford's graduates between 1971 and 1994, highlights the first of these trends – the realignment of the social élite behind the private sector in general and the Super Class in particular. Oxford graduates – for whom read their counterparts in Cambridge and London too – have decamped from the public sector *en masse*. The private–public ratio of 3:2 in 1971 had become 4:1 by 1996. Even these figures underestimate the switch. They exclude the large numbers going on from their first degree to study for post-graduate degrees: in the 1970s large numbers of post-grads were destined for university teaching; by the 1990s this was a minority pursuit. The 1971 figure also attributes the large Oxford entry into industry entirely to the private sector, although many in fact went to nationalized industries. The true 1971 ratio was probably closer to parity between the private and public sectors, against the 4:1 ratio of 1994. Medicine is Oxford's only growth occupation in the public sector, a career offering significant private earning potential for its élite.

The figures for Oxford's supply of new teachers is eloquent testimony to class segregation within the education system. Between 1971 and 1994 the number of Oxford graduates taking up teaching posts in the private sector (mainly the public schools) remained static, while the number going into state school teaching collapsed by nearly 60 per cent in numerical terms (and far further still, from 9.7 to 3.3 per cent, as a proportion of all graduate careers). At least a quarter as many Oxford graduates now go to teach in private schools as in state schools, although the public–private pupil ratio is 19:1 – a compelling commentary on the Super Class as meritocracy. And the true proportion is probably higher still, since most independent schools do not recruit only through the routes monitored by the university careers service and teacher training colleges.

Table 7 is a tale of the flight of England's top graduates to law, accountancy and 'commerce' – meaning, overwhelmingly, merchant banking, management consultancy and other City occupations. Barely 300 Oxford graduates went into these occupations combined in 1971; by 1994 the number was nearly 900, with the entry into commerce four times as large as in 1971 and by far the largest single destination for new Oxford graduates. The raw figures give only the broad picture. These excerpts from the 1994 report of Oxford's Careers Service add some light and shade:

> *Commerce*: 'The City institutions, notably the investment banks, drew huge numbers to their presentations: only the management consultants could equal their expectation of fifty or even a hundred attenders for every likely recruit. More than forty different banking institutions were involved here.'
>
> 'Only the management consultants, it seems, rivalled the glamour of the investment banks ... The 1994 total of sixty-nine marks an increase on previous years and represents an outstanding achievement for some highly talented undergraduates. They were joined by a dozen or so with higher degrees.'
>
> *Solicitors*: 'The well-known City firms still dominate the list ...'
>
> *Accountants*: 'Oxonians were the second largest contingent in the 1993–94 entry in the statistics produced by the Institute of Chartered Accountants.'
>
> *State school teaching*: 'While seventy-eight appears a low figure for training at secondary level, we can only report that press coverage of education and parental discouragement are two detractors among undergraduates who continue to attend our sessions on teaching.'
>
> *Local government*: 'Local government scarcely figured at all in 1994, except for one archivist and four workers at clerical level who were probably hoping in due course to move on to do something more stretching.'[44]

We are talking here about trends and dominant groups – about the mainsprings of the Super Class, without claiming that they are its sole sources of recruitment. As for what this means down the line, three more figures are indicative: virtually all recruits to the top London management consultancies come from Oxbridge; some three-quarters of judges have a public school and Oxbridge background; and a third of the new partners in the UK's top thirty law firms in 1995 were educated at Oxbridge.[45]

What, then, of the public sector élite? Many senior public professionals have long enjoyed significant private sector incomes, their scale poorly appreciated because they have been unpublished and typically downplayed. The public–private overlap takes one of two forms: a vertical division of *careers* split between the two sectors over time (the judicial model), and a horizontal division of *salaries* derived from the two sectors at the same time (the hospital consultants' model). This division is not altogether neat – judges, for instance, often sit on the bench as part-time Recorders before leaving the Bar, while NHS doctors can generally cultivate large private practices only once they have become consultants – but it is serviceable.

England's senior salaried judges – some 700 in the county courts and above – are virtually all recruited from the ranks of private sector QCs, in contrast to most continental states where the judiciary is a career public service. A high proportion of the 900-odd QCs at any one time will proceed to the bench: among those able and willing to do so, the real competition is for the level of judgeship. The best go to the High Court and perhaps higher thereafter, the rest become circuit judges. Judgeships typically come at about the age of fifty – i.e. after twenty or so high-earning years at the Bar, when many QCs are happy to exchange salary for prestige (senior judges still get automatic knighthoods) and a more relaxed lifestyle. Governments, anxious to sustain this regime for public and personal reasons (the Lord Chancellor is invariably a barrister), generally treat the Bar and judiciary with kid gloves. In 1990 the judges even successfully fought off modest proposals from a rare reform-minded Lord Chancellor (Lord Mackay – a Scot, significantly), which would have curbed some of the Bar's quainter restrictive practices. The

Bar raised a fighting fund of £1 million for a campaign led by Lord Lane, the Lord Chief Justice, who hailed the plans as 'one of the most sinister documents ever to emanate from government'.[46]

The military and media élites follow the judicial model. Journalists cross back and forth between the BBC and the private sector – John Birt being the classic case at the top level: enriched by a career in London Weekend Television, and recruited thence, at a fraction of the salary, to be director-general of the BBC. As for the armed forces, its officerships are increasingly seen by young aspiring professionals as training not for wars and decorations but for lucrative private sector careers. There has always been a steady flow of officers into the private sector, given short service commissions and early military retirement ages. The flow is now a flood. As one observer puts it, the 1980s saw the rise of the 'nine-to-five subaltern' drawn to the army 'by its career prospects rather than a sense of duty'. The army used to work on the basis of 60 per cent of subalterns serving as regulars and 40 per cent on short service commissions of three years. By 1990 a little over a quarter were regulars, and the proportion continues to fall.[47] By the mid-1990s the army was making a virtue out of necessity: its 1996 officer recruitment brochure was entitled *Army Officer: Training for Life in Leadership and Management Skills*, stressing the opportunities for gaining degrees 'or even membership of the élite chartered professions'.

The judicial career model is likely to spread further. Labour has floated the possibility of ambassadors recruited from the business world; such posts might prove highly attractive as fixed-term stints for top corporate executives. Similar practices could be extended to the rest of the senior civil service. Existing mandarins might be resistant, but the principle was conceded with the decision in the early 1990s to advertise top Whitehall posts – including, from 1995, permanent secretaryships – for open competition. The United States (whose public sector salaries are lower than Britain's, headed by President Clinton on a paltry $150,000) operates such a system. Top US public service jobs are treated as political spoils, but it would be possible to operate a similar system in the UK while retaining Whitehall's tradition of political impartiality.

Then there is the consultants' model. Under the generous terms of their misleadingly titled 'nine-elevenths' contracts, Britain's 21,000 NHS consultants have ample scope to develop their private practice. The best and/or most assiduous in sectors such as dermatology and gynaecology comfortably double their £50,000 – £65,000 NHS salary (in 1996) from private practice. In fields like public health and paediatrics, there is far less scope for private practice, and career choices are made accordingly. Like the judges, consultants are dealing with compliant ministers who – whatever the egalitarian rhetoric of the NHS – have always, since the launch of the NHS in 1948, accepted private practice as part of the deal to accommodate the higher medical professionals (a theme discussed further in Chapter 6). The Audit Commission, the public sector watchdog, has criticized the extraordinary laxity of the contractual arrangements for consultants,[48] finding that many managers have little idea how many hours their consultants devote to the NHS, let alone how much private work they do on top. But only marginal changes are likely: even a government keen to tackle what one senior Labour minister calls a 'public sector racket' would probably draw back from a pitched battle with the medical high command.[49]

The consultants' model is spreading, informally, to higher education. Professors and senior lecturers in applied subjects from economics and law to business studies and medicine regularly boost their income by private consultancy. Some economics lecturers at the LSE and Oxbridge earn high five- or even six-figure sums from consultancy – in some cases, ironically, from advising the privatized utilities. With both political parties committed to larger student contributions to higher education, and the old egalitarian salary structure for academics crumbling fast, private income is likely to boost academic salaries more broadly and formally, raising the roof at the top of academe and bringing the earnings hierarchy of British universities more closely into line with that of their US counterparts. As this happens, the new structure will reflect the pecking order of universities – headed by London and Oxbridge, descending through the old provincial institutions and redbrick down to the former polytechnics – which students and employers have always taken for granted, notwithstanding the changes of official title that have turned everything from Cambridge to South Bank Poly into 'universities'.

The life of the Super Class

London; servants; second homes; globalism; the best of private education, health and leisure; exotic foreign holidays; modern art; an almost total separation from public life; intermarriage between professionals with both partners on large incomes – these are the dominant themes in the life of the Super Class. Only a few can be drawn out here, although others are developed elsewhere in the book.

Christopher Lasch writes of the élite in the US: 'Their loyalties . . . are international rather than regional, national or local. They have more in common with their counterparts in Brussels or Hong Kong than with the masses of Americans not yet plugged into the network of global communications.'[50] The British picture is somewhat different. Parts of the Super Class are thoroughly international, trading or dealing in international markets, working abroad for part of a career. But as much or more of the class is thoroughly insular. And whether insular or international by career, when in Britain its members are overwhelmingly concentrated in London and a narrow range of occupations therein. A few other metropolitan centres – notably Manchester and Edinburgh – are outposts, but there is no British San Francisco or LA to match its New York, no Hamburg vying with a Frankfurt and Berlin. Consider just one ostensibly national profession: the law. Nearly half of all solicitors' firms are located in London and the south-east; 37 per cent of all solicitors work in London (one in five – 10,300 – in the City of London alone).[51] Half of the £6.6 billion in gross fees earned by solicitors in private practice in 1994 was earned in

London. Of the top thirty law firms, twenty-four are in London, including all of the top fourteen.[52] As for the Bar, of the 8,498 barristers in independent practice in England and Wales in 1995, two-thirds worked in London, with 85 per cent of all QCs being London-based.

This concentration in London has two effects, reinforcing the dominance and the distinctiveness of the Super Class. In the first place, most of its economic weight is exerted at the very heart of the nation's politics and culture, ensuring it strong political clout although few of its members engage directly in politics. The City, the West End and Westminster are the boundaries of opinion-forming Britain, including as part of the triangle the erratically growing Docklands, soon to be integrated fully by the Jubilee Line. Secondly, it enables the Super Class to separate itself physically from most of the country at no social cost. Britain beyond the Home Counties does not feature on its collective horizon: yet within that narrow sphere, the size of the Super Class is sufficiently large for it to have equipped itself with a highly developed infrastructure of private schools, hospitals and leisure facilities. History helped, of course: the English élite has been largely south-east-based since the Middle Ages, its institutions being handed on from one generation's élite to the next; but rarely has it been so exclusively London-based as today.

As for servants, education, marriages and lifestyle, the Horlick affair of early 1997 is a Super Class tale *par excellence*. Enter Ms Nicola Horlick, the dismissed 35-year-old fund manager at Morgan Grenfell intent on revenge over her former employer. Privately educated at Birkenhead High School, then Balliol College, Oxford. Annual salary £1.15 million, which she had been hoping to increase before being caught out seeking to transfer her valuable skills to another bank. Married to Tim, a head of corporate finance and investment banking at Salomon Brothers on a salary of several hundreds of thousands. Five children all under ten, with multiple nannies and housekeepers in attendance. A £1.3 million five-storey house in Stafford Terrace, Kensington, plus a second home in the country. Dubbed 'Superwoman', her response was indignant: 'I'm an ordinary woman doing an ordinary job,' she protested. 'People who say that sort of thing haven't tried it. I'm usually home by 6.30 p.m. and have until 8 p.m. every night with the children; and every weekend we all go down to our cottage in Hampshire. It helps that Tim is willing to play his part and even change the odd nappy now and again.'[53]

The servants are back, nowhere more numerous than in the homes of two-salary Super Class couples. As Henry Porter puts it: 'Domestic servants no longer enable leisure, as they did in the relaxed days of the Bellamy household in *Upstairs Downstairs*, but much longer hours at the office.'[54] Estimates put the number of foreign au pairs alone at 170,000, apart from the army of nannies, cleaners and gardeners who go unlogged. In the mid-1980s Mintel, the market researchers, estimated that £524 million a year was spent on cooks, cleaners, child minders and gardeners; by 1997 the figure was thought to be £4 billion. Agencies confirm that the demand for nannies, housekeepers, butlers, cooks, drivers and occasionally even gardeners, outstrips supply. A London nanny with good references can cost up to £20,000 a year, once tax, board and lodging, and the use of car and phone are included.

Two vignettes complete the picture. In mid-1996 the *FT* reported a boom in demand for country houses in the Home Counties. Manor houses in Hampshire were particularly sought after, an agent reporting average prices rising from £1.25m to £1.4m. 'The last two years has seen more confidence among businessmen and City professionals about the state of the economy,' said an agent.[55] Another claimed that the electronic superhighway meant 'professional people are seeking properties where they can install an office' and 'may spend only two days a week in London'. Some of the biggest demand was said to be 'close to public schools'. City bonuses were given as the main source of funds.

Appropriately, however, we end by revisiting the 'fat cats'. Not Cedric Brown, but the 1996 Annual General Meeting of privatized

Yorkshire Water, which had attracted the wrath of consumers and the water regulator the previous summer for leaving thousands of customers at the mercy of standpipes. There was the customary fuss about the latest pay and incentives package for the board, small shareholders directing their anger at the company's new chairman, Brandon Gough, the former head of accountancy firm Coopers and Lybrand. But the protests were not just about his pay – £120,000 for one day a week. Of far greater concern to them was that Yorkshire Water's new chairman had decided to continue living in Kent 'for personal reasons'.[56]

4. POLITICS

All middle class now?

The British People, being subject to fogs and possessing a powerful
middle class, require grave statesmen.

Benjamin Disraeli

Middle class, Middle England, middle of the road – the three vital
qualifications for success in national politics today. The result is
a House of Commons more uniform in appearance – socially and
ideologically – than any since the Great Reform Act of 1832
forced the aristocracy to share power with the Victorian middle
class and the Duke of Wellington complained of the first reformed
Commons that he had never seen so many shocking bad hats in
his life.

It has been a few decades in coming. Ever since Harold Wilson
demolished Sir Alec Douglas-Home – a fourteenth earl recruited
from the House of Lords to lead the Tories in 1963 – as an
out-of-touch aristocrat picked off the grouse moors, the Tories
have made a fetish of suburban leaders. 'Ability must be the test,
and ability is not to be measured by upper-class accents,' Wilson
proclaimed in one of his compelling 'New Britain' speeches before
the 1964 election.[1] Home was soon replaced by Heath, son of a
Broadstairs carpenter; Heath by Thatcher, daughter of a Grantham
grocer ('I sort of regard myself as a very normal, ordinary person
with all the right instinctive antennae,' she remarked[2]); and Thatcher
by Major, son of an itinerant actor and trapeze artist, who left school
at sixteen with a few modest O-levels. Even William Hague –
Magdalen College, Oxford, and president of the Union – glories
in his other *alma mater*: Richmond Comprehensive in Yorkshire.

Major's selection by Tory MPs in November 1990 was a
defining Tory moment. Class was far from decisive in the selection

of either Heath or Thatcher. Major, by contrast, ran above all on his class credentials – namely his lack of them. It was 'classless John' against Douglas Hurd 'the toff'. Mere attendance at Eton, and the trace of a matching accent, were enough to disqualify Hurd, however strongly he protested that he was the son of a tenant farmer and went to Eton as a scholarship boy. Major's celebrated 'classless society' remarks were made first in a campaign press conference, largely with the intention of shafting Hurd whom Major had to supplant immediately after Thatcher's resignation as the main contender against Heseltine. Final proof, perhaps, that the Conservative party had passed from the estates to the estate agents.

Meanwhile the Labour leadership was in rapid transit from Celtic firebrand to Oxbridge smoothy via Edinburgh barrister. Neil Kinnock, for all his courage in leading Labour from the abyss to respectability, was stereotyped by the English media and middle classes as a Welsh working-class windbag, and unstable to boot. Labour's 1992 defeat was largely attributed to the fact. In truth, Kinnock and Major were uncannily similar. 'Kinnock: the Journey', Hugh Hudson's brilliant 1987 election broadcast charting the rise of a dutiful, honest, popular working-class lad from the valleys, was such a success that Major did his own version in 1992, pointing out the sites of his boyhood Brixton from the back of a Rover. But for Major the class transition was more definite (he really had been a bank manager); and anyway, he was English, grey, Tory and MP for Huntingdon.

To be fully trusted, Labour had to find a leader from the English professional classes, with matching accent and image. Which is just what they did, by a circuitous route. In 1992 Kinnock gave way to John Smith, stolid bespectacled bank manager by appearance, Edinburgh advocate by training. The cultivated Edinburgh tones were an improvement on the Welsh lilt. But Smith was still, well, Scottish, and the party needed above all to reassure the Middle English. Smith's untimely death in May 1994 was Labour's defining moment. Cometh the hour, cometh the man. Public school, St John's College, Oxford, the Bar, married to a fellow barrister (soon to be QC), impeccably clipped Oxford accent, an English MP (the first to lead the party since Wilson), three young children, youthful (forty-one) but with J. F. K. dynamism – Tony Blair (always Tony, never Anthony) was everything Labour's image makers were striving to become. It was immaterial that his schooling was in Scotland. Fettes was a top public school incidentally located in Edinburgh; the accent and looks were right; and Blair himself has been in the modernizers' vanguard since his election to the Commons in 1983. As shadow Home Secretary before Smith's death, he made his mark with a skilful play on Middle England's crime paranoia ('Tough on crime, tough on the causes of crime'). Within months of taking the helm, he had ditched Clause Four of Labour's constitution, committing the party to public ownership. New Labour was proclaimed. The unions were soon being dismissed as fifty years out of date. By the spring of 1996 Blair was reassuring New York businessmen that Labour stood for the 'radical centre', in a speech making no mention of socialism or even the Left.[3]

The upshot of the New York speech was as symbolic as its content. The following morning John Prescott, Blair's blunt-spoken deputy, chosen in 1994 for his working-class trade union roots, declared on Radio Four's morning news programme *Today* that he was in fact middle class. 'People come to me and say you're a class warrior,' he said in response to a question about New Labour's appeal to Middle England. 'But by the nature of being an MP and the salary I earn I'm middle class. My roots, my background and the way I act is working class, but it would be hypocritical to say I'm anything else than middle class now.' Blair's spin doctors leaped on the remarks. 'John has turned himself from a class warrior into a class act,' came their response from New York.

Prescott's remarks precipitated a national inquisition on the class system, noted earlier. But their narrow political purpose was equally revealing. Desperate to oust the Tories, Labour leaders worried that for all their party's changes of policy, rhetoric, even name, and however great the opinion poll leads, they might still lose Middle England because of residual fears that Labour remained working class at heart. Prescott could not quite bring himself to proclaim the middle classless society, but he was anxious to place himself squarely within middle-class Middle England. It was all the more symbolic coming from one of Labour's authentic manual-worker trade union MPs, the only sizeable section of today's House of Commons which is manifestly not middle class by background. The view from the Commons gallery is equally revealing. Wellington could tell them apart by their hats. At the turn of the century Keir Hardie appeared in a cloth cap. Until the mid-1980s the suits and ties told the story, particularly the Eton, army, college and union neckwear. Nowadays the two front-benches, at least, are almost indistinguishable in their dark double-breasted suits and bright designer ties. The striking contrast comes from the growing band of women MPs – virtually all daughters of professionals, with accents to match.

Yet to say that Britain's politicians are 'all middle class now' obscures as much as it enlightens. Today's politicians may almost all look alike in social terms, but this uniformity is essentially superficial. Scrape the surface and the new political class is found to be riven by one of the deepest divides within contemporary Britain: the separation between public and private sector professionals. This public–private divide has become *the* essential differentiator between the two main political parties. A product of broad societal change – the decline of the old upper and manual classes, the post-war growth of the public sector, and the rise of the Super Class described in Chapter 3 – it represents a social division pregnant with potential for political conflict. In composition and mentality Labour has become the party of the public sector professionals; the Tories mostly represent the private sector, particularly the Super Class. British politics in the coming years will largely be shaped by this bifurcation.

Furthermore, the political élite as a whole – taking MPs from the two parties together – is recruited from a narrower social range than at any time since the First World War. The professional classes, whether public or private, have long dominated the Commons; but until the 1960s they co-existed with a large contingent of worker MPs on the Labour side, which has been progressively eliminated. The aristocracy too has vanished from the Commons. As for the Super Class, which has replaced it as an effective 'upper class', it may support the Conservative party but it is represented on the Tory benches in Parliament almost exclusively by its 'cadets' and not (as with the aristocracy of old) by its leaders. Several factors are at play: the demise of both the trade unions and a leisured upper class; the rise of women MPs; the poor remuneration (by Super Class standards) offered by politics; and the growing dominance of the professional politician. The result is the modern democratic paradox: a Parliament and political system less representative of society than at any time since Britain became a democracy.

Public Left, private Right

Nothing reveals more about the tensions within a society's élite than the composition of its legislature. The House of Commons is true to form. With the odd flamboyant exception – Nicholas Soames and a few unabashed upper crusts on one side, Dennis Skinner and a few ex-miners-and-proud-of-it on the other – social class has ceased to be a stark visible differentiator. A bastion of the professional classes which run society at large, the Commons looks as uniform as the morning assembly in a private school which has just started admitting girls. Yet this is a misleading impression, for in reality the Commons is a cockpit of competing public and private factions within the professional classes. To appreciate how this has come to be, we need to understand the forces which have transformed the political class in recent decades.

Until the Second World War a gaping social chasm divided the two sides of the Commons. Most Labour MPs were former manual workers and/or trade unionists, many of whom – a quarter as late as 1951 – had left school by the age of thirteen. When

Table 8: Education of Members of Parliament, 1951 and 1992

(percentages of MPs within each party)

	1951		1992	
	Con	Lab	Con	Lab
State school to age of twelve	1	26	–	3
State secondary school	23	53	38	82
Private ('public') school	75	20	62	15
Eton College	24	1	10	1
University	65	41	73	61
Oxford or Cambridge	52	19	45	16

Source: David Butler, *The British General Election of 1951* (1952), Ch. 3; David Butler and Dennis Kavanagh, *The British General Election of 1992* (1992), Ch. 10.

Ernest Bevin, the square-built former general secretary of the Transport Workers Union who dropped all his aitches, was appointed Foreign Secretary in 1945, it was said that the only other job he could have filled in the Foreign Office was that of porter. By contrast, the Tory benches were an amalgam of the blue-blooded aristocracy, barristers and wealthy industrialists. The public schools, particularly Eton, reigned supreme. Among the 420 Tory MPs sitting in 1939 there were only ten solicitors, eight accountants and four teachers. 'The Conservative Party is indeed exclusive,' noted one critic, 'excluding entirely members of nearly all the main occupations from becoming Conservative Members of Parliament.'[4]

The post-war decades saw a progressive blurring of this social divide. Clement Attlee (Haileybury and University College, Oxford) blunted the edges of the one authentically socialist government in British history (1945–51). A grammar school and Oxbridge élite rapidly colonized Labour's frontbench, directing the 1964 and 1974 Labour governments under the leadership of Harold Wilson (Wirral Grammar and Jesus College, Oxford), whose lieutenants included Denis Healey (Bradford Grammar and

Balliol College, Oxford) and Roy Jenkins (Abersychan Grammar and Balliol, and later Chancellor of Oxford University). The major public schools also produced a notable post-war Labour élite: Hugh Gaitskell, Douglas Jay and Richard Crossman were all Wykehamists. Yet Labour's parliamentary party remained substantially working class by background. The 'workers' provided around 40 per cent of Labour MPs in the 1950s, and the proportion declined only gradually thereafter. Even at the top Labour was an uneasy social coalition. James Callaghan, a minor tax official turned trade unionist who left school at fifteen, quietly resented the social pretensions of Jenkins and Healey, but overtook them to become Wilson's successor as prime minister in 1976.

On the Tory side the expanding class of the post-war decades was that of the up-and-coming private sector professionals, particularly business executives, who co-existed with an older Tory élite of barristers, company owner-managers and knights of the shire.[5] This social coalition was graphically exhibited by the Heath and early Thatcher leaderships: Heath (Chatham House Grammar, Ramsgate, followed by the inevitable Balliol), supported by Sir Alec Douglas-Home (Eton, heir to an earldom, a third-class degree from Christ Church, Oxford, and a spell as a first-class cricketer) and Willie Whitelaw (bluff Rugby–Cambridge son of a railway company director); while Thatcher (Grantham High and Somerville College, Oxford) gave the top posts in her first Cabinet to the sixth Lord Carrington (Eton and Sandhurst), Sir Geoffrey Howe (Winchester, Cambridge and the Bar) and Whitelaw, whom she had defeated for the Tory leadership.

Until the early 1980s the class character of the two major parties was therefore clearly distinct. Both were social coalitions. They overlapped significantly at élite level, notably through the common Oxbridge experience of the public and grammar school boys holding most of the top jobs in successive Cabinets (a Balliol man was either Prime Minister or Chancellor for twenty of the twenty-four years between 1955 and 1979). Yet taken as a whole, the two parties in the Commons were *and looked* classes apart.

Those of their leaders failing to act the part paid the price: witness the damage inflicted on Roy Jenkins' Labour leadership prospects by his sybaritic lifestyle. 'I don't see why only Tories should enjoy the good things in life,' he told one interviewer in the late 1960s: the trade union barons and most Labour MPs were unimpressed.

All the while, however, the social divide between the solid mass of the Labour and Tory MPs was apparently narrowing. Election by election after the mid-1960s, salaried professionals took over seats vacated by defeat or retirement on both sides of the House. On the Labour benches the process was slowed by the post-1979 lurch to the left and the rout of 1983, which pushed the party into its northern and Scottish industrial (increasingly *ex*-industrial) heartlands. But by the 1987 election, when only twelve of the sixty-nine new Labour MPs returned were former manual workers,[6] Labour was back on track. By the mid-1990s the two main parties in Parliament were more look-alike than at any time since Labour became the principal Opposition to the Tories in 1918. The same was true of party activists in the country at large. Studies of Labour and Tory party members in the early 1990s found school teachers to be the single largest occupational group in both parties.[7]

More than four-fifths of today's MPs have professional, executive or managerial backgrounds, compared with less than one-third of the working population at large (see Table 9). Gone almost entirely on the Tory side is the old aristocracy. And going at a rapid rate are Labour's authentic working-class trade unionists, down to barely one in five of all Labour MPs by 1996, the smallest proportion since the party's foundation in 1900. Even that rump is diminishing fast, hastened by the rapid decline of union influence in constituency parties, the introduction of one-member-one-vote ballots of party members to select new candidates, and a large rise in the number of women MPs through female-only shortlists (virtually all the women selected are professionals).[8] On the Tory side the change has been less stark, because the presence of professionals and business leaders was larger at the outset. Of

Table 9: Social background of Members of Parliament, 1951 and 1992
(percentages of MPs within each party)

	1951 Con	1951 Lab	1992 Con	1992 Lab
Public professional				
University/post-eighteen teaching	1	8	2	14
School teaching	–	6	5	14
Armed services	10	1	4	–
Civil service/local government	3	3	3	6
Doctors	1	3	1	1
Private professional/business				
Barristers/solicitors	22	14	18	6
Company director	24	3	11	–
Company executive	6	2	22	3
Commerce (banking, etc.)	6	4	3	–
Farmers	5	1	3	1
Other private professional	3	–	5	1
'Private means'	8	–	–	–
Public/private				
Manual workers	–	37	1	22
Misc. white collar	1	4	3	13
Politician/political organizer	4	2	6	9
Totals				
Private professional/business	66	24	62	11
Public professional	15	21	15	35
Public prof. + 'public/private' groups	20	64	25	79

Source: David Butler, *The British General Election of 1951* (1952), Ch. 3; David Butler and Dennis Kavanagh, *The British General Election of 1992* (1992), Ch. 10.

Tory MPs elected in 1992, nearly two-thirds hailed from private schools and virtually all had a professional, commercial or business background. Yet behind such bald figures the Conservative parliamentary party has become steadily less exclusive. The proportion of Etonians, one in ten in 1992, was down by more than half since the 1950s, the decline being part of a wider shift away from the top Clarendon schools and Oxbridge and towards a wider range of independent schools and provincial universities. Comparing today's two frontbenches, the most immediately striking difference is not the class but the regional balance, Labour's dominated by accents from Scotland, the Tory's from the Home Counties.

The ideological convergence of the two parties in the 1990s must be seen in this context. Mainstream Labour and Tory rhetoric (post-Thatcher, at any rate) rejects the notion of necessary, let alone desirable class conflict. Both parties laud a classless 'one nation' and peddle identical catchwords of choice, markets and opportunity. A recurrent theme of Tony Blair's speeches is the end of party competition in the form of fundamentally conflicting ideologies. In Britain, as in all democracies, the convergence has largely been of Left converging on Right – on a Right represented by a Conservative party which for decades has pitched its appeal squarely at respectable, employed, home-owning (or wanting to be) Middle England, without jeopardizing that minimum degree of support needed from other social groups and regions. Looked at thus, it is unsurprising that European integration and devolution to Scotland should have become the key issues dividing the parties before the 1997 election: policies beyond the old Left–Right divide, addressing England's relationship with its neighbours.

It would be easy, but mistaken, to stop there and proclaim an end to serious social – as opposed to regional – divisions at the heart of British politics. Mistaken, because the social consensus of the late 1990s is far more fragile than it appears, founded not on a unity of interests and aspirations among social élites but on a precarious compromise born of the dominance of the private sector professional and managerial élite under the long period of Tory rule after 1979. By contrast, New Labour is the political voice of the public sector professionals: in his quest for power, Tony Blair studiously avoided challenging the private élite, but in government his readiness and capacity to contain the aspirations of Labour's public sector élite will be sorely tested.

Like all explanatory frameworks, this public–private division of the political class is necessarily broad-brush. Labour has its barristers and bankers, just as the Tories have their dons and doctors. Moreover, below the professional level this public–private division ceases to apply: although some of the lower private sector groups, notably the small-scale self-employed, are largely Tory, most non-professional white- and blue-collar employees cannot be neatly categorized. Trade unionists, for instance, largely assemble behind Labour irrespective of public or private sector. Yet these lower social groups are poorly represented in Parliament, and it remains true that the essential division between the contemporary Labour and Tory élites is between public and private sector professionals, with the values and core interests of the two groups, particularly their disposition for and against high state welfare spending, uniting them to larger social groups below.

The public–private division between Labour and Tory MPs is evident at every level – schooling, career patterns and lifestyles.[9] Moreover, the division has become more, not less, pronounced in recent decades, as illustrated by Tables 8 and 9, which compare the social composition of the House of Commons of 1992 with that of 1951. The 1992 picture remains valid: although the 1997 election brought a massive shift of seats from the Tories to Labour, the social make-up of the two parties in Parliament altered barely at all – a testament to the strength of the class divisions separating them.

Sixty-two per cent of Tory MPs returned in the 1992 election were private school educated, against 15 per cent of Labour MPs. The Labour public school contingent was significantly lower in the 1990s than in the 1950s, due to the post-war expansion of state secondary education, which made a far smaller impact on the Tory than on the Labour side (see Table 8). One in three of all Tory MPs in 1992 was a former or serving company executive (112 in all), against a paltry ten Labour MPs (3.7 per cent). As for the leading private sector professions, the law and accountancy claimed almost one in four Tory MPs in 1992, but fewer than one in ten on the Labour side. Here again the Labour proportion was sharply lower than a generation ago: in 1951 fully 14 per cent of Labour MPs were lawyers. In 1992 nearly one in three of all Labour MPs was a former school, college or university teacher (twice the proportion of the 1950s), against one in fifteen on the Tory side.

Taking all MPs together, a solid three-quarters of Tories count as private sector middle class, facing a solid three-quarters of Labour MPs who are either public sector middle class or have trade union, local government, clerical or manual worker backgrounds and have come as MPs to adopt a broadly public sector professional mentality (John Prescott, by frank admission, is in this latter class). Tony Blair is quite candid about being a class misfit. 'With my class background,' he told an interviewer after his election as Labour leader, 'if all I had wanted to do was to exercise power I could and would – let's be blunt about this – have joined another party.'[10]

MPs' lifestyles are divided on the same public/private lines. Tories generally send their children to independent schools. Labour MPs with a professional background generally used to do so too. In 1956 the senior Labour MP and barrister Hartley Shawcross declared: 'I do not know a single member of the Labour Party, who can afford to do so, who does not send his children to a public school.'[11] When in 1965 Harold Wilson offered Roy Jenkins the Ministry of Education and a seat in the Cabinet, Jenkins declined it partly because 'all three of our children were at fee-paying schools and . . . this was surely an obstacle to being Minister of Education in a Labour government', only for Wilson to respond: 'So were mine.'[12] Within a decade, however, independent education became out of bounds for any Labour MP aspiring to the frontbench, let alone one aiming to become Education Secretary, thanks to the battles over the phasing out of the direct-grant schools and the abolition of the state grammar schools. This remains true even under Tony Blair – witness the controversy, within as much as beyond Labour ranks, at the decisions of Blair and Harriet Harman to send their children to selective state schools miles away from their inner London homes.

Private schools and the other appurtenances of a Super Class lifestyle do not come cheap, and Tory MPs readily exploit their private sector contacts to help foot the bill, insofar as the rules of ministerial and parliamentary conduct allow them to do so. The tightening up of these rules in 1996, following the scandal of Tory MPs accepting cash for questions and forging unhealthily close links with lobbying companies, was a serious source of angst on the Tory side. The resulting reforms – particularly the new rule requiring declarations not just of outside interests (as previously) but also of outside income – served only to demonstrate the extent of Tory dependence on private remuneration. In 1996 the Conservatives declared extra-parliamentary income of £2 million, four times as much as all the other parties in the House of Commons put together – despite the fact that many Tory MPs, led by David Mellor with his ten private sector consultancies, refused to declare much of their income on the grounds that it was unconnected to their parliamentary duties.[13]

No issue exposes the public–private dimension of the Commons more graphically than parliamentary pay, the subject of periodic parliamentary rows and deep soul-searching among MPs. For Tory MPs with large private incomes or well-paid spouses (of which there are many) the parliamentary salary is merely the icing on the cake. But for many Tories, and virtually all Labour MPs, it is their livelihood, and tensions flare whenever it comes to discretionary decisions on the question of uprating.

The 1996 pay round was a classic case. First came the report of the independent Senior Salaries Review Body, chaired by Sir Michael Perry, chairman of consumer goods group Unilever, whose own remuneration in the previous year totalled £2.84 million (£700,000 in basic salary, £91,950 in benefits, £84,000 in performance-related pay and £1.96 million in pension contribution).[14] Perry and his colleagues recommended a 26 per cent increase in MPs' basic salary, taking it from £34,085 to £43,000. Cabinet ministers were to gain more still, their pay rising from £69,651 to £103,000, with the prime minister ascending from

£84,217 to £143,000. For MPs the SSRB's rationale was to bring them into line with counterparts 'in the public sector/professional arena: head teachers, police superintendents, doctors, civil servants'.[15] For senior ministers the review body looked beyond the public sector, where it could not find satisfactory comparitors, to corporate jobs held to be of similar weight. For the prime minister it lighted on the chief executive of 'a huge multinational company in a sector (such as oil) requiring massive capital investment and exerting a clear influence on the world economy'.[16] On this basis it came up with a basic salary of £450,000 for the prime minister and £375,000 for Cabinet ministers, taking no account of the corporate sector's bonuses, enhanced benefits and share options (which had increased Sir Michael Perry's annual remuneration to over £2 million). Here, of course, the comparability exercise broke down, since there could be no question of hiking a Cabinet minister's pay from £69,651 to £375,000. The SSRB simply declared it not in the 'public interest' that Cabinet posts be 'undervalued' and recommended rises of a far more modest 50 to 80 per cent.[17]

John Major and his Cabinet colleagues, anxious about the impact on public sector pay, not to mention the coming general election, rejected the SSRB recommendations. Instead, they substituted a 3 per cent rise for MPs and ministers, but allowed Tory MPs a free vote on the issue. On the Labour side Tony Blair endorsed the 3 per cent, but also allowed a free vote. On both frontbenches there was a tacit willingness to let backbenchers vote through more – some in the shadow Cabinet campaigned openly for the whole hog – provided the leadership was not directly implicated. And so it was. On the floor of the Commons, the full increases were carried by a massive majority (317 to 168) following a highly charged debate. Tony Newton, speaking for the government, asked MPs to consider the increases 'in relation to their impact on the wider aims of public policy', particularly the need for 'firm control of public spending'.[18] But as one Conservative MP muttered privately, 'No Tory can live on £34,000 a year.'[19] Even in the formal debate, another Tory claimed, darkly, that previous pay increases for MPs had been emasculated under the influence of 'a number of people with large private incomes'. On the Labour side, the argument centred, tellingly, on the justice of narrowing the differential between MPs and senior public staff.

So much for the House of Commons. The public/private divide penetrates to the heart of the two parties outside Parliament. We noted earlier that teachers are the single largest occupational category among the membership of both parties. The second largest among Tories is financial service workers, including accountants, underwriters, brokers and tax specialists.[20] On the Labour side, by contrast, fully two-thirds of all party members are in public sector employment, extending from teaching to local government, health, civil service (particularly clerical grades) and state industrial sectors[21] – about four times the proportion among the workforce as a whole. Even this underestimates the scale of the division, which is far greater among party activists. Surveys of party conference delegates show the Tories dividing about three to one in favour of the private sector, while Labour tilts three to two towards the public sector.[22] Within Labour local politics the public sector trade unions remain a powerful force, not these days through their conference block votes but through the dominant role their members, led by local union officials, play within the party as party officers and local councillors. Moreover, Labour councils deal day-by-day as employers with the local government and teaching unions, both dominated by Labour activists. Tory local politics is a world apart. The public sector middle class is represented within Tory ranks only by individuals, often not even belonging to a trade union; and in practice the public sector is not as strong as the raw figures about teachers suggest, since the chairmen of local associations are drawn disproportionately from private sector professional activists (mostly retired).[23] Constituency chairmen are the prime movers in local Tory politics, particularly in the selection of Tory candidates; and as a US political scientist puts it, 'He who can make nominations is the owner of the party.'[24]

This acute public–private division between party activists is of fairly recent provenance. The top private sector professions have always been overwhelmingly Tory both in terms of voters and activists, but until the 1980s public sector professionals were also significantly more Tory in their voting habits than the electorate at large, and fairly evenly split between the parties in terms of activists. Until the 1970s, for every 'leftie' poly or university lecturer – the polys and redbricks were still in their infancy and did not come to dominate higher education until the 1980s – there was an actively Tory grammar school teacher or Oxbridge don; and so on along the chain of public sector professional employment from local government officers to hospital doctors. After all, these people defined themselves as middle class and professional: in salary, aspirations, esteem and lifestyle there was little difference between them and their private sector counterparts in, say, banks or accountancy firms, while there were massive differences between them and the unionized working class on all scores. And the Tories were the middle-class party *par excellence*. The 1966 election, won by Labour with a landslide margin over the Conservatives of 48.9 to 41.4 per cent of the total vote, saw the Tories retain a solid 61 per cent of the salaried middle classes.[25]

Tory middle-class hegemony started to weaken in the 1970s. One aspect of the party's collapse in 1974 after the disastrous miners' strikes (in October 1974 the Tory share of the vote fell to 36.7 per cent) was a sizeable desertion by the middle class to the eminently bourgeois Liberals, who took a quarter of the salariat vote. This was only a temporary shift: the Liberals remained a fringe party with a tiny membership, and in 1979 the Tories were back up to 61 per cent of the salariat. But it prepared the way for what, in retrospect, appears to be the veritable watershed: the formation of the Social Democratic party in 1981. Launched with its credit card membership and telephone hotlines just as the public and private sector middle classes were sharply diverging, socially and economically, the ultra-respectable SDP, in alliance with the Liberals, rapidly became the political voice of the public sector professionals. Both anti-Tory and anti-Labour in rhetoric, it spoke for the increasingly distinct identity of a public professional class resenting its growing inferiority of income and status *vis-à-vis* the private sector, which it largely blamed on the Tories, but equally hostile to a Labour party dominated by the manual trade unions and left-wing militants. By the mid-1980s the first phase of this realignment – the detachment of a large bloc of public sector professionals from the Tories to the SDP/Liberals – was completed. In the 1987 election private sector professionals voted 57 per cent Tory, while their public sector counterparts split 40–32–26 between Tory–SDP/Liberal–Labour.[26] Labour was third preference even among teachers, of whom only 28 per cent supported Labour, with the Tories and SDP/Liberal Alliance vying together in the mid-30s per cent.[27]

Dr David Owen – always 'Dr Owen', an NHS doctor and eloquently proud of it – was the public professionals' mascot of the 1980s, even for many of those voting Tory. The authoritative book on the rise and fall of the SDP constructs this identikit SDP member from party surveys in the early 1980s (notice that the words 'class' and 'sector' each recur three times in a single paragraph):

The typical Social Democrat was a middle-class family man (man, not woman) in his late thirties or early forties. He had a mortgage and lived in a suburb, a commuter village or one of the market or cathedral towns of southern England. He had moved into the area from another town to get a better job and would probably move again for promotion. His own parents were not poor but were of modest means, on the border between the 'respectable' working class and the lower middle class. He had passed the eleven-plus, had gone to grammar school and had done well enough at school to enter university. He had just escaped national service. After school or university he had launched himself fairly successfully on a professional or managerial career. If he worked in the private sector, it was probably in the service rather than manufacturing sector and on the 'staff' rather than the 'line' side of the organization. But he was more likely to work in the public sector, whether in a nationalized industry, the civil service, a local authority, a university or a hospital. He belonged to a professional association or a white-collar union, but without much enthusiasm, and he was certainly not a union activist.

In fact, until he joined the SDP he was not much of a joiner at all, being too busy furthering his career ... even as an SDP member he was not particularly active, preferring to write out cheques for the party than to pound the pavements.[28]

A principal theme of the study is the 'upwardly mobile' character of SDP members.[29] Although the higher professional and managerial dominance among SDP activists in the 1980s was only slightly greater than in the Conservative and Liberal parties, a far higher proportion had risen from working-class or lower-middle-class beginnings (65 per cent against 43 per cent for the Tories and 44 per cent for Labour). Education was the key. SDP members were archetypal meritocrats: twice as many SDP activists had remained in education beyond eighteen as their Tory and Labour counterparts. Of the party's parliamentary candidates in the 1983 and 1987 elections, three-quarters were graduates, while the proportion drawn from the education sector was three times greater than among Tory candidates, with proportionately six times as many university lecturers. Unsurprisingly, therefore, although insistently moderate in self-image and rhetoric, SDP members were notably statist. The beneficiaries of Butler's 1944 Education Act, Beveridge's social security system and Bevan's National Health Service, they mostly supported higher income tax, a wealth tax, national incomes policies, and Keynesian-style reflation through state investment. The authors of the study conclude that the SDP 'was as much the party of a class as the Conservative and Labour parties were', its class being the public sector professionals, spilling over into the private sector service occupations.[30] Tellingly, asked for their second party preference, SDP activists were far more likely to opt for Labour than Tory.

Hopes of a three-party system with a meritocratic professional SDP holding the balance between Tories and Labour collapsed when the Thatcher government was re-elected for a third time in 1987. Some form of Lib-Labbery might have ensued. But David Owen committed political suicide rather than merge his pristine professional SDP with the (as he saw it) sandals-and-beards Liberals, which had to be the first step on that road. The SDP disintegrated. Ultimately the Liberal Democrats under Paddy Ashdown revived to become a respectable third party, but they lost a third of the electoral support, half of the members, and virtually all the credibility achieved by the SDP–Liberal Alliance at its peak.

Where did these voters and activists go? The answer, critical to understanding class politics in the 1990s, is that they transferred *en masse* to Labour. Among party activists this was not primarily a matter of individuals changing allegiance: the number doing so was small, for long before the appearance of Tony Blair most of the SDP's 'political virgin' members had returned to furthering their careers. Rather, it was their social equivalents of the mid-1990s who, in far larger numbers, joined New Labour in a fit of political enthusiasm reminiscent of the early days of the SDP. It was emphatically New Labour they were joining: not Old working-class Labour, but a party which, under Tony Blair, had taken on many of the characteristics of the SDP, down to its credit card promotions, one-member-one-vote postal ballots and revamped Clause Four replacing state socialism with a non-sectarian commitment to social justice. As yet there are no social studies of the estimated 200,000 members recruited to New Labour under Tony Blair's leadership (or 'revolution' as two of his stalwarts describe it[31]), but observation of local Labour meetings bears this out. New Labour has a hegemonic hold over the public sector, consummating a political realignment which began in earnest with the launch of the SDP in 1981. The difference is that New Labour has embraced the public sector élite without losing its trade union ballast. This is a source of its electoral strength, but is also bound to lead to tension as the party evolves in government.

In summary, two fairly clear-cut social divisions are apparent within the political class, one vertical *between* the parties, the other horizontal *within* the parties. The vertical division is the broad public–private separation between Labour and the Tories at all levels – among MPs, activists and members. The horizontal division is the separation within the parties between élite and mass, with the élite professional groups within the public and private sectors colonizing the parliamentary representation of the two parties, while the activists and members represent a wider cross-section of the two sectors. Thus on the Tory side, MPs are drawn overwhelmingly from the Super Class professions (although most of those going into the Commons have, by the nature of political life, not progressed far up their earlier career ladders), while the party at large gives voice to the far larger swathe of private sector white-collar, self-employed and lesser professional workers. On the Labour side, the secondary teachers, lecturers, and former union and public professional administrators hold sway, while the party membership is more representative of the public sector at large, particularly the unionized working and clerical classes whose leaders retain an institutionalized standing within the party.

Put thus, the dual tension at the heart of modern politics becomes clear. On the one hand there is the battle within the political élite, essentially between the Super Class and the senior ranks of public professionals. On the other hand there is acute tension between those élites and the broader ranks of party supporters on each side, whose interests may be only loosely related to them. For instance, the mass of NHS ancillary staff, whose unions are part of the Labour party, want a better deal for the public sector; but they have little interest in narrowing the differential between NHS doctors and managers and their private sector counterparts, which is the prime aim of the public professionals within the NHS. On the Tory side similar tensions are revealed by the bitter controversy over the 'fat cats', with many a shopkeeping or clerical banking Tory member aghast at the explosion in pay at the top, while the Tory élite adamantly refuses to consider curbing practices which are quite acceptable to most Tory MPs and their friends.

The most potent of these tensions are those within the state sector, since the grievances held by those at the top and bottom of the public sector have been heightened by two decades of political alienation. While private professional salaries took off in the 1980s, public salaries remained capped by Tory governments desperate to constrain public spending and cut direct taxation, mainly for the benefit of top taxpayers in the private sector. While the private professionals decamped from the state sector in droves – not just to their private schools and hospitals, but to their private health clubs and exclusive foreign holiday resorts – the public professionals were forced to make do with public services and more mediocre private goods. And, at the bottom of the tree, compulsory competitive tendering and similar initiatives widened differentials even within the public sector, as manual and clerical grades found their real conditions worsening *vis-à-vis* the professionals in their own sector.

The political repercussions are profound. All groups within the public sector look to Labour for a better deal, but whether a New Labour government will or can deliver is highly problematic. But restraints on public sector pay and investment will be acute under Labour, and pressure to contain taxation will be intense. A number of scenarios are conceivable. Labour could try to resist, appease or reform. Resistance would sooner or later lead to serious confrontation. Appeasement, meaning progressively higher real public sector remuneration, would be equally fraught given competing political pressures. As for reform, the only obviously viable course would be the progressive marketization of public services, enabling teachers, public sector managers and university lecturers, for instance, to go the way of health service consultants, drawing income from the public and private sectors by redrawing the boundaries between the two (a process discussed further in Chapter 3). But accomplishing such reforms will be highly controversial within the Labour party and the public sector groups affected. Like all social struggles, the battle within the professional classes will throw up some unlikely allies and adversaries.

The politics of exclusion

So far we have considered divisions within the political class at large. Equally important, however, are the forces uniting the political élite as a whole and dividing it from wider British society. Two forces are paramount: the continuing strength of the Establishment tradition, and the strong and growing sway of the career politician. Taken together with the decline of social deference within society as a whole, and low levels of confidence as to the social and economic strength of the country at large, the upshot is sharply rising levels of popular disillusion with politicians.

Starting with Exclusive Britain, it is important to distinguish between trends and their starting point. Because the contemporary trend is towards a *less* exclusive political class, that does not make today's élite *non*-exclusive. Far from it. A brief glance at a list of senior politicians and their educational background reveals the continuing proximity of England's traditional élite institutions to the centres of power in contemporary Britain. Lords, public schools, Oxbridge: all continue to play a formative role in the construction of Britain's governing class. The next chapter describes the remarkable vitality of Crown and Lords, the quintessential class of the past. A Marquess of Salisbury, or heir to the title, has served in almost every Tory government since 1866 – including John Major's.

Look at the Labour party's élite. Although largely public sector by education, Tony Blair's private school upbringing is far less exceptional on the Labour side than is John Major's non-university education on the Tory side. One in seven Labour MPs in 1992 went to private school, twice the proportion among the population as a whole. Two-thirds of Labour MPs went to university, one in four of them to Oxbridge. Nor are exclusive roots a Left–Right divide within the party – viz. Tony Benn, alias Anthony Wedgwood-Benn, son of a viscount, educated at Westminster School and New College, Oxford, president of the Oxford Union, whose leading acolyte in the 1980s was Michael Meacher, also of public school and New College, Oxford.

As for the Tories, John Major was the exception to almost every social and educational characteristic of the government he led. He was the only member of his own Cabinet who did not go to university. Of the other twenty-two (in 1995), sixteen were Oxbridge-educated, and a majority went to private schools – including four Etonians, all of them sons of peers. Eton's sway may be declining on the Tory benches in the Commons, but this should not disguise the fact that it still furnishes one in ten of all Tory MPs, nearly a fifth of the last Tory Cabinet, and more than one-third of the membership of the House of Lords (including life peers). And the influence of the independent schools is likely to grow on the Tory benches. Consider the so-called 'Cambridge mafia' which took over much of the Tory leadership in the early 1990s. Although formed by Cambridge university, most of its members made it to Cambridge from state grammar schools – Kenneth Clarke from Nottingham High, Michael Howard from Llanelli Grammar, Norman Fowler from King Edward VI Grammar School, Chelmsford, to name just the leaders. With the decline of the state grammar schools and the meritocratic transformation of the independent sector, the dominance of the private sector will reassert itself within the Tory leadership.

Then there are the permanent secretaries, who run Whitehall whichever party commandeers the ministerial red boxes. The

Whitehall Companion entry for Sir Robin Butler, Cabinet Secretary and head of the home civil service since 1988, says it all: '*Education*: Harrow School, University College, Oxford (classics). *Decorations*: CVO 1986, KCB 1988, GCB 1992. *Clubs*: Anglo-Belgian, Athenaeum, Brooks's, United Oxford and Cambridge. *Recreations*: competitive games, opera.' Taking the eighteen permanent secretaries together, as of mid-1995,[32] two-thirds were educated at Oxbridge, with grammar and private schools equally represented. The average age was fifty-four, with classicists outnumbering economists by nearly two-to-one. Almost all had joined Whitehall by their mid-twenties and spent no more than a year or two outside the civil service thereafter. Every so often the government launches an initiative to broaden the basis of civil service recruitment: in July 1996 there was one to attract more graduates with 'relevant' training, drawn from a broader age-range and university background. It was a carbon copy of the recommendations of the Fulton Report of 1968, replicated in a host of schemes in the thirty years between.

This is but one facet of a recurrent theme in this book: the renovation of England's old élite institutions since the late 1960s. British government has much of the appearance of a meritocracy, for the country's top politicians and civil servants are mostly the products of its top academic institutions and leading professions. Yet, as we saw graphically in Chapter 2, to equate Britain's élite with a social meritocracy is to beg fundamental questions about its initial recruitment.

To some extent the second force making for an exclusive political class – the rise of the career politician – is the flip side of this coin. For to succeed in politics from outside the Establishment, utter dedication to a political career is required. These are not either/or categories: nowadays even most politicians with pristine Oxbridge pedigrees also treat politics as a full-time career; but without the right background, nothing less than single-minded devotion to advancement will propel the aspiring politician into the Commons and up the ministerial ladder.

Consider John Major. Famously lacking degrees, connections, even A-levels, he could hardly have been further from the charmed circle. Yet as a career politician he is a contemporary role model. According to his best biographer, 'as soon as young John Major began to think, he began to think about politics'[33] (as, too, did William Hague). Major himself says that his ambition to become an MP was formed at the age of thirteen on a visit to the House of Commons – arranged at his own initiative, so great was his enthusiasm. On his sixteenth birthday he joined the Young Conservatives (the earliest age allowed); at twenty-one he fought his first local council election (the earliest age allowed); by twenty-five, in 1968, he was a councillor in the London borough of Lambeth, climbing methodically through the ranks to become chairman of the housing committee. By now he had gone into banking, rising to become head of public affairs at Standard Chartered, a job on a clear track to the Super Class, providing time and opportunities for cultivating political contacts. In 1974, aged thirty-one, he fought an unwinnable parliamentary seat in Camden, entering the Commons five years later, in Mrs Thatcher's first term, as MP for the safe Tory seat of Huntingdon. After a spell on the backbenches came the whips' office, a junior ministerial office, and the lowest job in the Cabinet as Chief Secretary to the Treasury. The rest is history. All in all, a textbook case of what Lord Nolan describes in his 1995 report on parliamentary conduct as 'the onward march of the professional politician'.[34]

Professional politicians are hardly a new breed. Hereditary monarchies and aristocracies justified themselves partly in terms of the virtue of schooling individuals in the art of government from youth. Yet therein lies the rub. Democracies are supposed to be different, with government in the hands of the many, not the few; and those many being fully representative of the governed. Instead, the professional politicians have taken over, proficient at winning elections and often therefore at discerning the popular mood, but none the less conceiving of power largely as a commodity for personal reward and advancement. *Primary Colors,* the brilliant portrayal of the 1992 Clinton campaign for the Democratic nomination, depicts the obsessive professional politician now recognizable in all democratic societies, not least Britain. 'Never has the full-time politician flourished so much,' writes Peter Riddell of *The Times* in his study of the rise of the British career politician.[35] A mid-1990s survey of more than 300 MPs showed that Tory MPs elected before 1979 had spent barely 4.7 per cent of their total years of work experience before entering the Commons in professional political activity. The proportion rose to more than 10 per cent for those elected in 1987, and will certainly be far higher in future. It was higher still on the Labour side, rising from around a tenth of those elected before 1979 to over a quarter for the 1987 cohort.

Riddell's analysis of candidates selected for the 1997 election underlines the inexorable rise of the political careerist.[36] He estimates that nearly half of the new Tory candidates picked for what were considered winnable seats had long been 'fully committed to politics' – in many cases having never done anything much else to speak of – by working as special advisers to ministers, party officials, lobbyists, assistants to MPs or full-time councillors. It was a similar picture on the Labour side, if trade union policy officers and officials are included, although with Labour out of office and a large proportion of its winnable seats far distant from London, the range of politically compatible occupations was larger. As for those who have done other jobs, most hail from so-called 'brokerage occupations'[37] providing the working flexibility, generous vacations, interrupted career paths, networks, income and technical skills useful for promoting political ambitions. Typical brokerage careers include the Bar (viz. Tony Blair, Ken Clarke, Malcolm Rifkind, Michael Howard), journalism (Peter Mandelson) and university research (Gordon Brown). In line with our earlier analysis, the brokerage careers of Labour MPs tend to be in the public sector and those of Tories in the private sector, but they have in common the avenues they open to the politically ambitious.

There is, perhaps, little to surprise us in the success of the careerists. However hostile public opinion to politicians in general, local selection committees responsible for choosing candidates are inevitably impressed by those displaying virtuoso political skills as a speaker, dynamic campaigner and policy expert, and the political brokerage careers cultivate them. Some claim that the rise of career politicians is inevitable and even desirable for a further reason: because politics, like other occupations, has become more professional than ever before. Riddell quotes a former Conservative minister as claiming that 'the increasing complications of government require a more specialist training' than formerly. This is a dubious proposition: the elemental functions of government and political representation have changed little over time, and certainly not over the recent decades which have witnessed the ascendancy of career politicians. Politics has become an all-consuming career because an increasing number of its practitioners has treated it as such; and by raising the threshold for participation, they have only further discouraged – or disabled – the non-careerists from taking part.

This is an international trend. In some respects, notably in the sophistication of campaign techniques and the financial self-sufficiency of the political class, it is less developed in Britain than elsewhere, notably in the US and Germany. However, it is particularly stark in Britain, because of the extraordinary isolation of Britain's political élite from the people it governs, an isolation brought about by the country's institutional structure. Virtually all the politics that matters in Britain depends upon the House of Commons. Ministers must be MPs or peers; the Lords has only a minor residual role; and local government is emasculated to the point of irrelevance as a forum for political decisions. And there are no forms of direct democracy in Britain besides occasional referendums (only one of which, the 1975 referendum over European Community membership, has involved the country as a whole).

Accordingly the only significant say a British citizen has over his or her government is through a single vote, once every four or five years, in an election for the House of Commons, when as likely as not s/he will send to the Commons a career politician whose prime, perhaps sole, motivation is to climb the ministerial ladder. The contrast with the US is particularly striking. Most of the politics that matters to the American voter takes place at state level or lower. Virtually all those exercising executive, legislative and judicial power are either directly elected or (as with Supreme Court judges) subject to a relatively open political appointments process in which public opinion plays an often decisive role. Candidates for election are generally chosen in primary elections involving the voters at large. Referendums are frequent at state and local level.

The US is, in short, an *open* democracy, while the UK is an extremely *closed* one. This is not to say that the US has a system of government which, in all respects, is notably preferable: US politics, too, is dominated by obsessive professionals from Bill Clinton downwards; and it is hard to contend, by measures of social cohesion or relative prosperity that America is decisively better governed than Britain. Even Germany's more sophisticated democratic structure, which can fairly claim to have produced more prosperity than Britain's, has not prevented the rise of deep popular disillusion with politicians. The issue, rather, is the accessibility of politics to the people, and the perception on the part of the mass of citizens that they can influence their own governments. In Britain, acute social segregation and the lack of aspiration among the lower classes co-exist with a pervasive sense of political impotence and it is hard to believe the two are unconnected.

British government has been aptly described by Lord Hailsham, the longest-serving Cabinet minister since the war, as an 'elective dictatorship'. The dominance of the careerists is one face of the dictatorship, and the strength of class divisions partly a consequence.

5. CROWN AND LORDS

The class of the past

The question, I suppose, has to be faced – what are dukes *for*?

Hugh Montgomery-Massingberd

The daily Court and Social page of *The Times*, sandwiched between the obituaries and letters to the editor, is a must read for those in search of Britain's *ancien régime*. It is headed by the Court Circular, a daily record of the royal family's official engagements and appointments. The entry for 1 May 1996 yields this information, under the heading BUCKINGHAM PALACE:

> The Queen has been graciously pleased to appoint Earl Percy and Lord Eskdaill to be Pages of Honour to Her Majesty in succession to the Hon. Edward Lowther and the Hon. Simon Ramsay . . . The Lady Elton has succeeded the Hon. Mary Morrison as Lady-in-Waiting to Her Majesty.

Some elucidation is required. Pages of honour are boys who assist Her Majesty at state occasions such as the State Opening of Parliament, dressed in elaborate Court uniforms. Ladies-in-waiting attend the Queen on a daily basis, always one step behind Her Majesty to gather up the bouquets of flowers and deal with personal matters. Earl Percy was, in 1996, the eleven-year-old son and heir of the twelfth Duke of Northumberland; Lord Eskdaill the grandson of the ninth Duke of Buccleuch and Queensberry. (The twenty-four non-royal dukedoms are the pinnacle of Britain's hereditary aristocracy: Queensberry was created in 1684, North-umberland in 1766.) The Honourables Edward Lowther and Simon Ramsay were sons of earls, Lowther being a classmate of Prince William's at Eton College, where young Percy and Eskdaill may be expected to follow. Lady Elton was the wife of Lord Elton, a hereditary baron and former Tory minister in the House of Lords; the Hon. Mary Morrison was the daughter of Lord Margadale, another hereditary peer and ex-minister.

Coincidentally the next-door column of the same day's *Times*, under the heading 'latest wills', contained an entry for 'the eleventh Duke of Northumberland of Alnwick Castle, Northumberland'. This was Earl Percy's uncle, who had died unmarried leaving estate valued at £5,364,631 net to his brother. That figure would have excluded the value of Alnwick and the Northumberlands' other estates, held privately in trusts.

A vignette of Britain's thriving *ancien régime* in the mid-1990s. Presided over by the world's grandest monarchy, rich in hereditary titles and possessions, entrenched in institutions from Eton to the House of Lords, it remains formidable. As the *Economist* remarked in 1992 of Britain's 'evolving not disappearing' class divisions: 'Feudal stratification lives on. The class of the past remains stronger in Britain than in most other countries, thanks to the monarchy, to the endurance of the landed gentry and to the private school system which perpetuates upper-class apartheid.'[1]

It is, moreover, quite wrong to suppose that Crown and Lords have steadily weakened. From time to time – notably during the *annus horribilis* of 1992 when Windsor Castle caught fire and the Queen had to pay tax and endure intimate revelations about the breakdown of her sons' marriages – it has looked that way. But taking a longer view, the class of the past remains stronger now than on the eve of the Second World War. The Abdication Crisis of 1936 left the Crown reeling; until the 1950s the House of Lords appeared on the verge of extinction, along with the hereditary aristocracy which comprised it. 'Everything is going now: before long I shall also have to go,' George VI remarked fatalistically to Vita Sackville-West in 1948 on hearing that her family home of Knole in Kent had been taken over by the National Trust.[2] In the 1960s the royal children were despatched to Gordonstoun, not Eton, in a deliberate bid to put some distance between the monarchy and England's other citadels of privilege. Nowadays even these inhibitions have gone. Prince William is at Eton, where new money mixes with old and academic standards are at an all-time high, while the Conservative party proclaims the hereditary peerage a bulwark of British democracy for the twenty-first century in the face of Labour threats to their voting rights in the House of Lords.

It is essential, then, to make sense of Britain's class of the past. Why did it survive? How has it adapted? What is its impact on contemporary society? This chapter restricts itself to the two most important branches of the *ancien régime*: the royal family and the peerage, comprising the two grandest and oldest surviving institutions of the British state – the monarchy and the House of Lords.

Windsor sclerosis

One canard should be quashed immediately: any idea that the monarchy is essentially unimportant, a distraction from the serious business of government and society.

This notion is deeply rooted in political discourse, dating back to Walter Bagehot's celebrated *English Constitution*, which has been a sacred constitutional text for more than a century. Bagehot's interpretation of the constitution rested on a fundamental distinction between its 'dignified' and 'efficient' elements.[3] The Crown and Lords he placed unambiguously in the dignified camp. Indeed, Bagehot's monarchy was little more than innocent amusement for an ill-educated populace. Explaining how 'the actions of a retired widow [Queen Victoria] and an unemployed youth [the Prince of Wales] become of such importance', he resorted to pop psychology. 'A *family* on the throne is an interesting idea', making government 'intelligible' to 'crowds of people scarcely more civilized than the majority of two thousand years ago', while 'the women – one half of the human race at least – care fifty times more for a marriage than a ministry'. 'No feeling,' he added, 'could seem more childish than the enthusiasm of the English at the marriage of the Prince of Wales' – a remark as true of 1981 as of

1863, and equally valid for 1996 if 'divorce' is substituted for 'marriage'.

Bagehot, a great rationalist editor of the *Economist*, dismissed the monarchy as a dignified relic because he wished it to be so. Yet his own arguments belie his conclusion. An institution able to command the degree of popular obsession achieved by the monarchy then and now could scarcely be dignified in the sense of inconsequential. Charisma is a form of power, as Max Weber explained long ago. Add to its charismatic power the royal family's wealth, its influence over policy and government, its status at the head of the honours system and the hereditary aristocracy, and the monarchy becomes every bit as 'efficient' as most departments of state. Indeed, it *is* a department of state, for the Court and royal household are an enterprise as elaborate and relentless about self-promotion as any Whitehall ministry.

To appreciate the monarchy's social and political sway, consider what Britain would be like without it. In the first place, the institution would have to be abolished. Were the Crown truly of little account, this would be as easy as splitting the Department of the Environment – a laughable proposition, as Australia's republican movement is demonstrating, even though only narrow constitutional issues are at stake there. If, none the less, the Crown were abolished, the constitutional order, the practice of public life, the concept of 'news', and the status and formalities of an entire titled élite, would be transformed. Sue Townsend touched this nerve in her best-selling novel *The Queen and I* (1992), imagining the life of the royal family on a council estate under a republican regime.

Buckingham Palace will not be vacant in the foreseeable future. More illuminating, then, than imagining the Queen in a Lambeth tower block is to set the royal family alongside its real continental counterparts. The contrast between the House of Windsor and Europe's 'bicycling monarchs' is a cliché; and like many clichés it disguises the starkness of the difference, which amounts to far more than informality in style and ceremonial.[4] Of Europe's seven other monarchs, only one (Juan Carlos of Spain) heads an even semi-functioning titled aristocracy, and only one (Beatrix of the Netherlands) is in the Windsors' wealth league. Even there, Juan Carlos maintains a tiny Court, while Beatrix – daughter of Queen Juliana, the authentic cyclist – is centre neither of an elaborate court nor of an aristocracy. Beatrix never wears a crown, changes her personal staff (except the gardeners) every few years, and is dubbed 'the general manager of the Kingdom of Holland' by the Dutch government's spokesman. For the rest, Queens Sonja of Norway and Silvia of Sweden are unpretentious daughters of industrialists, Sweden's constitution was rewritten in 1975 to remove all the executive prerogatives of the Crown, while the five other monarchies have written constitutions going almost as far. Queen Margrethe of Denmark studied at five European universities and acts as a national patron of the arts and archaeology. Albert II of Belgium works from a Brussels town house known simply as Number 16, Rue Brederode, while Juan Carlos inhabits a modest hunting lodge outside Madrid, using the sumptuous Palacio Real only for state occasions. No European monarchy besides Britain's still regularly confers heraldic or aristocratic titles beyond the royal family.

Europe's crowned heads also have as much in common with Britain's. The point is not that the British monarchy is in all respects different from its continental counterparts: they, in truth, are very different from each other. The point, rather, is that the House of Windsor has modernized itself in virtually none of the respects noted of the others. It has stuck to its aristocracy, its Court, its imperial pomp, its private fortune, and to a Victorian conception of national leadership comprising little more than pomp plus patronage of the state Church, charities and the armed forces. It is this peculiar case of Windsor sclerosis which sets the British monarchy apart, making it so powerful an agent of old class.

Historically, sclerosis is an uncharacteristic state for the British monarchy. Until the early part of this century, Britain's sovereigns were the best royal adapters in the world: unlike the Bourbons, they learned well. Subject to elected parliaments and shrewd ministers, most monarchs reigning after the Restoration of 1660 were careful to keep in tune with élite opinion. The eighteenth-century Hanoverians – from whom Elizabeth II is directly descended – forged a stable and viable constitutional monarchy, which Queen Victoria, over her sixty-four-year reign (1837–1901), transformed into the nation's most popular institution. It was brilliantly contrived. A studied 'reinvention of tradition' added a popular pageant of mock medieval ritual to the Crown's increasingly formal political functions.[5] Disraeli conferred a quasi-imperial aura, proclaiming Victoria Empress of India at the height of Britain's imperial expansion. The growing charitable role of the royal family developed a 'cult of benevolence', giving the Crown leadership of a powerful philanthropic movement embracing old and new wealth.[6] Victoria's last decades saw the granting of peerages and knighthoods to the *nouveaux riches* (including Jews), converting the honours system into a still more effective instrument for uniting old and new wealth within traditional hierarchy.

But that, to a remarkable degree, is where Britain's royal evolution stopped. A century after its founder's demise, the Victorian monarchy still reigns. Elizabeth II makes her annual peregrination, with a staff of eighty, between three of Victoria's huge mansions – Buckingham Palace, Windsor Castle and Balmoral – and one of her son's – Edward VII's Sandringham. Outside London dogs, horses and shooting are the main royal preoccupations. The Empress of India has become Head of the Commonwealth, devoting herself to a set of imperial connections increasingly irrelevant to Britain, while taking until 1965 to make a first state visit to Germany.[7] Peerages and knighthoods are distributed in greater profusion than ever before, mostly on class lines. The century's new order of honours is named after the British Empire – 'deliberately instituted to be the order of chivalry of British democracy', as David Cannadine notes,[8] and divided into five class-related subdivisions headed by 'knight commanders'. John Major's much-vaunted invitation to the public to nominate honorands produced a few more local worthies as MBEs, but otherwise it is business as normal. The Supreme Governor of the Church of England largely ignores the other denominations and faiths whose followers massively outnumber the practising Anglicans. The range of royal patronage has broadened, to include even Aids and sexual abuse organizations under the wing of the Princess of Wales in her vocation as 'Queen of Hearts'. But it is essentially the same unchanging philanthropic and 'awayday' routine, the royal progress conducted by royal yacht, royal train, royal plane, Rolls Royce – with receptions hosted by Lords Lieutenant, a collection of ageing, mostly titled, grandees (of forty-six male English Lords Lieutenant in 1990, thirty were Etonians).[9] As for culture, the only activity notably favoured by the Queen is horse-racing, centring on the Victorian ritual of Royal Ascot and managed for her by the seventh Earl of Carnarvon.

The persistence of the Victorian monarchy is a function not just of the Queen but of her governments, whose bidding she does in all public matters. From Churchill to Major, prime ministers have *wanted* a Gothic Revival monarchy, appealing to a mythicized, unchanging past, easing the transition from empire to Europe (although Lady Thatcher had little time for the Commonwealth, which caused friction), providing a valuable source of patronage, and protecting their executive power – a function of the royal prerogative in Britain's unwritten constitution – from pressure to limit its scope. Windsor sclerosis is manifestly not just a matter of royal conservatism, but of long-term government policy. And it shows little sign of changing. There is a deep irony here. Bagehot saw the monarchy 'as a *disguise*. It enables our real rulers to change without heedless people knowing it.' Now it is the opposite: a disguise enabling our real rulers *not* to change without heedless people worrying unduly.

A key aspect of this policy has been to leave the Court and the royal household, bastions of the old order, untouched; indeed positively to discourage reform by sanctioning bloated Civil List settlements and shielding the Crown from effective parliamentary or public scrutiny. The Queen's decision to pay tax on her private income, encouraged by a John Major anxious about the alarming – but, in retrospect, temporary – degree of public disquiet with the royal family, is the sole notable exception to this rule since 1945. A graphic exhibition of the monarchy's protected status came in 1971, when in response to a suggestion from a Commons committee examining the Civil List (itself highly unusual) that the royal household should be constituted as a government depart-ment and managed accordingly, Lord Cobbold, the Lord Cham-berlain, dismissed the idea as totally unacceptable. The royal household, he insisted, was 'in one sense a Department of State', but 'it is also a family administration and the two things are slightly intermingled'. He continued:

> It is almost an item of principle that the Queen regards these people as her own servants and they regard themselves as her servants. I think they have the idea of the dignity of the monarchy, which is supported by the idea that the Queen is controlling her household.[10]

And that remains the case.

In 1957 John Grigg (then Lord Altrincham) was hysterically attacked for suggesting, in a judicious assessment of the state of the monarchy, that the royal entourage was 'almost without exception the "tweedy" sort ... a tight little enclave of British ladies and gentlemen'.[11] Forty years on, so it remains. 'The palace ethos,' says one royal observer, 'is that of a Guards regiment.'[12] The household is presided over by the Lord Chamberlain (the seventh Lord Camoys), assisted by the Lord Steward (the fourth Viscount Ridley), the Master of the Horse (the third Lord Somer-leyton) and the Mistress of the Robes (the Duchess of Grafton), heading teams of ladies-in-waiting, women of the bedchamber, equerries and extra equerries (the last mostly senior military officers). Even necessary management reforms are kept within the magic circle as much as possible. Lord Camoys is the archetypal modern aristocrat, with dual membership of the Super Class as a former deputy chairman of both Barclays de Zoete Wedd, the merchant bank, and the auctioneers Sotheby's. So was his predecessor, the thirteenth Earl of Airlie, who became Lord Chamberlain in 1984 after thirty-four years in the blue-chip merchant bank Henry Schroder Wagg. Airlie appointed a new-style director of Finance and Property Services in 1990 to shake up the management of the palace, including such innovations as performance-related pay. His identity? Michael Peat: Eton, Oxford, then eleven years in KPMG Peat Marwick, the accountancy firm founded by his father.

The most important 'efficient' agent of the monarchy is the Queen's private secretary, who, together with the Cabinet Secretary and the prime minister's principal private secretary, forms what Peter Hennessy has dubbed the 'golden triangle' at the heart of the constitution.[13] The Queen's private secretaries since 1952 have, to a man, been professional courtiers by birth or breeding. The first was Sir Thomas Lascelles, educated at Marlborough and related to the royal family through his wife, the daughter of a viceroy of India. Then came Sir Michael Adeane, literally palace-bred as a grandson of Lord Stamfordham, who had been assistant private secretary to Queen Victoria and private secretary to George V. Progressing through Eton, Cambridge and the Coldstream Guards (his father's regiment), Adeane became an aide-de-camp to the governor-general of Canada, joined the royal household at the age of twenty-seven in 1937 as assistant private secretary to George VI, and finally retired as the Queen's private secretary in 1972 after twenty years in the job. Next came Colonel the Hon. Sir Michael Charteris, Eton, Sandhurst, grandson of an earl and a duke, who first joined Elizabeth as private secretary when she was still a princess. 'Choosing me was an act of pure nepotism,' he said of his first royal appointment.[14] On retiring, Charteris was appointed Provost of Eton, a residential post equivalent to chairman of the governors, where *inter alia* he can keep an eye on Prince William. The current private secretary, Sir Robert Fellowes – Eton, Scots Guards, the City – is Princess Diana's brother-in-law.

Looking back in 1992, Grigg thought he understated his case in 1957, underestimating the depth of Windsor sclerosis:

> After the Second World War the monarchy reverted to its pre-war routines almost as though nothing had happened, and virtually no changes were introduced by the Queen when she succeeded her father in 1952 ... Britain seemed to be compensating for loss of power in the world by lapsing into a state of collective make-believe, in which the hieratic aspects of the monarchy were grossly exaggerated.[15]

Are the 'hieratic aspects' on the way out? The younger royals disport themselves before the media without reserve. Their sexual mores are thoroughly modern. And Prince Charles, at least, has made a few half-hearted cultural forays. The best that can be said of the first two is that they reinforce Bagehot's view that a *'family on the throne'* is 'an interesting idea'. As for the third, it is hard to credit the Prince's architectural prejudices as a great advance in cultural patronage. His religious attitude – 'Defender of Faiths' – is more creative in its implications for the Crown as a focus of national unity, but so far it is largely tokenistic. More promising, perhaps, is the prince's entourage, drawn from a broader group than his mother's. Jonathan Dimbleby records – in a telling exhibition of how much in England comes down to schools – that in 1994 the Prince's senior staff included two former public school boys, three with grammar school backgrounds and two from comprehensives, 'which sharply delineates St James's from Buckingham Palace'.[16] On the other hand, Charles has few friends outside his own upper-class circle; his patronage is little more than fitful dabbling; and his lifestyle – yet more palaces and country estates; the annual round of polo, shooting and skiing – is as 'tweedy' as ever. Football, the leading national pastime, is an indicator of sorts. George V and George VI always attended the Cup Final. The Queen never goes. Charles went in 1995, as part of a campaign to refurbish his image, when he attempted to present the cup to the losers.

How much does Windsor sclerosis matter? The battle lines are sharply drawn. Anti-monarchists play variations on the theme of playwright John Osborne's famous charge that the Crown is 'the gold filling in a mouthful of decay'. Stephen Haseler, in a typical critique, claims it 'perpetuates a culture of backwardness in a nation desperately needing to modernize itself'.[17] The defence is best articulated by the Oxford historian Brian Harrison.[18] Noting that 'some sort of social gradation seems inevitable' whatever happens to the monarchy, he stresses the Crown's historic class-integrating role. The Victorian and Edwardian monarchy 'stabil-ized relations between aristocracy and middle class', while the twentieth-century monarchy has helped 'integrate organized labour' politically and socially. George V readily accepted Labour governments in the 1920s. George VI, as Duke of York, pioneered summer camps of working-class and public school boys. Under Elizabeth II 'the monarchy's social-class contacts and appeal have widened still further'. As evidence Harrison cites the broadening invitation list to Buckingham Palace garden parties (now attended by 35,000 a year), informal lunch parties enabling the Queen to meet 'leading figures from many walks of life', and the increasing numbers granted honours.

The problem with this 'class integrating' argument is one of dates. It is a persuasive interpretation of the century until 1945, comparing the British Crown with its continental counterparts, and with the fascist and communist tyrannies which replaced many of them. Beyond Ireland and the Irish, the British Crown also did a comparatively good job of racial integration in this period, aided by the fact that the dynasty was itself foreign and obviously so until it changed its name from Saxe-Coburg and Gotha to Windsor in 1917. Since the Second World War, however, the sclerotic House of Windsor, with its Victorian palaces, castles, rituals and flunkies, buttressed by a hereditary aristocracy, has powerfully sustained a self-regarding upper class which still, in the 1990s, underpins the *perception* of a rigid British class system. The Crown symbolizes old class – particularly for the poorly educated working class, for whom the royal family still serves, as Bagehot saw it, to make British government and society 'intelligible'. Intelligible, that is, as a land of 'them' and 'us'.

Note in this context the trifling examples cited by Harrison of Elizabeth II's attempts at social outreach: more honours, private lunches and frock-coated guests at palace garden parties. More telling are two remarks he makes in developing his case. He argues, first, that 'Monarchy seems secure enough in several European countries less class-conscious than our own.' True but, as we have noted, their monarchies are also far less class-conscious than Britain's. Secondly, after conceding that since the death of Prince Albert in 1860 the monarchy has been profoundly anti-intellectual, almost philistine, he responds: 'In its anti-intellectualism the British royal family once again reflects national traits.'[19] But here again, which is the cause and which the effect?

Aristocratic renaissance

The decades of Windsor sclerosis have seen not just the survival but the renaissance of the British aristocracy.

In 1945 the peerage seemed doomed – its titles, wealth, stately homes, social cachet and, most obviously anachronistic of all, its role as the second chamber of Parliament through the hereditary House of Lords. None felt this as strongly as the peers themselves, who mostly believed their days to be over as the core of a socially and politically significant 'upper class'. Facing unprecedented levels of taxation and fearing worse to come, with little public sympathy for their plight, there was a rush to sell estates or hand them over to the National Trust. Aristocratic Britain retreated into its shell, sticking closely to its caste institutions, notably Eton and the officers' messes of the aristocratic regiments. Even the selfless 'do gooders' had a hard time of it. Vita Sackville-West's husband, Harold Nicolson, a member of the National Trust executive and an oddball pro-Labour grandee, wrote in 1949: 'The present government (or rather their supporters) do not like the Trust because it is managed by aristocrats working on a part-time basis.'[20]

The House of Lords, dying in its sleep, symbolized the aristocracy's apparent euthanasia. It made no pretence of resistance to the flood of socialist legislation introduced by Attlee's government after the 1945 Labour landslide. The Tory peers hoisted the white flag, dignifying their retreat under the guise of a new parliamentary convention named after their leader Lord Salisbury (grandson of the last peer to be prime minister), which declared that the Upper House would not challenge any bill promised in the government's election manifesto. When, despite this, the peers threatened in 1948 to hold up the nationalization of the iron and steel industry – a measure known to be dividing Attlee's Cabinet – they succeeded only in provoking Labour to enact legislation halving the Lords' delaying power from two years to one. Ejection of the hereditary peers seemed a matter of time. Labour was bound to get round to it sooner or later, the only obstacle being its fear that a reformed second chamber might be better placed to resist left-wing governments. Ironically, as far back as 1911 the Tory leadership, confronted by Lloyd George's Liberal radicalism, had for just this reason supported replacing the Lords with a more representative assembly.[21]

Returned to office in 1951, Churchill and the Tories left the House of Lords alone, and the peers sank into still deeper somnolence. Since Labour had only a tiny number of peers, the Upper House contained no Opposition worth the name. Debates were short, votes rare, attendance pitiful. The only effective role played by the Lords was to enable a few of the abler Tory peers – notably Lords Home, Hailsham and Carrington – to advance to the Cabinet. Even that function looked set for redundancy when the Peerage Act of 1963, prompted by the long-running farce of Tony Benn's refusal to leave the Commons after succeeding his father as Viscount Stansgate in 1961, permitted hereditary peers to disclaim their titles. Lords Home and Hailsham promptly followed Benn and left for the Commons – in Home's case to become prime minister. The general assumption was that all politically able peers would in future follow them, destroying the last vestige of vitality in the House of Lords and making its replacement unavoidable.

Not so. Labour's 1964 victory marked an extraordinary turning of the tide. The cause can be traced back to a legislative ruse carried through in 1958 by Harold Macmillan, that most subtle and far-seeing of post-war prime ministers, enabling peerages to be granted to men and women for life. It was a neat trick. When Macmillan put the proposal to Hugh Gaitskell he found the Labour leader 'a little embarrassed – his party is again divided about all this'.[22] Understandably so, for by creating life peerages Macmillan cut away the main Labour objection to entering the House of Lords, while shrewdly anticipating that most Labour MPs would jump at the chance of retiring there. It thus offered a means to revive the Lords as an institution, while safeguarding the hereditary peerage as its principal component. Even the decision to allow female life peers was an inspired Conservative step, opening the Upper House to women while not affecting the male descent of hereditary peerages.

The Life Peerages Act fulfilled all Macmillan's hopes. Tellingly, it was a Labour, not a Tory, honours list (Wilson's 'lavender list' of 1976) which did more than anything since Lloyd George to bring the honours system into disrepute. Wilson used life peerages shamelessly as an instrument of personal and party patronage, while claiming to be 'modern' by refraining from creating new hereditary peerages. By 1979 Labour had 180 life peers in the Lords. In the process the Lords revived, acquiring the cut-and-thrust of a two-party assembly for the first time this century (Labour and Liberal Democrat peers, mostly former MPs, are a loquacious lot). This was a vital factor in the failure of Wilson's attempt to reform the Upper House in the late 1960s. Labour's 1968–9 reform scheme was itself a testament to the rehabilitation of the Lords: far from eliminating the hereditary peers, Wilson proposed that they remain as speaking (but not voting) members, with votes going to a reconstituted class of life peers. Even this modest reform failed to pass the Commons (unsurprisingly the Lords loved it). To explain its defeat much is usually made of an unholy Commons alliance between Enoch Powell on the right and Michael Foot on the left. Yet there was a far more basic reason. The Lords now *worked*. It was no longer an undeniable farce which no self-respecting non-Tory government could continue. Most important of all, it worked for the Labour party – for the party's élite, that is, which had a large stake in the Lords through life peerages. A jibe of the 1970s was that while half of all Labour MPs wanted to abolish the Lords, the other half were desperate to join it. In fact, the proportion in favour of joining was nearer nine to one, for those given the chance. Every member of the 1979 Labour Cabinet bar two (Michael Foot and Albert Booth) accepted a peerage after leaving the Commons, and there was no serious political pressure on the Thatcher or Major governments to engage in reform.

Nothing demonstrated the Lords' newfound vitality better than the periodic creation, from the 1960s, of batches of so-called 'working' peers – politicians nominated for peerages by the three main party leaders to assist with the legislative work of the Upper House. Fifty years ago the term 'working peer' would have been an oxymoron worthy of Evelyn Waugh. By the 1980s working peers accounted for most of the active debaters in the Lords, and party leaders were besieged by candidates wanting to become working Lords and Baronesses. About three-quarters of today's 370 life peers are former MPs and/or party nominees, and average daily attendance in the Lords is well over 350. Turn-out is helped by generous Lords attendance allowances, another innovation of the 1960s. Peers can claim up to £139 a day (as of mid-1996), plus travelling expenses, for attending the Lords, however briefly (walking into the chamber is enough), providing an income of up to £14,000 a year for peers 'attending' two-thirds of sittings. Needless to say, almost all the working peers think that the Lords does a splendid job, irrespective of party. *Liberal Democrat News* runs a weekly slot extolling the weighty speeches of the party's peers, while competition is intense among Labour's lords and ladies for the twenty-odd ministerial slots for peers available under Tony Blair.

The Lords is a classic case of survival through co-option, a process evident in so many other of England's old class institutions encountered in this book. The life peers have steadily increased in number, rising from 3 per cent in 1960 to 15 per cent in 1970 and more than one-third in 1997. The life peers now make up well over half of the regular attenders and debaters. Observed from the gallery, the House of Lords looks and sounds like a hybrid of the House of Commons and the Jockey Club – excluding most of the members under the age of fifty. Yet for the 'true blue' aristocracy, co-option of large numbers of politicians as life peers has been a small price to pay for survival intact. After all, they have been co-opting for centuries: the hereditary peerage grew from barely 200 in the late eighteenth century to 750 by the 1950s, before the passage of the Life Peerages Act.

The effect has been not only to preserve the coherence of the peerage as a class (no other aristocratic élite in the world is so easily defined by membership of a parliamentary chamber), but to preserve a substantial political base for the old aristocracy into the 1990s. When the Conservatives are in office this base extends from the Lords to the heart of government, since convention and the exigencies of parliamentary management require that more than twenty of the hundred-odd ministerial posts be reserved for peers. In 1996 the Leader of the House of Lords, with a seat in the Cabinet, was Viscount Cranborne, heir to the sixth Marquess of Salisbury, great-great-grandson of the Lord Salisbury who was prime minister a century ago, and descendant of the chief ministers to Elizabeth I and James I. Another eleven hereditary peers – four earls, two viscounts and five barons – were also members of the government, in addition to ten life peers holding office. Then there was the quangocracy. Two of the five government-appointed quangos distributing the National Lottery billions intended for 'good causes' were run by hereditary peers (the Earl of Gowrie at the Arts Council and Lord Rothschild at the National Heritage Memorial Fund), and the list goes on. Tellingly, in the past twenty years only one peer has used the 1963 Peerage Act to disclaim his title – and that was the special case of Lord James Douglas Hamilton, a Tory MP and junior Scottish Office minister when he succeeded in 1995 to the earldom of Selkirk, who remained in the Commons rather than cause John Major an embarrassing by-election.

The aristocracy's renaissance through adaptation and co-option is evident far beyond the Lords. As we shall see in later chapters, its caste-forming institutions, notably Eton and the army, have embraced new social forces as effectively as the House of Lords itself without losing their exclusive character. Nine in ten hereditary peers are public school educated, and well over half went to Eton.[23] The old aristocracy continues to function as an adjunct to monarchy. The 1980s saw the *Tatler* revive, while *Hello!* maga-zine, one of the big publishing successes of the decade, is practically a journal of photographic record for the aristocracy's matrimonial and leisure activities. *Hello!* lumps the peers in with pop stars and sports idols, and its tone is mocking as much as fawning – which is no less a commentary on the aristocracy's continued social force.

The word 'caste' is apposite, for the hereditary peerage is best understood as a caste conferring large social prestige and advantages on its 755 members by virtue of their belonging to a highly select and virtually closed order (new peerage creations now almost invariably being for life only). Its standing still has much to do with inherited wealth, as we shall see in a moment. But it is also a function of caste privilege – the combination of titles, schooling, the House of Lords and associated social prestige, which is a powerful boon even to those hereditary peers lacking broad acres. Consider Lord Gowrie, the chairman of the Arts Council mentioned earlier. 'Grey' Gowrie inherited an earldom at the age of sixteen in 1955. A recent creation (his grandfather was a governor-general), it came with little wealth, but Gowrie was sent to Eton, proceeded to Balliol, where he edited one of Oxford's literary magazines and cultivated a reputation as something of a romantic dandy and poet. After Oxford he started out as a lecturer in English literature, published a slim volume of poems, and became a modern art dealer. Then he took his seat in the House of Lords. Spotted as a young articulate Tory, he was made a junior whip under Heath, propelled to be a minister of state (just below the Cabinet) by Thatcher in 1979 at the age of forty; and after stints in Northern Ireland and Employment, he was appointed Minister for the Arts, gaining a seat in the Cabinet by 1985. He resigned, famously remarking that he could not live in central London on a ministerial salary, and reappeared in short order as chairman of Sotheby's for a salary reportedly five times as large.[24] All of which made him a natural ministerial choice to chair the Arts Council for England (unpaid) when the decision to reinvent it as a lottery 'good cause' in 1994 made it one of the nation's foremost cultural baronies. It is futile to speculate about the fate of the talented and charming Gowrie minus an earldom. The point is that his career, spent circulating the heights of Britain's political and cultural establishment, cannot be understood apart from his inherited title, Eton and the House of Lords. Each career is unique, but hundreds of peers circulate equally smoothly across politics, the cultural establishment, the City and the professions.

The hereditary peerage remains an élite of great inherited wealth. Among its large landowners, this wealth is stupendous in scale. National land ownership figures are not published, or even properly collated, but a 1994 study claimed that Britain's ten largest individual landowners, most of them peers, owned 1.5 million acres between them – the pinnacle of the 1 per cent of the population estimated by a late-1970s royal commission to own half of the land in Britain.[25] Then there are central London's great urban landlords, headed by the sixth Duke of Westminster, the seventh Earl Cadogan, the ninth Viscount Portman and the ninth Lord Howard de Walden. Here again, salvation came almost fortuitously in the post-war decades. In the 1940s and early 1950s, it was expected that what socialist taxation and anti-landlord legislation did not accomplish by force, low morale and the National Trust would achieve by stealth. Not a bit of it. Virtually all the great country houses still in private hands by the mid-1950s remain so today. So do most of the great estates, fortified by the unforeseen rise in land and art values, a tax and legislative regime more favourable to the super rich than at any time since 1939, and huge state handouts to farmers and landowners courtesy of the European Union's Common Agricultural Policy – a policy originally designed to sustain continental Europe's indigent mass of small-scale cultivators.

The title of a recent book by Peter Mandler says it all: *The Fall and Rise of the Stately Home*. And how did it happen? Inherited wealth was a prerequisite, of course. But far more important has been the success of the stately home owners, most of them peers, in reinventing themselves as custodians of the 'national heritage'. The rise of the National Trust is one dimension. Set up a century ago to safeguard places of outstanding natural (not man-made) beauty, the Trust came under patrician control in the inter-war years. After the Second World War its attention turned to country house preservation, under powers gained in 1937 (through the efforts of the Marquess of Lothian) enabling the Trust to accept country houses with endowments while allowing the former owners to remain as tenants.[26] Assuming this role hesitantly at first, the Trust took it forward after the war with growing confidence.

Meanwhile, the great private owners started aping the Trust by opening their stately homes to the public, obviating the need for them to part with their estates in the first place. The pioneer was the sixth Marquess of Bath, who in 1946 inherited the dilapidated, 118-roomed mansion of Longleat in Wiltshire together with £700,000 worth of death duties. Selling much of the land, he kept the core estate intact and opened the house as a West Country showplace in 1949 – the first stately home to admit visitors on a regular, paying basis.[27] By the mid-1950s a quarter of a million paying visitors a year were flocking to Longleat, and Lord Bath was – and his son still is – employing as large a staff as their ancestors a century before. Lord Montagu of Beaulieu launched his motoring museum in 1952; the thirteenth Duke of Bedford opened Woburn Abbey in 1955, its grounds soon a safari park replete with lions, tigers and baboons tearing down every car aerial within sight. So unfolded a pattern of English middle-class family recreation which has thrived ever since. Between 1950 and 1965 some 600 houses were opened to the public, headed by Chatsworth (eleventh Duke of Devonshire), Blenheim (eleventh Duke of Marlborough), Hatfield (sixth Marquess of Salisbury), Arundel (seventeenth Duke of Norfolk) and other stately houses still firmly in the hands of their aristocratic owners. A consensus reigns as to the desirability of the status quo (who wants to see the destruction of England's great houses?), creating a more popular role for the aristocracy than conceivable at any time since Lloyd George famously derided the peers before the First World War as '600 men chosen at random from among the ranks of the unemployed'. By 1996 the chairman of the Conservative party could deride plans to reform the House of Lords as 'driven by class envy'.[28]

The status of the hereditary peerage as a political class remains uncertain. Tony Blair's Labour party has pledged to remove it from the House of Lords, leaving the life peers to run the Upper House unaided. This appears set to happen. Yet even if it does, the continuation of a House of Lords with wholly titled inmates – as envisaged by Labour – will limit the social damage to the hereditary peerage. And no one is seriously proposing to take away the hereditary peers' titles, houses or wealth.

In any event, the old aristocracy remains remarkably bullish. And not just as custodians of the national heritage. In 1995 three of their grander number, led by the seventh Earl of Carnarvon (the aforementioned racing manager to the Queen, lord of Highclere Castle near Newbury and former chairman of Hampshire County Council) published one of the most robust defences of the hereditary House of Lords forthcoming since the advent of democracy. Characteristically, they co-opted a distinguished life peer (Lord

Bancroft, a former head of the civil service) and a former official of the House of Lords to help with the job.

Carnarvon and his colleagues began, disarmingly, by declaring that 'The hereditary members of the present House of Lords – who are well aware of its shortcomings – would vote themselves into history with barely a backward glance in favour of a reformed House which was more effective, and whose composition commended wider acceptance, than the present one.' They proceeded, however, to highlight all manner of serious obstacles to reform, and all sorts of great advantages in the status quo. The Lords is 'an organism rather than a machine'. A reformed second chamber might upset a delicate constitutional balance achieved over the centuries between Crown, Upper House and Commons. It might even undermine the monarchy 'since the Crown and the House of Lords have remained associated with each other ... and a radical reform of the one may affect the other'. Hereditary peers 'discharge their duties as public servants, according to their lights'. If abolished, gone would be their 'distinctive contribution' produced by having a 'random element' in political life, as in the Athenian and Venetian constitutions. The Lords would be left in the hands of professional politicians – 'the ultimate quango indeed', and one unlikely to be popular. Furthermore, ejecting the hereditary peers 'would not actually do very much about our pattern of privilege' (an argument also deployed by defenders of the royal status quo). 'It could be argued that it would be largely cosmetic [while] one of the things which has distinguished our society has been the continuity of institutions encouraging those who are born with advantages to use those advantages in public life.'[29]

The merits of Lord Carnarvon's case are neither here nor there. The outstanding fact is that a defence of a parliamentary chamber dominated by hereditary aristocrats can be made in Britain with such conviction and plausibility at the end of the twentieth century.

PART THREE

Conditions

The clearest links with the excess burden of ill health are: low income, unhealthy behaviour and poor housing and environmental amenities.

Sir Donald Acheson, government Chief Medical Officer, 1991

If the inner city is like a chemistry lab full of dangerous social reagents, the dump estate is the test-tube where they are most corrosively combined.

Paul Harrison, *Inside the Inner City*, 1985

6. HEALTH

Class in microcosm

> The National Health Service is the closest thing the English have to a religion, with those who practise in it regarding themselves as a priesthood.
>
> Nigel Lawson, *The View from Number Eleven*, 1992

The National Health Service was born on 5 July 1948. Launched by Aneurin Bevan and the post-war Labour government with all the fanfare accorded to the National Lottery in the 1990s, it quickly embedded itself in the nation's affections. Fifty years on, continuously renewed, it has become a microcosm of Britain's new class structure. As both the largest employer in the land, and the single most important pillar of the welfare state – and the only one spanning all classes in nearly equal degree – it faithfully exhibits the full range and dynamics of Britain's new class hierarchy.

This chapter examines the NHS from these two class dimensions. The opening section is devoted to the NHS as a social institution, with 979,081 employees[1] – almost 3.5 per cent of all those in work in the country at large.[2] At the top of the NHS are the hospital-based consultants (at the very top are the consultants of the London teaching hospitals), although they are often to be found away from their hospitals in their private consulting rooms – or on the golf course. Below the consultants is the upper middle class of the medical profession – the senior managers, who may earn as much as the consultants but who are the *nouveaux riches* of the service. Next comes the middle middle class, the GPs – some through choice, some because they have not quite made it. An increasing number of these are female – often because women realize pretty soon that they are unlikely to make it up the hospital career ladder. There is then a dramatic drop to the skilled, lower middle class: the nurses, therapists, technologists and technicians, who are mainly female. And below them is the proletariat – the auxiliary, ancillary and service personnel, who are overwhelmingly female.

In the second section we look at the NHS as a social service delivering health care. As a *National* Health Service, it exists to treat us all. In theory we should all have access to health care according to need, not class. In practice needs are defined largely by class; so are the doctors and other professionals charged with meeting them; so is the distribution of resources for the purpose. And so, unsurprisingly, is the health of the nation – fifty years after the birth of the supposedly classless NHS.

Doctoral distinctions

The powerful medical profession of today is a recent phenomenon. A century ago it was neither well rewarded nor well regarded.

In the nineteenth century, physicians, surgeons and the despised apothecaries plied their trade as equals in law, although enjoying widely differing public esteem. Over time they became identified simply as general medical practitioners. In 1858 Parliament created a single register for all practitioners and a single council to coordinate medical education. Since then, the growth in the power and influence of doctors has been unrelenting. In 1869 it was still possible to write that 'Medicine has ever been and is now the most despised of all the professions which liberally educated men are expected to enter.'[3] By the First World War this had changed, thanks to improvements in the quality of medicine and its practitioners. In severely limiting the numbers of practitioners, which dropped from 30,000 in 1841 to 11,000 in 1858, the new council began the process of increasing the power and prestige of those fortunate enough to gain admission. As David Owen, a medical doctor who first rose to public prominence as Minister for Health, puts it:

In medicine, as in all walks of life, the principles of economic liberalism vied with the forces of social protectionism. As the demand for medical care increased, the individual medical practitioner became less dependent on the patronage of a few wealthy patients. Whereas in the eighteenth century the patient was the dominant figure in the relationship with the doctor, by the middle of the nineteenth century their roles were reversed.[4]

By the turn of the century, the medical class structure had reshaped itself. At the top were physicians and surgeons, of upper-middle-class origin and with a university education behind them. Their energies were directed towards those who paid their bills – the wealthy – although they found treating the poor in voluntary hospitals provided useful teaching material for their centres of learning. They practised under the auspices of the Royal College of Physicians, a self-regulatory body which governed the profession much as the Royal Colleges still do today.

The majority of health professionals were apothecaries and general practitioners. They serviced the working classes and new middle class, but the latter only in competition with the surgeons and physicians in the outpatient departments of voluntary hospitals, where they were paid on a fee-for-service basis. Workers were treated mostly through their thriving friendly societies, and apothecaries and general practitioners were paid primarily on a capitation fee basis. The Poor Law looked after the rest. Those who treated them worked in foul Poor Law hospital conditions with little reward; and those who were treated had to undertake a humiliating means test and satisfy the 'relieving officer'. As the health analyst Vicente Navarro puts it: 'At the top (was) the upper class doctor serving the upper class and, at the bottom, the apothecaries serving the working class and the poor, with both groups competing on a rather unequal basis for the emerging middle class clientele.'[5] All the while, doctors – even the most lowly – shrewdly insisted that they remained independent contractors, selling their services, rather than salaried *fonctionnaires*. The profession remained independent and self-governing – and thus, in the public mind, pure and well-intentioned. As the prestige of medicine rose (almost everyone now accepted that medicine worked) the early twentieth century became a 'golden age', to quote David Owen: 'The medical profession, through organization and effective lobbying, had by then shaped the medical system itself, so that education, payment and conditions of service buttressed its professional sovereignty instead of undermining it.'[6]

This exclusive regime could not last. Bismarck's introduction in Germany of national insurance in the 1880s pointed the way towards a new order, and Lloyd George's national insurance scheme of 1911 represented a tentative first step on the same road for Britain. By the 1930s the scheme's flaws – less than half of the population of 46 million were covered by National Insurance – generated demands for a further move towards a universal, single health care scheme. Plans for a national health scheme were developed in the 1920s and 1930s (a 1926 Royal Commission, for instance, recommended a tax-based system) so that by the 1940s what Rudolf Klein has called a 'sedimentary consensus' had built up behind the introduction of a new national system.[7] The war heightened this further. Hence the Beveridge committee, and the extraordinary enthusiasm which greeted its report when it was published in December 1942. Although not dealing explicitly with the introduction of a health service, Beveridge declared that disease was one of the five great social evils, along with want, ignorance, squalor and idleness. Two years later, a White Paper, *A National Health Service*, recommended 'a comprehensive service covering every branch of medical and allied activity'. Free at point of use, treatment would be paid for out of taxation. The British Medical Association, the doctor's professional lobby group, reacted with horror, their fears fuelled by the Socialist Medical Association having earlier called for a salaried medical profession under the control of local authorities. All the White Paper amounted to, argued the BMA, was a smokescreen for state control – loss of their independence, and with that loss of their ability to control their own careers and incomes.

But the tide was irreversible; and once Labour had been elected in 1945 with a landslide majority, the question was not *whether* but *how* a system of universal health care would be introduced.

For the medical profession it was a fraught period. A string of measures culminated in the 1946 National Health Act. In effect 3,000 hospitals were nationalized and controlled by twenty regional hospital boards. The Act was to come into effect on 5 July 1948 – so Bevan, the Minister of Health, had two years to persuade doctors to join the scheme. In 1946 a poll of doctors found that 66 per cent were implacably opposed to what they saw as the consequent loss of their independence.[8] As the BMA put it: 'The Association regards the points at issue as not bargaining points but signs of the doctor being a free man, free to practise his science and art in his patients' best interests ... (W)e must not yield on any of the points which collectively or individually spell the end of the doctors' freedom.'[9]

The doctors were intransigent. But since everyone knew that their real objection was a fear of loss of earning power, Bevan adopted the same tactic used by other nationalizing ministers of the day. He bought off their opposition by 'stuffing their mouths with gold'. The key to a settlement, as he correctly saw it, lay with the top echelon of physicians (who worked mainly in private practice and the voluntary hospitals), represented by the Royal Colleges. Bevan knew that if he could secure the backing of this élite he would have plenty of time to buy off the middle class of the profession – the GPs. Without their backing, he would have no chance with the GPs. Hence the extraordinarily generous terms offered to – and still enjoyed by – consultants. Bevan allowed consultants to work part time in the NHS and at the same time charge fees to private patients, as well as using private 'pay beds' in NHS hospitals from where they could simultaneously supervise their NHS and private patients. So successful was this tactic that, while the BMA held rancorous protest meetings about the Bill, the Royal Colleges gave lavish dinners for members of the government.

In setting up the NHS Bevan followed the pattern developed under previous governments, with one great difference: the nationalization of the voluntary hospitals. Many were greatly in debt, their future hanging in the balance until the NHS took them over. But the need for nationalization was all part of the plot, according to Barbara Castle: 'Nye asked Lord Moran (President of the Royal College of Physicians – dubbed by the BMA "Corkscrew Charlie" so close was he to Bevan) how he would attract first-rate consultants into the peripheral provincial hospitals. When Moran replied that consultants would go there if they got an interesting job and if their financial future was secured by a proper salary, Nye paused and then said, "Only the State could pay those salaries. This would mean the nationalization of hospitals." And nationalize them he did.'[10] So nationalization was not, as the BMA referred to it at the time, 'the largest seizure of property since Henry VIII confiscated the monasteries',[11] but was rather a fundamental part of the bargain between Bevan and the medical élite. Bevan's decision to create a national hospital service simultaneously achieved his aim of equal access to the best medical care regardless of income, and satisfied the consultants.

Although the struggle for their acceptance of the system was protracted, the GPs themselves were in many ways easier to deal with. Money spoke power, and Bevan engineered an ingenious solution of a capitation fee *combined with* a basic salary. With their mouths stuffed too, and their resistance futile now that consultants had joined the new order, the BMA backed down in May 1948. By December, 21 million people had received free treatment. Bevan now had different worries: 'the ceaseless cascade of medicine which is pouring down British throats'.[12] As one GP complained: 'One would think the people saved up their illnesses for the first free day.'[13]

This 'ceaseless cascade' was, perhaps paradoxically, crucial to the underpinning of the NHS as a British institution. Far from it being the working-class ghetto that some had predicted, the middle classes, who had found the pre-war system as piecemeal and unsatisfactory as the poor, were tremendous beneficiaries. As Nick Timmins stresses in his magisterial history of the welfare state, one of the defining features of the 1940s was the bringing of the middle classes 'into the net' – they no longer had to pay the market cost of private health care or take out insurance.[14] This cross-class ethos has maintained the NHS in its uniquely popular place among the public services ever since. As the professional classes today increasingly opt out of public services such as education, public transport and social care, the GP's surgery remains one of the few institutions used by all, even though a private alternative exists. Most inner-city GPs' surgeries will have the residents of the plush terraces sitting alongside the local council estate tenants.

There is no denying, then, that the NHS has to some extent subverted the class segregation which reigns across most of British society. But its success should not blind us to its limits. The old medical hierarchy was as much institutionalized as reformed by Bevan's NHS.

Like most hierarchies with old roots, today's medical profession is obsessed with correct titles, and has constructed a variety of complicated rules of address. On qualification a medical graduate asserts the title 'Doctor'. This is no more justified than 'Carpenter Smith', or 'Banker Jones', for a medical degree is a Bachelorhood of Medicine, not a Doctorate. But we are not just ordinary professionals; we are doctors, and merit a special status. After five years' further study the doctor can become a surgeon. He has moved on even from the upper middle class and become a breed apart – a true aristocrat of the profession. No longer can he be identified with the ordinary ranks of the profession. So, in a glorious piece of inverted snobbery, he reverts to the title 'Mr'. He is sufficiently eminent not to need to preface his name.

That is how it is today. In the old days, however, the surgical 'Mr' had a more obvious derivation. Surgeons were looked down on by physicians as mere quacks who blundered around with sharp instruments. Surgery could be carried out by any old mister – and was (hence barbers whose shops were marked with a red and white striped pole).

This hierarchical nomenclature reflects the organization of a highly exclusive and strict hierarchical profession. The consultants at the top are members of the Super Class which we described in Chapter 3. And as we saw in Chapter 2, Britain's education system ensures that year after year, generation after generation, the medical profession clones itself. In 1993, for example, 74.7 per cent of applicants to medical school had parents from the professions. Only 1.1 per cent of applicants had parents who were unskilled – and a mere 9.5 per cent had manually skilled parents.[15] Indeed, a BMA study of a statistically representative group of medical graduates in 1995 showed that 38 per cent had been educated at independent schools – the same figure as for state comprehensive schools; while 17 per cent – almost one in five of the new medical graduates – were educated at the few remaining state grammar schools – an astonishingly high figure given that there are only 174 grammar schools, against 2,876 comprehensives in England.[16] Eighteen per cent came from medically qualified families, in which one or both parents are doctors.[17]

Although in the past the primary qualification required to attend medical school was a private income (just as with the Bar), so that five years of penury and an initial low income were not a problem, competition for places is now fiercer than in almost any other profession. 'There are so many of them that you can select those with the personal qualities you are looking for,' says the dean of one medical school. 'Those you select will then be able to get through their exams as well as playing the clarinet, batting for the cricket eleven.'[18] It is, after all, vital that only the 'right sort of chaps' are selected. (Although, as with the public school system we encountered in Chapter 2, increasingly the 'right sort of chaps' are female – around half of all new entrants to medical school are now women.)

Back to the internal hierarchy. After registration – graduation – the newly qualified doctor will spend three more years in training as senior house officer (SHO) in various hospital departments. Those who wish to become surgeons will seek SHO posts with surgical teams as a form of apprenticeship. They will also have to take Parts I and II of the Fellowship of the Royal College of Surgeons exam, which has a pass rate of only 25–30 per cent. About 40 per cent of medical students tend to express a preference for general practice – and in fact 60–70 per cent of doctors end up as GPs.

An SHO, whose appointment lasts about six months, is fractionally more senior than a houseman and is given a greater degree of responsibility. After a couple of appointments the SHO can scour the *British Medical Journal* for posts as a registrar. These last a year, usually renewed for a further year. After two years as a registrar, competition begins again for posts as a senior registrar, where one remains for another three years before applying for the position of consultant – and arrival.

For physicians the pattern is similar but with the aim of joining the Royal College of Physicians – again, a two-part exam, with a still lower pass rate than that of the RCS. But once in, all the successful candidate has gained is an entry ticket to the next level of competition – with fellow members of the RCP (or RCS for surgeons). Fellowship (whose consequent financial rewards put even the healthy incomes of ordinary consultants in the shade) rather than mere membership cannot come until years later, after a successful career as a consultant, and is awarded after a secret adjudication process.

Within this structure there is a further pecking order of the glamorous specialities, such as cardiology, heart surgery, neurology and neurosurgery at the top, and psychiatry, anaesthetics and geriatrics at the bottom. Public health and paediatrics – where relatively little private work is available – are the distinctly poor relations. And radiologists and pathologists are hardly considered doctors by some in the medical profession.

But the pecking order concerns more than status. Over 250 hospital consultants earn, from the NHS alone, £102,240 p.a.[19] And above that are those who are employed for specific talents that are in short supply in an area and who, according to one trust, earn 'up to £20,000 above the NHS maximum'.[20] Brian Hanson, chairman of Hartlepool and Peterlee Hospital Trust, has described the inflation in consultants' pay: 'It is a common problem nationwide that hospitals have in getting suitably qualified staff. Some trusts have hired consultants at double the going rate.'[21]

Ignore private practice income for a moment. NHS consultants are contracted with a basic salary from £42,000 to £54,000 in 1996. But any consultant who took home only his basic salary would be a very disappointed man (and man is what the overwhelming majority – 82 per cent – of them are). For, in what Ray Rowden, former director of the Institute of Health Services Management has described as 'the biggest fraud since the Mafia', consultants award each other merit payments of up to another £51,710.[22] Not *bonus* payments for good work, determined annually as in most comparable walks of life; but *merit* payments, approved once, and awarded for the rest of the career. And they do this through a system which, since its inception with the coming of the NHS, has remained secret, with unpublished criteria. There are four levels of payout, from the top A-plus award which doubles a consultant's pay, through the A award of £38,100 and the B award of £21,770 to the bottom C award of £10,000.[23] The internal market may have made great inroads into some areas of the NHS, but even the supposed army of all-powerful accountants and managers is, by the contract under which consultants are employed, kept in the dark about the scale of these awards (although managers in some areas have started to be given a say in the granting of C awards). The latest reliable estimate, collated in March 1993, shows that a total of 7,223 had been granted at a cost of £80 million. At any one time around 35 per cent of consultants hold an award, with 60 per cent holding one on retirement. In Wessex, 29.1 per cent of consultants held an award – compared with 57.7 per cent in London. The awards themselves reflect the profession's hierarchy: in 1992 there were twenty-six awards to consultants in general medicine, but none in geriatrics. Truly the 'old boy network' does wonders – and it is literally an old boy network; of the awards granted in 1993, 90.5 per cent went to men.[24] So great are the financial rewards available, and so skilled is the BMA at negotiating them, that it was little exaggeration when the then Health Secretary, Kenneth Clarke, remarked to the BMA that 'Every time I mention the word "reform", you reach for your wallet.'

Not all hospital doctors will reach the heights of consultancy and so a new post has recently been created – associate specialist. This is justified as a supposedly 'non career' post for those who want to work in hospitals but not as consultants. That is the theory. In practice such a person does not exist. The associate specialist is an associate specialist not because he has rejected consultancy but because consultancy has rejected him. By this means the profession has found a way of looking after those who are either not good enough to become consultants or who 'don't fit in'. Doctors from ethnic minority backgrounds are far less likely to be given consultant jobs than whites: after examining 418 vacancies in forty-five NHS Trusts, in 1991 and 1992, in three specialities where ethnic minorities were rare (general medicine, surgery and obstetrics) and two where they tend to be concentrated (psychiatry and geriatrics), the Commission for Racial Equality found that out of 147 consultant vacancies, 53 per cent of applicants were from ethnic minorities and 27 per cent of the appointments, and of 130 senior registrar vacancies, 37 per cent of applicants were from ethnic minorities and only 17 per cent of appointments. 'The disparities in success rates . . . were so marked and consistent, and the omission of procedural safeguards so routine, that the possibility of discrimination cannot be ignored,' as the CRE report put it.[25] So most associate specialists are foreign or female. And they end up doing the jobs no one else wants – a gynaecology associate specialist will, for instance, usually do a hospital's abortions.

Below this élite comes the medical middle class: the GPs. From the launch of the NHS, GPs were astute enough to use their muscle to avoid a salaried service, preferring to keep the perks of self-employment and payment on the basis of fees and allowances. There is thus a huge range in the take-home pay of GPs. The government sets an 'intended annual net remuneration' of £44,770, and expects take-home pay to average out at £50,410.[26] But as a guide to real pay the figure is of limited use. In 1995 10 per cent of GPs took home less than £24,000.[27] So just as there is a hierarchy of consultants, so there is with GPs. As one highly cynical in-house guide to the medical profession, the mistitled *Official Doctor/Patient Handbook* puts it: 'The range of pay is enormous, probably varying from as low as £20,000 for the struggling, often foreign, inner-city single-handed doctor with a very small list to as high as £100,000 for the slick, Home Counties, business oriented doctor who is running three nursing homes.'[28] Pay is supposedly determined by the number of patients on a GP's list, together with a multitude of other 'weighting' factors such as patients' age. But for those lucky enough to work in a large rural area, dispensing their own prescriptions and with long car journeys (to take advantage of generous mileage allowances), income can increase by around 25 per cent.[29] Then there are the other perks, such as a salary allowance for a spouse's 'secretarial duties' and her pension scheme. Other services, such as night visits, childhood immunization, cervical screening programmes and various maternity service fees provide a welcome boost.

As for the bottom 10 per cent that earn so little, this is what one disgruntled GP had to say in 1995: 'Given the chance, I would leave the NHS faster than a heroin addict will steal your car stereo. What prevents me is that there is nowhere for me to go. Medical qualifications leave you spectacularly unqualified for anything else, unless, of course, you have previously untapped talents and can slide easily into a job on breakfast TV.'[30]

The varied status of GPs signals a more general point about class and status. Within society as a whole, the GP ranks high. It is not just the Jewish mother who wants her daughter to marry a doctor. But as we have seen, within the medical profession the GP, whatever he might earn, is very much the social poor relation – the solicitor to the specialist's QC – although the spread of fundholding has helped to improve the way consultants treat GPs: fundholding GPs have the power of the purse strings, a remarkably efficient catalyst to good manners. Whereas before the reforms GPs used to send consultants Christmas cards, now, it is said, it is the other way round.

Back to the hospital. The NHS is of course no longer run just by its doctors. That said, the power of managers and trust boards to rein back doctor control can be overstated. A trust chair who upsets the apple cart too much can be effectively forced out by his trust's consultants, as John Spiers, the crusading chairman of Brighton Healthcare Trust (and now, appropriately, chairman of the Patients' Association), found out when he tried to call doctors to account by pointing out the dramatic variations in successful treatments.

But managers' power has none the less increased dramatically – as has their pay. Before the NHS reforms of 1988 and the introduction of trusts, each unit had a general manager on about £35,000 p.a. Cleaners earned just *under* £6,000. Now, the average chief executive's pay is about £60,000, with some on over £100,000. Cleaners' pay has also increased. It is now just *over* £6,000. Since 1979 the pay of medical practitioners and nurses has improved, with doctors starting from an already high base. From an already low base, the position of porters and orderlies has deteriorated far more than that of the unskilled in the economy as a whole.[31]

A report published in February 1996 found that the average earnings rises of trust chief executives were running at more than twice the rate of nurses' over the year to March 1995.[32] While total remuneration of trust chief executives averaged a 7.6 per cent increase, NHS nurses' pay increased by only 3.2 per cent. Further, NHS managers tend to change jobs often – a quarter of all trusts had a change of chief executive during 1995. At one there were four different chief executives that year. Severance pay alone amounted to nearly £2.4 million in 1995.[33]

The NHS manager is *nouveau riche* in more than just a financial sense. As we have seen, doctors tend overwhelmingly to come from professional families. Most senior managers do so too, but it is a lot less surprising to find a manager from more modest social origins, such as Peter Griffiths, one of the architects of the reforms, and formerly chief executive of Guy's Hospital Trust – the hospital that was pivotal in the NHS reforms' success. Although the majority of senior managers are recruited through the NHS graduate training scheme, and come from the traditional universities (such as Ken Jarrold, director of Human Resources for the NHS Executive, and Barbara Stocking, director of Oxford and Anglia Region, both Cambridge graduates), quite a few did not even have degrees when they started as managers, and have only gained a qualification on the job – the almost ubiquitous MBA. This route to the top of their profession, however, does nothing to endear them to their exclusively university educated doctor colleagues.

This brings us to the largest single occupational group in the NHS, the nurses. Half of the nearly one million people who work for the NHS are nurses. Nine out of ten of these are women. Nurse salaries account for 27 per cent of total NHS spending. The rise in their status is new. For many years they were regarded as being just a step up from porters and orderlies, and quite separate from the 'medical professions'. The stereotype of 'devotion and obedience' which drove Florence Nightingale to anger is the traditional view. While the doctors' car park is considered essential, nurses need only travel in by bus. But as the traditional view changes, so nurses have begun to assert their case for higher status within the NHS. The modern teaching hospital nurse, with her new education – her A-levels (sometimes a degree) and her state of the art training undertaken through a college of higher education – is too qualified to waste her time on emptying bedpans, dressing wounds and preventing bedsores. That is now for the ancillary staff. 'The nurse,' writes the cynic in the *Official Doctor/Patient Handbook*, 'who should be doing the nursing sits at the nursing station pretending to be a doctor . . . The nurses . . . are sitting at their consoles pretending to read ECGs and to interpret complex biochemical investigations. They do not take responsibility for these "interpretations" but drive the doctors mad with their helpful suggestions.'[34]

The NHS has more women employees than any comparable organization. Women represent 78 per cent of non-medical staff and 45 per cent of general managers. Yet women and their needs are still under-represented in decision making. Perhaps that is because they account for only 28 per cent of chief executives and senior managers and 18 per cent of consultants.[35] And there are almost no black or ethnic minority managers. Those women who do make it to the top have as a group far fewer family ties than their male colleagues. Among top NHS managers, 50 per cent of women but only 7 per cent of men have no children.[36] Among support staff, however, 85.9 per cent of clerical workers and 61.5 per cent of ancillary staff are female.[37]

So if we look at the NHS from the inside – if we look at how it is structured, and at those who work in it – we can see that it is indeed a fair microcosm of Britain's class structure. Just as the classless society is itself a myth, so too is the comforting classless NHS.

Health by class – I
The very title, *National* Health Service, would lead one to think that health outcomes are broadly similar across the population. Certainly, the health of the population as a whole has improved over recent years. In 1991, for example, a baby boy could expect to live to seventy-three and a girl to seventy-nine – an improvement in a decade of two years.[38] Indeed, 50 per cent of boys and 66 per cent of girls now have a life expectancy of eighty.[39] Other measures, such as height and dental health, are similarly improved.

And as mortality rates from infectious diseases have declined, deaths in childhood are that much rarer.

But such global figures, much beloved by politicians parading the achievements of the NHS, deceive as much as they enlighten. As Margaret Whitehead, one of Britain's leading health analysts, has put it:

> Lower occupational groups have been found to experience more illness which is both chronic and incapacitating. Although it is taken for granted that sickness will happen to almost everyone sooner or later, it seems that lower occupational groups experience it earlier and this must be seen as a major inequality in a welfare society. Other indirect measures of affluence and poverty, such as household-based classifications and employment status, also highlight inequalities in health. Owner-occupiers continue to have lower rates of illness and death than private tenants, who in turn have lower rates than local authority housing tenants. It is well known and confirmed in recent studies, that the unemployed have much poorer health than those with jobs. It is also now beyond question that unemployment causes a deterioration in mental health and there is increasing evidence that the same is true of physical health . . . The overall North/South regional differences in health in Britain are still evident, but what is now becoming apparent is the great inequality in health which can exist between small areas in the same region. Areas suffering social and material deprivation have been found to have much poorer health profiles than neighbouring affluent areas.[40]

In practical terms this means that:

- There would be 42,000 fewer deaths each year for people aged sixteen to seventy-four if the death rate of people with manual jobs were the same as for those in non-manual occupations.
- A child from an unskilled social class is twice as likely to die

before the age of fifteen as a child with a professional father.
- Premature deaths among people with unskilled occupations cause the loss of nearly three times as many years of potential life among men, and twice as many among women, as they do among professionals.
- If the whole population had experienced the same death rate as the non-manual classes there would have been 700 fewer stillbirths and 1,500 fewer deaths in the first year of life in England and Wales in 1988.
- The prevalence of angina was almost twice as high among middle-aged men in manual occupations compared with non-manual in 1987.[41]

Almost all health indicators confirm the association between the prevalence of ill health and poor social and economic circumstances. The 1981 census revealed, for instance, that the premature death rate was twice as high in the lowest social class as in the highest. Using the Registrar General's classification, the life expectancy for a child with parents in social class V (unskilled manual) is over seven years shorter than for a child whose parents are in social class I (professional). Male manual workers have premature death rates 45 per cent higher than non-manual workers, and women 43 per cent higher. The number of premature deaths associated with manual work is greater than the total number of deaths from strokes, infectious diseases, accidents, lung cancer and other respiratory diseases combined.[42] And children in social class V are four times more likely to suffer accidental death than those in class I.[43] Another way of looking at the evidence is to say that men in social class V lose 114 years of potential life per 1,000 population against thirty-nine years in class I, reflecting the higher mortality rates due to accidents and violence among young men. People in unskilled occupations and their children are twice as likely to die prematurely as professionals.[44]

So much for the classless society.

It is striking that these socio-economic differences in mortality are not confined to a few diseases which one might expect to find associated with particular occupations or lifestyles. Of the sixty-six 'major list' causes of death among men, sixty-two are more common in social groups IV and V than among all others – and of the seventy major causes for women, sixty-four are more common in groups IV and V. Again, a 25-year-old unemployed unskilled man living in council housing had a 17 per cent probability of having a limiting, long-term illness – three times higher than a man working in a professional job and who owns his own home. Women living in a council house had 30 per cent higher odds of a similar limiting, long-term illness than owner-occupiers. Worse still, unemployed women had a 78 per cent higher chance and housewives a 68 per cent higher chance of such an illness than employed women.[45]

Wide class differences in life expectancy have been reported since the first accurate data was collected in 1921 by the Registrar General. *The Black Report on Inequalities in Health*, published in 1980, argued that there had been a continuing widening of these differences since 1951. *The Health Divide* report repeated this in 1987. But the key question is this: are people less healthy because they are socially deprived and living in poorer circumstances, or are they where they are because they are less healthy? The common sense assumption – that income provides the prerequisites for health, such as shelter, food and warmth – would tend to support the view that poverty determines health. A study of sixty-five families living on supplementary benefit in 1980, for instance, found that some parents went without food to provide more for their children,[46] and a study of 1,000 low-income people in the North in 1984 showed that a quarter did not have a main meal every day, with a third citing cost as the reason,[47] a finding confirmed by a recent report which showed that a 'healthy' shopping basket was £5 a week more expensive for low-income families than an 'unhealthy' one – representing 20 per cent of total weekly food expenditure.[48]

In contrast, the view that poor health causes poverty is supported by evidence which shows, for instance, that childhood hospitalization and short stature prejudice a person's chances of upward social mobility, and that chronic illness later in life limits job choices and opportunities.[49] The public health expert David Barker's examination of 20,000 adults with known birth weights shows that low birth weight is a crucial determinant of health in later life. He shows that babies who were small at birth, because of poor nutrition in the womb, have an increased risk of heart disease, strokes, diabetes and hypertension.[50] Even in the 1950s it was clear that there was a relationship between maternal health, social mobility at marriage and the various outcomes of pregnancy. Women who were taller and in better health than other members of their social class were both more likely to marry higher up the social scale and to have lower rates of prematurity, stillbirths and first-week infant deaths.[51]

We need first to consider what we mean by health. There are many measures of a nation's health, from mortality rates, through morbidity rates, to sickness-absence rates. Each of these is relevant, but none gives the complete picture, for each has its own problems. Mortality rate alone, for instance, gives no weight to chronic illness, whereas morbidity rate alone ignores congenital and other permanently incapacitating conditions. So one needs to look at the broader picture.

The cause of every death in Britain is registered – along with the occupation of the deceased. By taking the number of deaths in each class and dividing it by the total number of people in that class, one can estimate class differences in mortality. Thus we know that men and women in class V have a two and a half times greater chance of dying before retirement than those in class I.[52] Age by age, such class differences recur: at any age those in class V have a higher rate of death than their better-off counterparts. During the first month of life, the risk of death in unskilled families is double that in professional families. In the first year of life, for the death of every one male child of professional parents, two boys with skilled manual worker parents and three with unskilled manual worker parents will die. The ratio is still higher for girls.[53]

Why do they die? Accidents, which account for 30 per cent of childhood deaths, are ten times more likely to kill boys from class V (from fire, falls or drowning) than those from class I. The corresponding ratio of deaths caused to young pedestrians by cars is more than seven to one.[54]

Arguments about rates of death across the regions rage, based on the same evidence. The traditional (and still widely held) view is that the South of England (under a line from the Wash to the Bristol Channel) is far healthier than the North.[55] Premature mortality among Northern males is 26 per cent higher than in East Anglia, for instance, and among females in the North it is 21 per cent higher than in the South West.[56] But analysis of the same figures by Illsley and Le Grand, two of the more open-minded social scientists, has found instead that 'simple conclusions about the persistence of a north/south divide are not justified'.[57]

But what is certainly true is that within relatively poor areas there is widening inequality. The poorest areas in the North, for example, have been found to be 'increasingly coming adrift from the experience of the rest of the population . . . Mortality experience in poor areas continues to lag far behind average national experience, particularly in middle age', according to the *British Medical Journal*. 'In the poorest 10 per cent of wards, mortality in 1989–91 among men aged 45–54 and women aged 55–64 was equivalent to national levels of mortality last experienced in the late 1940s, while among women aged 45–54 and men aged 55–64 the equivalent national rates occurred in the early 1950s.'[58] Similarly, urban areas in the North West and Inner London have high premature mortality, while areas with low mortality tend to be in the South. Mortality in Manchester, for instance, is two and a half times higher than that in Elmbridge.[59]

Again, if one looks at the overall impact of the twenty most common causes of death by counting the number of times a locality features with high mortality, the most frequently mentioned are areas such as South Wales, Greater Manchester, Merseyside, Tyneside, Teesside and Greater London – the only one in the South.[60] To take the big picture, the gap between the health of the richest and poorest is greatest in the North, where mortality in classes IV and V is 188 per cent of that for class I and II men, and 170 per cent for women.[61]

Health by class – II

We will look more closely at housing in the next chapter. But one cannot separate housing from health. The social investigator Edwin Chadwick, reporting on the conditions of the urban poor in the 1880s, first highlighted the state of housing and those who were housed. Many nineteenth-century social reformers were concerned with the housing stock. Today the importance remains, but the problems have changed, as Sir Donald Acheson, formerly the Chief Medical Officer at the Department of Health, has written:

> Nowadays, the relation between housing and health is mediated in subtler ways than in Chadwick's time. Illness is brought about by factors such as faulty design (which contributes to falls and fires in the home), inadequate heating and lighting (which is also linked to falls), damp (which is related to the growth of moulds and mites and thus linked to chest diseases including asthma), and lack of safe amenities for recreation. Houses with multiple occupancy (bedsits, converted flats and bed-and-breakfast hotels) may be particularly hazardous especially when the supporting services such as sanitation and fire escapes are overburdened and families have to share washing, toilet, food storage, and cooking facilities.[62]

When not at home, those in jobs spend the majority of their time at work, and working conditions can have a vital influence on health. Occupational health experts have found that a wide range of diseases are associated with hazards such as chemicals, dust and noise, which are obviously more prevalent among manual workers. The same is true for accidents at work. The greater one's exposure to possible risk, the more likely one is to suffer.[63] Similarly, monotonous, repetitive tasks, close supervision and the inability to deal with personal matters during work – all characteristic of the worst paid and lowest status jobs – have been shown to result in increased output of 'stress hormones' and are thus linked with an increased risk of coronary heart disease.[64] And, of course, manual work is usually more physically demanding, noisier and more dangerous than the work of professionals and managers. Incidentally, the health service hierarchy we discussed earlier shows itself again here. Relative to other men in England and Wales, mortality in the 1980s was significantly lower among dentists, doctors, opticians and physiotherapists and significantly higher among hospital porters, male nurses and ambulancemen.[65]

What about those without jobs? Since low income is so closely associated with poor health, it is hardly surprising that there is a strong relationship between unemployment and poor health. To return to the question we posed earlier (does poverty cause ill health or vice versa?), a study of over 6,000 men for the British Regional Heart Study, for instance, found 'increased mortality in men experiencing a loss of employment ... After adjusting for a wide range of background variables including social class, health, behaviour, and health status before loss of employment ... (the result) suggests a causal effect.'[66] Those men who reported some interruption to their employment had almost double the risk of dying prematurely, after adjusting for a range of factors (such as unemployment being caused by ill health), than those who were continuously employed.[67]

Unemployment is also closely associated with higher morbidity rates. The evidence is overwhelming that the unemployed have lower levels of psychological well-being, a higher risk of depression, anxiety, poor self-esteem, neurotic disorders and disturbed sleep.[68] The unemployed frequently face stigma and loss of status, as well as a loss of structure to their lives. Researchers in Oxford in 1979–82 found that the attempted suicide rates for unemployed men were twelve to fifteen times higher than those for employed men, and were particularly high for the long-term unemployed. Unemployed men are 30 per cent more likely to report chronic illness;[69] unemployed women had chronic illness ratios 28 per cent above the average for all women.[70] Indeed, the 1996 edition of *Social Trends* – a publication of the government statistical service – confirmed 'the significantly raised mortality of the unemployed in comparison to all men of working age'.[71] A 1990 analysis of a sample of more than 500,000 people drawn from the 1971 census showed that premature death rates were 37 per cent higher than average among unemployed men. It also found that 20 per cent of unemployed men and 38 per cent of unemployed women had suffered a neurotic disorder during the week before the census. Among people with full-time jobs the rates were only 10 per cent and 16 per cent respectively. Five times as many unemployed as employed women suffered from depressive disorders.[72]

There is an argument that those in disadvantaged circumstances – the lower social classes – suffer poor health because they are more likely to adopt health-threatening behaviour, such as smoking. Certainly, there is a clear and direct relationship between smoking and socio-economic status, with rates of smoking highest among the poorest. Nineteenth-century analyses of the poor health of workers and their families concentrated upon dirt, squalor and bad hygiene. Although they played a role in their own right (as causes of, for instance, TB), they were also indicative of other factors which were still more important, such as poor nutrition and chronic exhaustion. The story may well be the same nowadays. Although cigarette smoking and high blood fats are most common among groups which are most likely to have heart attacks, the chances of their having one are far greater than would be expected on the basis of these risks alone. Take smoking. Now that the evidence that smoking damages health is so clear and so well known (smoking increases the risks of most major causes of death, such as lung cancer and heart disease, and smokers are twenty times more likely to die of lung cancer than non-smokers[73]), one would have expected to see a fall in the number of smokers overall, as indeed there has been. Yet that decline has been more rapid among the more affluent, so that smoking is now predominantly a habit of the poor: three times as many people in unskilled occupations smoke as in professional jobs. Indeed, particularly high smoking rates are found among people who are unemployed and among young adults with children – especially single parents (nearly 70 per cent of single parents with low incomes, no qualifications and living in council housing smoke).[74] In 1988 16 per cent of professional men and 17 per cent of professional women smoked, compared with 33 per cent for both in 1972. Again, in 1988 43 per cent of unskilled men and 39 per cent of unskilled women smoked, compared with 64 per cent and 42 per cent in 1972. Overall, the 1992 General Household Survey showed that almost half (46 per cent) of the unemployed smoked, compared with 29 per cent of those with jobs.[75]

The most recent survey reveals that half of single parents and three-quarters of couples on income support typically spend a fifth of the disposable section of their income support on cigarettes. Thus, a very large share of social security benefits given to families with low incomes is given straight back to the Treasury through excise tax.[76]

Although there is a similar variation in alcohol consumption between social groups, the story is much more complex than for smoking. There are more heavy drinkers among non-manual than manual workers. For instance, 14 per cent of professional women consume more than the recommended safe limit, compared with only 8 per cent of semi-skilled and unskilled women. It is a similar story with men.[77] In 1988 the level of consumption by men by region showed high levels in the North, North West and Wales, and lower in Scotland, East Anglia and the South West.[78]

Equally important is the persistence, despite the existence of the NHS, of inequalities in access to health care. A study of Newcastle in 1985 showed that dental services were more widely available to residents of affluent areas than to those of the poor areas designated 'priority' by the Department of Health.[79] That was before the effective privatization of dental care. And analyses of GP consultations have shown that higher social class patients receive more explanations and details of their treatment than lower social class patients,[80] that the middle classes spend more time on average with their GP than those with working-class backgrounds,[81] and that there is clear evidence that classes I and II are more likely to be referred to specialists by their GP than classes IV and V.[82] In 1993 there were 8.4 full-time GPs per 10,000 patients in Manchester, compared with only 5.6 in Rotherham.[83] As we have shown, the most disadvantaged members of society often have the poorest access to health care either in absolute terms or relative to their needs, through a combination of both practical factors (such as the absence of a car) and more entrenched causes. Julian Le Grand has shown, for example, that (relative to need) professional and managerial groups receive over 40 per cent more NHS spending per person than those in semi- and unskilled jobs.[84] And those in the highest income groups who report their health as 'not good' use 2 per cent more GP services and 17 per cent more in-patient services than those in the lowest groups.[85] It is much the same for primary care. Individuals from areas with high deprivation have a low uptake of immunization[86] and there is a lower utilization of health promotion clinics among poorer social and economic groups.[87] Researchers in Glasgow found that clinical investigations for heart disease were performed more frequently on patients from more affluent neighbourhoods[88] – despite their having a lower incidence of such disease.

The nation's attachment to the NHS is a fascinating phenomenon. If not the 'English religion' which Nigel Lawson dubbed it, the NHS is certainly a shrine before which most of the population genuflect as a matter of course. They do so because of a deep-seated belief that health care is somehow a commodity above the market; and because they believe that the NHS has in fact made it so –

that equal treatment is made available to all, regardless of wealth and status. Yet in reality the NHS owes its effectiveness and popularity in large part to the fact that it is *not* egalitarian. The comfortably off revere the NHS in no small part because they get a good bargain out of it, and are thus happy to feel good about themselves by continuing to pay for what they are told is a subsidy to the poor. The poor see it, with all its imperfections, as one of the few public services in which they can have confidence of reasonable treatment. We are back, again, to the myth of the classless society – the myth of equal opportunity crowding out the reality of segregation by class. But at least, in this case, those at the bottom have gained.

7. HOUSING

Where do you live?

Up to the mid-1950s council blocks were in the main four or five storeys, no different in style and scale from the private blocks in north Westminster, for example. Suddenly the skyline of every large town and city was disfigured by these 'welfare blocks'. The middle classes didn't mind paying for council housing. What they did mind was being literally overshadowed by welfare housing that was destroying their skylines.

Jack Straw, quoted in Nicholas Timmins, *The Five Giants*, 1996

In 1991 British Telecom introduced its 071 and 081 codes for London. Who knows how many trees died so that newspaper style pages could print scores of articles, all with the same message: 081 spelt social death. Estate agents reported home-owners flooding them with calls, concerned that the new 081 prefix would wipe thousands off the value of their houses. For in middle-class Britain in the 1990s, it is not *how* you live – we are all home-owners now – but *where* you live. Indeed, a recent *Scotsman* poll found that more than one in three people (36 per cent) regarded where we live as a key indicator of class.[1]

Is this any different from the way it used to be? In 1933 J. B. Priestley remarked in his *English Journey* that the real divisions were not between the prosperous South and the declining North but between the inner cities and manufacturing towns and the new outer suburbs. Beyond the picture-book English idyll and the Dickensian urban squalor was a new England:

This is the England of arterial and by-pass roads, of filling stations and factories that look like exhibition buildings, of giant cinemas and dance halls and cafés, bungalows with tiny garages, cocktail bars, Woolworth's, motor coaches, wireless, hiking, factory girls looking like actresses, greyhound-racing and dirt tracks, swimming pools, and everything given away for cigarette coupons.

This was, Priestley continued, 'as near to a classless society as we have got yet'. Yet, of course, it was only 'classless' because it was cordoned off from the other classes. Seen as part of the wider landscape, suburbia was no more than an institutional separation of the expanding middle class. In the traditional countryside the rich at least mixed with the poor, and in nineteenth-century industrial towns the boss lived in 'the big house on the hill' and looked over his workers literally and metaphorically.

The rise of the suburb changed all that. Now you lived in the area, as well as the house, you could afford. As Harold Perkin puts it,

> The classes and subclasses sorted themselves out more neatly than ever before into single-class enclaves which did not know or speak to each other. The life of the stockbroker belt with its big cars and detached houses and private infant schools was more remote from the white-collar semi-detached private estate than ever the squire was from the village almshouses or the cotton spinner from his operatives' cottages.[2]

Segregation by area has been more than a century in the making. Back in the 1880s, Lord Salisbury, the first Conservative leader obliged to fight mass elections, discovered large pockets of 'Villa Toryism' ripe for mobilizing in the exclusive districts of the major cities. The rise and fall of council housing, and the expansion of urban Britain, have changed old patterns dramatically, but the reality of segregation continues intact.

The subtlety of these social and housing distinctions is, however, always changing. Take an area like Cricklewood, in north-west London. Cricklewood is the deserving butt of a score of Alan Coren columns. But it used to have an important – in terms of social standing, irreplaceable – asset: it could be all things to all people. To yuppies concerned to impress their friends it could, when giving directions to visit, be described as West Hampstead. To those who wanted working-class street cred it could be described as Kilburn. To the real working class, it was a mass of tower blocks in shocking condition. A similar phenomenon applies to Bayswater. To the trendy it is Notting Hill. To the 'grunge chic' it is Paddington. The introduction of the 081 code added a new dimension. From then on you were either 071 and a part of the metropolitan circle, or you were 081 and suburban and, well, a bit out of it all.

Until recently there was a similar divide across Britain as a whole. If you lived north of an imaginary line from the Wash to the Bristol Channel (until you got to Scotland where civilization began again) – 'North of Watford' – you were a rugby-league-watching, bitter-drinking, pigeon-racing coal miner. Or rather, you were according to the London-based arbiters of taste. The fact that Manchester, for instance, was a leading financial centre, and had in its environs some of the most splendid and expensive houses in the country, was irrelevant. Certainly this appeared to be the view of the former Health Minister, Edwina Currie – a northern lass with a gift for controversy. Responding in 1986 to a study commissioned by the North Regional Health Authority which attributed premature death, excess morbidity and low birth weights in the North to poverty and unemployment, she argued that: 'I honestly don't think the problem has anything to do with poverty. My family grew up in Liverpool and they didn't have two beans but, as a result of good food, good family and good rest, they grew up fit and well. The problem very often for people is, I think, just ignorance and failing to realize that they do have some control over their lives.'[3] The remarks were interpreted as saying that stupid northerners existed on chip butties whilst sensible southerners breakfasted on muesli.

This view that the comfortable, civilized South was for 'U people' and the frozen, industrial North 'non-U' (to borrow Nancy

Mitford's terminology), has a long history. But like Priestley's 'classless suburbia', this too could be turned on its head: 'When you go into the industrial North,' wrote Orwell in 1937 in *The Road to Wigan Pier*,

> you are entering a strange country. This is partly because of certain real differences which do exist, but still more because of the North–South antithesis which has been rubbed into us for such a long time past. There exists in England a curious cult of Northernness, a sort of Northern snobbishness. A Yorkshireman in the South will always take care to let you know that he regards you as an inferior. If you ask why, he will explain that it is only in the North that life is 'real' life, that the industrial work done in the North is the only 'real' work, that the North is inhabited by 'real' people, the South merely by *rentiers* and their parasites.[4]

Plus ça change. One has only to listen to Fred Trueman on *Test Match Special* to hear the same story. As David Smith points out in his book about the North–South divide, *Coronation Street*, a soap opera that has if anything increased its popularity over the years, revels in 'gritty northern reality'.[5] Its provenance is not for a second in doubt, even though it contains its share of yuppies and fast cars. This perception of the North is based, according to a northern academic, on

> deep-rooted antagonisms – between the centre and the prov-inces, and between a supposed affluent middle-class South and deprived working-class North. Legendary conflicts and misconceptions made the North an easy subject for music-hall jokes or, latterly, a place and a people easily lampooned in the television sitcom. And inaccurate perceptions are further reinforced by powerful representations of the North in the past – the setting of *When the Boat Comes In* or Catherine Cookson's Tyneside of the 1920s. The rapidly expanding heritage industry – of Beamish, steam railways and other

industrial relics – has added to the sense of a region living for the past and even living *in* the past: a backward area. Small wonder, then, that southerners may have images of the North which are outdated, a landscape of pits, shipyards and steelworks, complete with Andy Capp and his whippets.[6]

The 1980s recession, which in popular mythology barely touched the South, reinforced this divide, condemning the North to an even more intense battering at the hands of the style merchants. But the 1990s recession had a very different impact. Southern England was hit the hardest. It was no longer possible for Essex man to regard himself as being somehow privileged and superior for living in the sunny uplands of Billericay. 'I used to think how lucky we were to escape from the North, where all it ever did was rain,' remarked one contemplative Harlow resident. 'Now I wonder why we ever left. Back home there was a sense of community. Here it's every man for himself and bugger the rest – and when everyone is looking to get the same job it can get pretty unpleasant.'[7] While house prices in London and the South East fell steepest during the early 1990s, those in the North actually rose. But this was only a modest swing of the pendulum. The importance of living not just in the right part of town but in the right town itself remains. It's not just that 0171 is superior to 0181, but that London is superior to the Wirral. The introduction of the council tax in 1992 provided a ready reckoner of such social standing. By placing every property in the country in common bands it made it possible to determine at a glance the most desirable areas of the country. Kensington & Chelsea, with nearly 20 per cent of properties worth over £320,000 (Band H), is the country's most exclusive neighbourhood. Elmbridge in Surrey is the most consistently superior area, having virtually nothing worth less than £40,000 and 5 per cent of properties over £320,000.[8] Table 10, listing the fourteen local authorities with the highest proportion of Band H properties, is a directory of where to find the Super Class described in Chapter 3. One has to go down to

Table 10: Local authorities with the highest proportion of houses in Band H (above £320,000)

	%
Kensington & Chelsea	17.8
Westminster	12.8
South Buckinghamshire	5.9
Elmbridge, Surrey	5.1
Chiltern, Bucks	4.7
Camden, London	4.6
Three Rivers, Herts	4.0
Tandridge, Surrey	3.9
Waverley, Surrey	3.9
Richmond upon Thames	3.3
Barnet, London	2.9
Guildford, Surrey	2.9
Hammersmith, London	2.9
Mole Valley, Surrey	2.7

Source: Greg Hadfield and Mark Skipworth, *Class: Where do you stand?*, 1994.

forty-third in the pecking order to find the first northern council, Ribble Valley in Lancashire – a traditional farming area – with 1.3 per cent of properties worth over £320,000.

Rural idylls and urban ghettos

Housing is about far more than bricks and mortar. It is also about a lot more than mere chicness. The nature of one's housing is a primary determinant of class membership – whether the Super Class, the Under Class, or the classes in between. Every country has its poor, and in every country there are barriers of varying strength which prevent those born into poverty from escaping it. But in Britain those barriers are not so much obstacles along the way as limits to the very road down which one may travel. In Chapter 1 we argued that one of the defining features of the

British class structure is that, to a large extent, where you are born, metaphorically, determines where you end up. Such is the importance of housing in this process that one can leave out the metaphor. Quite literally, where you are born determines to a large extent where you die, both geographically and as a member of society.

If Disraeli was right to speak of two nations in the nineteenth century, so those two nations remain as starkly divided as ever today in the field of housing. On the one hand is the middle class discussed above, with its problems of taste, space and geography. The layers within it are, relatively, great. But in absolute terms the divisions are as nothing compared with the chasm separating the broad mass of the middle and lower classes. For on the other hand are those for whom choices such as West Hampstead versus Cricklewood are a mystery, those for whom choice is between one council flat and another – in the unlikely event of their being able to get a transfer. It is easy to forget, when considering the dramatic increase in owner occupation over the past two decades, that 32 per cent of the population – almost a third – still rent their properties.[9]

These two nations exist side by side and on top of each other. In London streets, for instance, middle-class terraced and detached houses at one end and a council estate at the other is a common sight. The council residents have to pass by the middle-class houses to get around the city. But the middle classes have no call ever to enter the estate – indeed, they go out of their way to avoid it, and ban their children from going there, let alone playing with the council estate children.

Increasingly the wealthy are not content with this city life and are moving further and further out. The Super Class moves just at weekends, by buying second homes which give it the best of both worlds – the convenience of the city in the week, and the rural idyll at weekends. If one of the main attractions of suburbia is that one can't bring up children in the city, and this is thought to outweigh the huge downside of living in the suburbs

– boredom – then a city week and a country weekend delivers on both counts. And if the children are at boarding school anyway, there is no worry about bringing them up in the city during the week.

But for professional, middle-class Britain apart from the Super Class, two homes are simply too costly. So a move to the suburbs is unavoidable. After managing to avoid it for generations, Britain is at last beginning to copy the American urban sprawl: 27,000 acres of land – an area of countryside the size of Bristol – are swallowed up by new buildings every year,[10] so that by 2050 it is estimated that 20 per cent of the land area of England will be urban.[11] This is a particularly southern problem – the North and Scotland are barely affected.

Why this intense pressure for expansion? One might think it simply a matter of finding space to house an ever increasing population. But the demographics show that the population is growing only very slowly. It is not the number of people living in England that matters but how many households they comprise. Government actuaries predict that there will be 4.4 million more households in 2016 than in 1991.[12] Increasingly, couples split up, children move out of the parental home, and houses once thought of as being large enough for a family are felt to be unsuitably small.

But the invasion of the country is more than a reaction to pressure of space. The rural idyll has a strong pull – about 300 people move out of cities and into the country every day, causing an annual outflow of 100,000 (this despite the fact that the population of Greater London is, after reaching a low in the mid-1980s, rising again).[13] The average net annual migration from the South East – the traditional middle-class focal point – rose from 5,000 in the mid-1980s to 60,000 by 1989.[14] Millions have migrated from British cities since the Second World War. Hugh Pearman, the architecture correspondent of the *Sunday Times*, has written extensively of this new countryside, and class is integral to his description:

The usual reasons for leaving are high crime levels, poor schools, pollution and expense. As the middle classes choose to leave – typically when a child nears secondary school age – the cities are left to the poor, who have much less choice in the matter, and the very rich, who can afford fine apartments in the centre and usually have a country home as well. Once the social balance is upset, trouble results. Those who have quit to live in the country may well commute back to the city by car to work, so increasing pollution. Thus, they help to worsen the urban problems that drove them out in the first place, at the same time helping to spoil the countryside a little more.[15]

With the dash to the country gathering pace, so areas such as Kent, Surrey, Essex, Buckinghamshire and Berkshire, which had in the past offered a trade-off between space, greenery and relatively cheap house prices against distance from the centre of London, lost even the advantages of space and house price. And so the boundaries of the commuter stretched even further out into areas such as Cambridgeshire, Dorset and Oxford.

As the demand to escape London increased, and the pressure of space in existing bolt-holes grew too great, so developers turned instead to the creation of entire new towns under the umbrella organization Consortium Developments, consisting of all the leading builders. The towns would comprise around 5,000 homes over around one square mile, housing 12,000–15,000 people. The Department of the Environment's White Paper in 1988 broadly welcomed this push, but expressed a preference for schemes of 200–1,000 homes, housing 500–2,000 people. Although the 1990s slump slowed things down, even in 1992 planning consents were given for nearly 1,200 housing schemes in the South East.[16]

It is the scale, not the fact, of this scramble to the country which is novel, reflecting the class-based aspect of the rural–city divide. Ebenezer Howard's vision of the garden city, *Tomorrow, a Peaceful Path to Real Reform*, was published in 1898 and republished in 1902 as *Garden Cities of Tomorrow*. It prompted the construction of towns such as Welwyn and Milton Keynes, which were conceived of as 'classless', for which one should read (as we described at the beginning of the chapter) 'for one class' – the middle, suburban class. Howard disliked his native London so much that he believed everyone should be transferred to new towns of no more than 30,000 people with garden-like layouts and countryside environs. Sir John Betjeman's paean to Metroland was prompted by the suburban growth of areas bordering the Metropolitan Line. 'In England,' argues the social researcher Ken Worpole, 'city dwellers have a greater passion for houses and gardens (than Europeans). They persist in believing this rural myth and have spent years trying to turn cities into the countryside. Now they are turning the countryside into cities.'[17]

In *The Creative City*, Charles Landray traces much of the dissatisfaction with the city to the Industrial Revolution. Begun in Britain, it had a far more immediate and pronounced effect here than elsewhere, where developers had the opportunity to learn from our mistakes. Large parts of previously open cities were transformed into unhygienic slums. On the continent, in contrast,

> Cities became places where you could celebrate some sense of liberation, as you can see in the works of Baudelaire and Manet. Dickens merely depicts them as grim points of exploitation, by contrast. And merchants who made their fortunes from steam or steel here merely aped the aristocracy – and built country mansions. Cities were for the poor.[18]

The essential paradox of city life, and the search for rural bliss, is that we have, as Matthew d'Ancona of the *Sunday Telegraph* has pointed out, long associated the idea of the city with

> the ideal of harmonious community. From Augustine's *City of God* to Le Corbusier's Radiant City notion of urban modernity (which approved Howard's garden image but combined it with high density twenty-four-storey blocks, allowing 95 per

cent of a city to be landscaped) and the opening scene of Woody Allen's *Manhattan*, we have conjured up ideals of urban existence. What these dreams have in common is the faith that we are capable of finding happiness on earth in the streets, squares, and parks of cities.[19]

So it is not that we despise cities: what we despise, and seek to escape, is what we see as the warped city; the features of the city that we relish inflated to the *nth* degree and in the process turned from assets to disasters.

The upshot of this obsession with the countryside and migration thereto is that a new, additional middle-class home base is emerging, which defines itself not by traditional factors such as metropolitan chic but by 'quality of life'. Negatives, such as crime, pollution, cost of living and poor social facilities weigh heavily against cities in analyses by organizations such as the Glasgow-based Quality of Life group. The 'urban nightmare' view of the city stretches from Shelley's description of hell as being 'a city very much like London – a populous and smoky city', through Cobbett's condemnation of London as 'the Great Wen', in his *Rural Rides* of 1830, to the more modern version in Tom Wolfe's *Bonfire of the Vanities*. They represent a common theme: that cities are made up of two groups – the well-off, who can afford to make the city habitable, and the rest, who must suffer all that the city throws at them. Sherman McCoy, the anti-hero of Wolfe's modern classic, seeks 'insulation' from the city, and uses his wealth to construct barriers between his existence and the rest of the city's – a more extreme, if none the less recognizable picture of the typical British city experience. And to the extent that the 1990s has seen a city renaissance – such as Glasgow's Mayfest, Manchester's Metro and London's acclamation by *Newsweek* as the trendiest city in the world – it has been on this segregated basis.

In terms of social standing home ownership, or (in younger people) the aspiration to it, is a prerequisite for admission to mainstream middle-class society. Yet even among these seekers after middle-class housing romance, most 'home-owners' are in reality 'home-leasers', burdened with mortgages and far more tied down than the small number who rent. More than half of all mortgages outstanding in 1995, for instance, were advances for over 90 per cent of the equity.[20] Very few people really own their property. The majority have simply exchanged one form of landlord for another: the building society. And beyond that, it is the peculiar nature of England's (as opposed to Scotland's) feudal society that, even once the mortgage is paid off, few people literally own their properties, for most are merely leaseholders (albeit often with leases that will expire long after they do) still subject to the whims of their freeholder (who is often the scion of one of the very same feudal families who owned the land centuries ago), and still obliged to pay an annual 'ground rent'. Despite this, home-leasers are perceived to be home-owners, and to be worth as much as the value of their home even if part of it is 'negative equity' and the whole of it a mere leasehold. Since the introduction of feudalism, status has been indelibly associated with – dependent upon, even – property ownership.

The role of housing as an indicator of class has, like the structure of housing itself, changed dramatically over the past century (see Table 11). Until the Second World War very few people owned their houses. Private rented accommodation was, for all but the toffest of the toffs, the norm. The De Walden properties, for instance, which comprise one of the most widespread and valuable portfolios to this day, were rented to many of the country's leading Establishment figures. Today they are – apart from those occupied by the De Waldens themselves – rented to the likes of employment agencies and management consultants. The archetypal middle- and upper-class families who had rented them in the past now own their own properties in the posh suburbs of London such as Esher or, if they are seriously rich, Bishop's Avenue in Hampstead.

For the immediate post-war period, the new indicator of class was owner occupation. The rise of council (or 'social', to use the jargon) housing and the continued existence of private rented

Table 11: Housing tenure in Great Britain, 1945–96 (percentage of all households)

	Public rented	Owner-occupied	Private rented*
1945	12	26	62
1951	18	29	53
1961	27	43	31
1969	30	49	21
1971	31	53	16
1979	32	55	13
1985	25	62	13
1991	20	67	13
1996	18	67	15

*including Housing Associations
Sources: M. Boddy, *The Building Societies* (Macmillan, 1980); *Housing and Construction Statistics* (HMSO, 1980 and 1996).

accommodation, which together accounted for 71 per cent of dwellings in 1951, meant that the new owner-occupiers were now the breed apart.

But the picture that would emerge today had already, with hindsight, become clear. Prompted by a variety of factors (such as Mrs Thatcher's pursuit of the 'right to buy'), the rise of the owner-occupier became unstoppable. Even in 1979, before the 'Thatcher effect', the proportion of people renting had fallen from the 1951 figure of 71 per cent to 45 per cent. To know that someone owns their own home today tells you nothing about their place on the social scale other than that they are not part of the core working class or Underclass who rent from the council.

As home ownership has increased – in 1951 4 million homes were owner occupied, by 1988 there were 14.7 million, a rise from 29 per cent to 65 per cent of housing stock – so its status has changed.[21] The property price boom of the 1980s turned the established order of class and property on its head. Those who had invested all their often small savings and income in modest homes in the South East, who were proud and happy with their small semis, suddenly found that they were sitting on a metaphorical gold mine, and were able to sell up and fund a comfortable retirement on the proceeds. Others moved away into areas where property prices had yet to take off, and were able to live in homes beyond their previous imaginings.

Many were simply lucky to buy before the price boom and were for a short time sitting on a paper valuation that appeared to make them asset rich, or were able to sell and move up the scale. For others, whose financial status and job would previously have 'entitled' them to a fine house or flat in a desirable location, the escalation in prices forced them to make do with what they could afford. Others again bought at the outer limits of their capabilities to keep up with the Joneses. When the boom became a crash they faced disaster, trapped in properties they couldn't sell, and whose value had fallen way below the loans that had been taken out on them, which they could in any case barely afford to pay.

But beyond the see-saw of the 1980s and 1990s boom and bust, the house has long been regarded as more than a status symbol. It is somehow thought metaphysically to represent the essence of an 'asset'. No one today thinks of flats and houses as mere consumer goods, designed to fulfil a function like washing machines or cars. When, as the historian Martin Pawley has pointed out, the vast majority of people rented their homes – less than fifty years ago – they did so 'under terms of tenure that were actually far less arduous than those enjoyed by the drivers of company cars today. It is interesting to remember this when people argue that ownership is a "privileged" or "democratic" form of tenure, while rental is "oppressive" or "feudal".'[22] The comparison with cars is telling, for houses like cars are critical purveyors of status and security, reflecting class divisions as surely as schools, accents and dress.

Consider also the *sort* of houses in which people live. For one thing, no one who has really arrived wants to live in a new house. Period – character – houses are the sign of success. Indeed, virtually all new upmarket houses in Britain produced by builders such as Barratt, Wimpey and Charles Church are 'mock' this or that past architectural style. Mock Tudor was particularly popular during the 1980s housing boom. If status in housing was about no more than the size of mortgage one could afford, the demand would be for modern, functional homes. Instead, it is for old, often badly designed houses. This is relative, of course. If the decision is between buying a house built twenty years ago or today, today's will always win. The older house will simply be a tattier version of the newer one. But if it is between one built seventy-five to a hundred years ago and today, the older house will often be said to possess the character that today's lacks.

Beyond age, the type of accommodation is what really counts. Terraced houses are, with the exception of areas such as Bath and Belgravia, reminiscent of everything that city evacuees hate about cities – poverty, age and monotony: *Coronation Street* writ nation-wide. The flat is more indeterminate, and depends greatly on location. The high-rise flat is the archetypal horror property: a 1985 study showed that ten of the poorest local authorities accounted for 43 per cent of the country's 4,570 tower blocks.[23] But the penthouse or mansion block flat can be an aspiration in itself. Jeffrey Archer does not live in a penthouse overlooking the Thames because he is stuck there by the council, but as a mark of supreme wealth and status.

The standard symbol of moderate success is the suburban semi-detached house. Just as the terraced houses of *Coronation Street* offer a uniformity that replicates itself from Manchester to Macclesfield, so the image of suburbia is row upon row of the semi-detached – millions of houses with their nice gardens and functional front patios, a brilliant and lasting combination of privacy and community.

The symbol of real success is the fully detached house. Although there are fine gradations of semis, it is only with the detached house that one sees real projections of advancement, outside the crescents, closes and mewses of Islington, Notting Hill, Belgravia and their like in other cities such as Edgbaston in Birmingham and Morningside in Edinburgh. The detached house can be anything from a three-bedroomed box in Surbiton to Highclere Castle or the Duke and Duchess of York's Sunninghill Park. Fergie's former home raises another subtle distinction. Our houses reflect our social standing. And that means aristocrats living in aristocrats' homes. So when the Yorks had a *new* home designed and built in Sunningdale – a grander version of the piles to be found in the wealthier suburbs of all American cities – the tabloids reflected the nation's horror at the prospect of members of the royal family living in anything so vulgar. If the Earl of Carnarvon was prepared to allow car salesmen to hold mock medieval banquets at Highclere Castle, using the receipts to pay for the castle's upkeep so that he could carry on living there, surely we expected more of royalty than a house soon dubbed South York, after its supposed similarity to the soap *Dallas*'s Southfork ranch – a far cry from Balmoral, Sandringham and Windsor Castle. Similarly, when it was announced that Fergie was to rent a stable block at South York for herself and her daughters, Bea and Eugenie, it was not the bizarre fact that she was to live in the stable block of her former house, next to her former husband, Andrew, that attracted press attention but rather that she was going to *rent* it.

It is not only royals who get into trouble for living in the wrong place. In June 1996 the *Daily Mail* reported the story of businessman Michael Pollock, his £215,000 home and his BMW: 'He couldn't wait to move in. But that proved rather difficult when he tried to put his car in the garage. The company director found that the 5-series BMW would not squeeze through its doors ... A spokesman for the developers said: "The garages have been designed and constructed for use by a suitable range of cars, similar to a Fiesta or a Mini Metro."'[24] Evidently, it was not appropriate for Mr Pollock to drive a BMW. His class, as reflected in his house, allowed him nothing grander than a Mini Metro.

Then there are the myriad changes in neighbourhoods which go to make up that other *leitmotif* of the 1980s: gentrification.

Previously working-class, often run-down, properties and areas are taken over by the moneyed for the size and age of their houses and their proximity to city amenities. Just as Islington includes more than its fair share of sink estates, so these sit uneasily next to streets such as Richmond Crescent which house barristers, City bankers and (until his move to Downing Street) Tony Blair. As a sign of false exclusivity, these new residents often give their areas nicknames to show how the place has changed. Thus, in London, Stockwell becomes St Ockwell, Cricklewood, Crick-le-Bois and Clapham is pronounced Clarm. The *Financial Times*' property page has even taken to referring to the south Manchester commuter belt as 'North Surrey'. Gradually, houses in these gentrified areas become desirable and, as with Albert Dock in Liverpool or Notting Hill in London, the area takes on a real new identity and becomes a sign of status in itself. Sometimes it completely changes name in the process – large parts of Holloway are now Islington; anything desirable in Kilburn is Maida Vale; and so on throughout London.

But the message of a house is about still more than this. Décor and furnishings can cover up a multitude of sins, or can reveal that the occupants of a seven-room detached house are little more than upstarts. As Alan Clark famously reports, Michael Jopling, a traditional Tory toff, remarked of Michael Heseltine that the man was obviously not a proper gent because he had 'bought all his own furniture'.[25] Further evidence of the Duchess of York's *arriviste* status was provided by the double whammy revelation that she *rented* her South York *reproduction* antique furniture.[26] Still worse, the Yorks chose an interior designer specifically to fill the house in chintzy, sub-Laura Ashley, mock-country house style.

The middle classes may not inherit their furniture, but their desire to ape 'old' money manifests itself potently in collections of antiques and an avid fascination with the BBC's *Antiques Roadshow*. The rise of Laura Ashley in the 1980s – to the point where there seemed to be a Laura Ashley shop on every southern high street – was a direct result of this craving to share the now uniform middle-class, middle-brow taste for 'traditional' flowery wallpaper and reproduction furniture (even if manufactured in Taiwan). Developers' show homes tell the story: white sofas, effete table lamps and wrought-iron dining chairs. The message is unmistakable. Particularly revealing is the use of net curtains, from the paisley-style patterned to the cascading ruffles. The very wealthy classes seldom resort to them because they don't need them: their houses aren't overlooked. The same is true for those of the middle class who live in detached houses with grounds that set them apart from the street. For everyone else they are the only barrier from the rest of the neighbourhood.[27]

From tower block hell to potted plant heaven

Ever shrinking as the proportion of social rented accommodation may be, its impact on society is no less diminished. A fifth of households in England, and a quarter in Scotland, live in council properties, even after Margaret Thatcher's bargain price sale of council properties to their occupiers in the 1980s. People who live in council housing have higher rates of mortality than those who rent from private landlords, who in turn have higher rates than owner-occupiers.[28] The healthiest members of society are those who own both a home and at least two cars; the unhealthiest are those who rent from the council and have no car – which indicates not just low socio-economic status but also the lack of ready access to health care.[29]

The link between housing status and health status being now so clearly established, it is astonishing that it is not a crucial consideration in health policy. A study in Gateshead in 1983 looked at eight council house estates, from the best in the area to the worst. It found 'marked and consistent differences in self-reported health between individuals from different areas. People from "bad" housing areas reported poorer health, more long-standing illness, more recent illness, and more symptoms of depression than those living in "good" housing areas.'[30] People in 'bad' housing areas reported more respiratory conditions than those in 'good' housing.[31]

Taking classes at large, cardio-respiratory mortality and morbidity get worse with each rung down the social ladder. The further down the ladder one goes, of course, the worse one's housing is likely to be. Cold, damp housing is far more likely to be a problem for the poor, and both increase the heart's work load and thus the occurrence of such illness.[32] In Liverpool it was found that unsatisfactory housing conditions on one estate contributed to high rates of infectious disease, respiratory disease and mental illness. One source of infection was traced to a common phenomenon – unhygienic mobile food vans which residents used because there were no shops on the estate. And respiratory illness was made more widespread by the common practice of drying clothes indoors because of inadequate facilities.[33] So it should come as no surprise that when 1,000 residents on a poor council estate in Bristol were asked in 1993 what they thought would most improve their health, the most common replies were 'better housing' (30 per cent) and 'a better environment' (15 per cent).[34]

A 1996 report by the Royal Institution of Chartered Surveyors concluded that poor housing kills thousands of people every year, and that most of the 1.5 million homes officially categorized as 'unfit for human habitation' are occupied, with consequences such as chronic chest disease and hypothermia. Well over 2.5 million homes suffer severe dampness; children in damp homes are prone to respiratory disease, gastro-intestinal complaints, dysentery, fatigue and nervousness. As the report concludes: 'Poor housing has been shown to contribute towards a range of physical conditions including influenza, tuberculosis, some cancers and respiratory conditions ... The inability of households to heat their housing adequately is contributing to a large number of deaths.'[35]

This aspect – the risk to the elderly during the winter of respiratory infection and hypothermia, as well as stroke, heart disease and accidents – is well documented. Above average levels of mortality for England and Wales during the winter months are estimated at 40,000. For each degree Celsius by which the winter is colder than average, there are some 8,000 extra deaths.[36] Trying to maintain a satisfactory temperature in inadequate housing is a vicious circle: those with least to spend on heating usually live in homes that are the most difficult and expensive to heat. The poor spend twice as much as a percentage of total income on heating as the rest of the population.[37] This works in reverse, too. Lack of access to proper refrigeration (a common trait in poor housing) increases the likelihood of gastro-intestinal illness.

The plain fact is that where you are born largely determines where you end up. The National Child Development Study found a direct relationship between housing situation in childhood (measured by tenure and overcrowding) and seventeen aspects of adult life:

> Those whose families were owner-occupiers at seven, eleven and sixteen, and similarly those who were not in crowded homes at those ages, were more likely, compared with those who were local authority tenants (or in crowded homes) at all three ages: to be in higher-status occupations at twenty-three; to have higher family incomes, particularly when family situation is taken into account; to have experienced less unemployment, both currently and since completing education; to have higher qualifications; and to rate their health highly. They were less likely to have married and/or have children; to have left home and formed an independent household; to be on a council waiting list; and to have moved home frequently.[38]

The *condition* of housing is another dimension of the class divide. The quality of housing has steadily improved throughout the century. The number of dwellings lacking basic amenities in 1991 was only 1 per cent (205,000 homes) of the total housing stock, compared with 2.5 per cent (463,000 homes) in 1986.[39] Similarly, the number of properties deemed unfit for human habitation is down from the 1986 figure of 1.66 million to 1.5 million (7.6 per cent). Worryingly high as this nevertheless is, a third of such homes required less than £500 spent on them to achieve fitness.[40]

Social housing has a long pedigree. Victorian industrialists and landowners provided housing for many of their operatives and labourers; Lloyd George promised state-provided 'Homes Fit For Heroes' as long ago as 1918; and over the next sixty years, governments of all political persuasions sought to provide housing if not for heroes, then at least for the unheroic unable adequately to provide for themselves. Clearing city slums was their prime objective. Cities had grown with frightening speed in the nineteenth century: in 1801 only 20 per cent of the population lived in areas with a population over 5,000. By 1851 the proportion was 54 per cent.[41] It was the transformation of urban life, and the oppressive slum conditions that often accompanied it, that spawned the idea of the rural idyll. As populations grew, dwellings were subdivided, leading to overcrowding and appalling sanitary conditions. In the first half of the nineteenth century, for instance, over 25,000 people in Liverpool lived in cellars which flooded whenever the tide came in.[42] As Engels wrote of St Giles in London in 1844: 'The houses are occupied from cellar to garret, filthy within and without, and their appearance is such that no human being could possibly wish to live in them ... Filth and tottering ruins surpass all description.'[43] But it was only when the effects of these conditions started to be felt by those who didn't live in them that a push – a moral outrage – for improvement began. The spread of cholera was thus at once the greatest misery and the greatest saviour of slum dwellers. The Public Health Act of 1848 represented the first steps in a whole series of measures which had by 1914 led to street cleaning, and proper municipal sewage and water systems. 'Homes Fit For Heroes' was the culmination of decades of growing pressure for government action to tackle the housing of the working classes. As the king himself put it in 1919: 'While the housing of the working classes has always been a question of the greatest social importance, never has it been so important as now. It is not too much to say that an adequate solution of the housing question is the foundation of all social progress.'[44]

Post-Second World War housing policy none the less marked a significant departure in policy. In the nineteenth century fore-runners of today's Housing Associations, such as the Guinness and Peabody Trusts, constructed blocks which aimed to give a 5 per cent return to their investors and to demonstrate that the private sector could provide affordable, decent housing for the working class. Yet rents were usually still too high for the poorest households, and the better-off working class tended to occupy these model dwellings. Attlee's post-war Labour government, however, believed that council estates should be engineered to represent a social mix rather than a ghetto of the poor, and ordered its housing policies accordingly – repealing, for instance, the statutory restriction of council housing to the 'working classes' in 1949 and instead setting as its objective the creation of 'balanced communities'. Far from questioning this goal, the Tories promised to promote it more vigorously still. When Harold Macmillan was appointed Conservative Housing Minister in 1951 his criteria for success was a further extension of the council house building programme to 300,000 units a year.

Yet 'balanced communities' are just what most of the grand designs of the 1950s and 1960s did *not* engineer. The classic study written by Jane Jacobs in 1961, *The Life of Great American Cities*, considered why it was that areas supposedly possessed of all the virtues were disintegrating, and apparently unviable areas were spontaneously growing and developing. Her conclusion was unsettling to traditional views. Successful city neighbourhoods were close-textured, high-density assemblages of mixed land uses, where many people lived within walking distance of many varied destinations and there was a constant coming and going along the streets, the whole pattern converging naturally to produce a firm social structure. Unsuccessful neighbourhoods were often the direct result of planning decisions designed to create such a structure.

The same was true of Britain. As John Major put it of his native Lambeth in a 1995 lecture:

In the fifties and sixties I saw terraces not far from where I lived demolished. Communities, albeit poor, were re-housed in tower blocks that were modern, clean, sanitary, spacious but also soulless. The best of intentions produced the worst of results . . . I saw the mistakes that were made by politicians and bureaucrats believing they could do it all: the ghetto estates, the stunted opportunities. These mistakes stemmed from an essentially socialist approach: top down planning . . . One of the major challenges we still face is the continuing legacy of large scale, sub-standard public housing estates – some in inner cities, some outside . . . Many were built as solutions to inner-city problems; ironically, they have now become major contributors to the problem. There they stand – grey, sullen, concrete wastelands, set apart from the rest of the community, robbing people of ambition, of self-respect.[45]

(He went on to say: 'When I spoke about the classless society it was people like that I had in mind,' an odd observation since tower blocks are hardly the evocation of classlessness.) The demarcation of land use into large units – huge schools, large shopping areas, industrial estates and cultural complexes, for instance – made for few areas within walking distance of each other. The circle of contacts thus tended to remain small, and there was no forum in which a widely accepted set of social mores could develop.

Council housing is now the ghetto of the poor. Since the introduction of the 'right to buy' policy by the Thatcher government in 1980, better-off social renters have left the council sector. Combined with the virtual cessation of new building by councils since the mid-1980s (at the direction of central government), this has meant that only the most needy have remained in, let alone entered the sector. Over a third of families lived in council housing in the late 1970s, when (even after the figure had slipped) around 170,000 homes a year were completed. The figure for 1993 was

3,000. As an Institute for Fiscal Studies report puts it: 'Being a council or Housing Association tenant is now one of the best available indicators of being poor: tenants in the social sector are overwhelmingly to be found at the bottom of the income distribution in a way that was just not the case prior to the 1980s.'[46] Conversely, most of the council properties sold under the 'right to buy' are in the 'better' – i.e. non working-class – areas, ensuring that they, too, become more socially homogenous in the process.

This rise in owner occupation, combined with the virtual extinction of private renting as a long-term housing provider (from 90 per cent of all households in 1919 to 9.2 per cent in 1988,[47] most of whom are low-income, non-family households and DSS bed and breakfast tenants), has radically changed the complexion of the market. The reasons for the change are various. Rent control restricted rents and reduced profits; security of tenure made renting a risky and illiquid investment; taxation and housing subsidies discriminated against private renting; tax treatment of owner-occupiers made ownership far more tax efficient; and real post-war house price inflation made ownership attractive. And for those who could not otherwise afford to buy, 'right to buy' legislation gave them the opportunity. In 1961 owner occupation accounted for 22 per cent of families. By the late 1970s the share had risen to 35 per cent. By 1993 the proportion had reached 50 per cent.[48]

The 'right to buy' legislation engineered a veritable housing revolution. Between 1980 and 1995 more than 1.6 million homes were bought, with an enormous annual figure for sales from the outset – 200,000 were sold in 1982 alone. Since most of those taking advantage of the legislation were middle-aged and better-off, with incomes around double those of other tenants, one of the main effects has been to return council housing to its former status as a ghetto for the poor. Of those who moved *out* in 1993–4, 32 per cent were couples with children, and 35 per cent childless couples. Only 4 per cent were single parents. A similar story is true of those moving *in* to social housing. Among the 123,000 lettings made by Housing Associations in 1994–5, for example, only a fifth were to families in which the head was in full-time work. Nearly a quarter were to single parents. The mirror image of this is the fall in the proportion of social renters who are couples with children – over half in the early 1960s but now less than a third.

Compounding this, the shortage of council accommodation has made it extremely difficult for those not defined as 'statutorily homeless' to get access to council housing. Around 40 per cent of new local authority tenancies are allocated to the statutory homeless (although the figure varies by region and is much higher in London). More than 80 per cent are housing benefit recipients. Over the past thirty years, as the IFS has shown, there has been a disproportionate growth in the number of over-sixties, unemployed, non-working lone parents, long-term sick and disabled households in the social rented sector. There has thus been a huge increase in the numbers dependent on social security benefits; by 1995 fully 95 per cent of families in social housing received state benefits. Indeed, state benefits are, for a quarter of tenants, the only source of income. Benefit income grew from less than 10 per cent of all social tenants' income in 1961 to 60 per cent in 1993, while the percentage of total social renters' income from employment fell from 84 per cent in 1961 to just over 30 per cent by 1996. Twenty years ago, if you wanted to find a poor family you had to ring a number of door bells of typical council flats before you found one. Today, arrive at a council estate, ring any bell, and you have probably found one.

The ghettoization of council housing is having profound social effects. Council estates have become dump estates. In sociologist Paul Harrison's words: 'If the inner city is like a chemistry lab full of dangerous social reagents, the dump estate is the test-tube where they are most corrosively combined.'[49] The estate, by its very nature, concentrates the social problems of the inner city in an even smaller and more intimate space. With the increased concentration of the disadvantaged that the 1980s has seen, there is a still greater problem. Harrison's study of sink estates in the 1980s showed that

> Once an estate acquires more than a certain proportion of disadvantaged tenants ... it can find itself trapped in a descending spiral which may continue until it is demolished or massively rehabilitated. The preponderance of single-parent families and families with conflicts caused by low income or unemployment weakens parental discipline, so vandalism and crime are more prevalent ... The estate acquires a reputation ... which discourages those with any hopes for their own future from even viewing a flat there.[50]

The only tenants willing to take up residence are those with no choice – the most desperate – who accentuate the ghetto-like atmosphere.

The vicious circle into which sink estates fall is further reflected by the fact that, according to recent evidence, the highest expenditure per dwelling on repair and maintenance is in affluent suburban areas, with the next highest spent in resort and coastal areas. The lowest amount is in declining industrial areas.[51]

Why did 1.6 million households – representing perhaps 4 million people – jump at the 'right to buy' offered to them by Margaret Thatcher? Was it all just to join in the great property-owning democracy bandwagon? Some doubtless leapt at the chance of home ownership as a means to further their independence. The discounts were a further incentive. But there was another powerful force at work. Local authorities were terrible landlords. Many tenants felt powerless both in relation to council decisions and to standards of repair and maintenance. No sooner had many people been given the opportunity to buy their council home than up sprung potted plants, new doors, fresh paint and an altogether more pleasant atmosphere on those estates – mainly terraced housing rather than tower blocks – which contained a sufficient number of owners to make a difference.

But it was not all joy. The volatility of house prices made the timing of the purchase crucial to the success of home ownership. Maggie Kennedy bought a vacant top-floor flat on the Doddington Estate in Battersea in 1988. Its value was assessed as £73,000 and the discounted purchase price was £51,100. In 1995 she was told she would not get £15,000 for it. 'My service charges have tripled. They were £400 a year in 1988 and they are £1,200 now. I have had a £2,000 bill for painting of corridors, not my own. There are people who have had bills of £18,000 and £12,000.'[52] The slump in prices applied, of course, to almost all houses during the 1990–92 recession – not just ex-council houses. But such marginal properties will not recover their value as fast as others – if they do at all.

If the Englishman's home is his castle, so too is it his inheritance. This applies to council tenants – who often pass their tenancies on to their children – but of course mainly to owners. As the patron saint of home-owners, Lady Thatcher, declared in 1979: 'It will give more of our people ... that prospect of handing something on to their children and grandchildren.'[53] Some of her political followers have stopped at almost nothing to dangle such prospects before the voters. Dame Shirley Porter, as Leader of Westminster Council in the 1980s, dreamt up a scandalous vote-buying strategy around the sale of strategically located council properties. As the District Auditor, Dr John Magill, put it in his damning report into the policy, Dame Shirley's 'top priority' was to secure success for the ruling Conservative group in the 1990 local elections. To do this she sought to increase the number of home-owners and to reduce the number of former homeless families in marginal electoral wards. A 'designated sales policy' was instituted in eight wards 'regarded as key to the Conservative Party retaining control of the council' in the sub-sequent borough elections.[54] Dame Shirley's Mayor Daley-style gerrymandering serves only to illustrate how housing was per-ceived by many in the 1980s. Home-owners – the vast majority of the population – are now 'our people', as Lady Thatcher put it; those who have something to conserve – and, more importantly perhaps, something to lose. Social renters were those without a proper stake in society, and thus deemed irredeemably Labour.

Late on in the housing boom of the 1980s, the inheritance factor began to arouse a lot of interest. One survey estimated in 1987 that the total value of newly purchased homes in estates was £6.5 billion, and that by 2000 the figure would stand at £24.3 billion. Although these estimates were at the height of the house price boom, they give a daunting sense of scale.[55] That is why John Major, as part of his avowed drive towards the classless society, talked confidently of wealth 'cascading down through the generations'. Hubris gave way to nemesis, and by the end of the ensuing recession in the mid-1990s no one much was talking of a cascade of wealth. The obsession transferred to the elderly having to sell their homes to finance long-term geriatric care, and how this was depriving heirs of their 'rightful' inheritance. The scale of the threat has been greatly overstated. More pertinently, the idea that a transfer of inheritance through the generations will obliterate class divisions is as quaint as can be. Those who have will pass it down – most likely to children who also have. The residents of the dump estates will not be endowing their children – many of whom live on the same estates – with similar advantages.

The view that housing represents the most perfect way of handing on a bequest to the next generation took off when the house price boom of the 1980s saw the value of many properties soar. But the boom was far from being the all-enveloping tidal wave of recent mythology. For one thing, the gap between the North and South – crudely, between houses with social status as added value, and the rest – widened. As the Halifax Building Society put it in 1988: 'The gap between average house prices in London and the rest of the country is wider than it has been in living memory.'[56] By the late 1980s average prices in London were double those in the North. The 1990–92 recession narrowed the gap, but it was still 1.59 times in 1992.[57] Indeed, reports emerged in 1995 that some properties more than maintained their values.

Savills, a specialist in 'prime' London property, said in 1995 that its own index showed that prices in its sector were only 3 per cent down from their pre-slump levels, and that there had been a 32 per cent rise since 1992.[58]

The picture has thus come full circle. At the turn of the century, 'social housing' was the ghetto of the poor. Council housing then lost much of its stigma, and became increasingly – although never fully – mixed. Today, those who can, own; those who can't, rent. No one chooses to live in a council house – especially if they are concerned to 'get on'.

For ownership means control, success, security and an inheritance. It is about far more than bricks and mortar. It is about status and membership of the middle class. The owner/renter divide is perhaps the sharpest reincarnation of Disraeli's two nations. No society that has any claim to classlessness can tolerate a situation where 67 per cent of householders – home-owners – have choice in their housing and control over their living conditions, but 18 per cent (almost one in five) – council tenants – effectively live where they are told, and must put up with whatever living conditions their council landlord happens to provide.

PART FOUR

Culture

Culture seeks to do away with classes; to make the best that has been thought and known in the world current everywhere; to make all men live in an atmosphere of sweetness and light, where they may use ideas, as it uses them itself, freely – nourished and not bound by them. This is the social idea; and men of culture are the true apostles of equality.

Matthew Arnold, *Culture and Anarchy* (1875)

Class differences within the family will play a big part. The grandfather, Angus, is quite working class, a miner who manned the picket lines and comes from the north. His son Chris is also from the north but has moved south. He is a builder who decided in the late seventies to set up by himself, and he and his wife Annie are lower middle class. But their children have had education and they've moved up. Holly, twenty-four, is a trainee lawyer. Her twin, Duncan, has opted out and is an entrepreneur who sets up music gigs.

Corinne Hollingworth, producer of Channel 5's new soap *Family Affairs*, interviewed in the *Independent*, 17 February 1997

We practise class distinctions even as we mouth our socially acceptable disgust. Snobbery courses through the leftish, *bien pensant* publishing party as surely as it does through Ascot or Henley. The wrong accent, the giveaway clothes are patronized and then avoided as rigorously in Bohemia as at Court.

Bryan Appleyard, *Independent*, 18 April 1996

8. LIFESTYLE

The BBC, sport and other varieties of social distinction

Those who aim to give the public what the public wants begin by underestimating the public taste; they end by debauching it.

T. S. Eliot, 1962

In 1944 Sir William Haley, the director-general of the BBC, set up the Third Programme to broadcast classical music and serious drama to the expectant masses. His rationale was a classic statement of the old Establishment view of the BBC, then barely beyond adolescence: 'I have always believed . . . that every civilised nation, culturally and educationally, is a pyramid with a lamentably broad base and a lamentably narrow tip.' The BBC's mission was to raise the tone as far as possible, with the Light Programme designed for the base, the Home Service for the middle and the Third Programme for the élite at the 'narrow tip'.[1]

The pyramid is still there. BBC Radio ascends from Radio 1 for the base to Radios 3 and 4 for the 'narrow tip' of today, with equivalent gradations between *Noel's House Party* and *Newsnight* on the two television channels. But the *content* and *purpose* have been transformed since Haley's day. No longer is Auntie out to raise the tone: her mission is to give the base what it wants – complete with Chris Evans complaining about Anne Frank's 'diarrhoea' on Radio 1 – so as to fight the commercial competition and protect its funding base: the licence fee. Otherwise, of course, there would be no money to sustain programming for the 'narrow tip'. Gone would be all those foreign and political correspondents, current affairs programmes and cultural gurus so vital to servicing the BBC's 'public service obligation'.

Nothing better exemplifies the changing cultural context of class in Britain than the evolution of the BBC, which is why we give it pride of place here. It leads on to sport, the second most revealing aspect of national life for class today, and thence to holidays, food, fashion and other give-away signs of class delineation – accepting that dozens of other aspects of modern life could have been used to paint the same picture.

Transforming Auntie

Lord Reith was blunt about the purpose of the BBC: it should 'lead, not follow'.[2] As to Reith's destination, A. J. P. Taylor, one of the early greats of television, remarked pithily that it was: '(to use) the brute force of monopoly to stamp Christian morality on the British people'.[3] This led to a somewhat cramped style, but it was a mission no one could challenge until competition reared its head in the mid-1950s. Not that 'Christian morality' should be confused with 'high culture'. 'One of the great troubles of broadcasting in this country,' wrote George Orwell in 1946, 'has been that no programme is regarded as economic unless it can appeal to millions of people, and that anything in the smallest degree highbrow provokes storms of indignation from ordinary radio users.'[4]

Forty years on, competition reigns supreme, and the style is anything but cramped. But the development of competition has been slow in coming. When commercial TV was launched in 1955, it was under carefully controlled conditions, with heavy regulation to ensure taste and quality. But as a tame, leashed ITV has given way to steadily more populist competitors, culminating in the launch of Sky and cable, the BBC had little choice but to respond in kind. In the 1960s BBC chiefs debated whether it was appropriate for the arbiter of the nation's taste to broadcast a documentary showing the royal family eating a barbecue. Even in the 1970s the state broadcaster remained choreographer-in-chief to the Wonderland Monarchy. By the 1990s we were in for *It's A Royal Knockout* and royal divorce by interview on prime-time television. A *cause célèbre* of 1957 illustrates perfectly the old BBC. Malcolm Muggeridge, the editor of *Punch* and a BBC regular, penned a cautiously anti-monarchy newspaper article apropos the Queen's visit to America. 'The impulses out of which snobbishness is born descend from the Queen, at the apex of the social pyramid,' it suggested. 'If it is considered – as I consider – that such a social set-up is obsolete and disadvantageous in the contemporary world, then the monarchy is to that extent undesirable.' In less ponderous vein, Muggeridge let his American readers into a secret: 'Duchesses find the Queen dowdy, frumpish and banal.'[5] The article shook the BBC to the core. 'On the one hand, the BBC was proud of its special relationship with royalty, and was prepared to put up with any amount of humiliation at the hands of the Palace to maintain it,' notes the historian Ben Pimlott in his biography of the Queen. 'On the other hand, the introduction of commercial TV in September 1955 and the rapid success of the new station in capturing audiences, had caused a division of opinion on the Board of Management about the old Reithian principle of obeisance to the Palace in return for a most-favoured-network status.'[6] Accordingly, Muggeridge was dropped. Harman Grisewood, the director of Current Affairs, dressed up the decision in a memo to the director-general by arguing that Muggeridge had been overused because of a 'journalistic urge' to go for the showy personality and a 'worrying tendency' to be too topical – a truly bizarre criticism from a director of Current Affairs.

In this process the class mission of the BBC has changed radically. Devoted in the first decades to narrowing, or at least transcending, old class divisions, it now glories in reflecting (and therefore reinforcing) the rawest of class prejudices. The old BBC fitted naturally into the Victorian and Edwardian tradition which established municipal museums and libraries up and down the country in an explicit attempt by legislators and town worthies to offer an improving alternative to traditional working-class amusements such as drinking. Edith and Tom Kelly, the leading historians of libraries, note not altogether flippantly that the Libraries Act of 1850 was intended not just 'for the cultivation of (working-class) minds, and the refinement of their tastes in science and art', as the Bill's sponsor, William Ewart Gladstone, put it, but also 'to head off drunkenness'.[7] In the process they also extended the provision of those services which the worthies themselves most valued. The early BBC saw itself in a similar role, intent on cementing all tastes to the BBC. It was a cultural crusade, but not of an exclusively – or even largely – cultural kind. As Orwell pointed out, not all culture was high culture: 'The existence of good bad literature – the fact that one can be amused or excited or even moved by a book that one's intellect simply refuses to take seriously – is a reminder that art is not the same thing as cerebration.'[8] If an evening dancing to the Joe Loss orchestra was a Friday night treat for the masses, then it would be *Friday Night Is Music Night* on the Light Programme. Similarly, if Saturday afternoon meant watching football on the terraces, so should Saturday evening mean *Match of the Day*.

The old BBC sought to solidify the nation. It was *our* BBC, the nickname 'Auntie' a reflection of its status as cultural aunt of the nation. Our leisure was shared in a common experience. During the war we all laughed at Tommy Handley; in the 1960s we all watched *Z Cars*. Those in charge were thus in a unique position to shape the tastes of the nation, and saw themselves in a suitably elevated role. The BBC consisted of professional producers making middlebrow programmes for middle-class viewers, financed by a licence fee, with the occasional nod either way to the highbrow and lowbrow. A look at any year's News Trainee intake – the most prestigious training scheme in broadcasting – shows how the BBC clones itself from year to year, with Oxbridge dominating the scheme.

The Swinging Sixties were the turning point. The ending of censorship, the new popular culture (the Beatles *et al.*), and the rise of commercial television transformed the BBC's world. Until then, the only nation the BBC had to serve was that which aspired upwards. The Reithian tradition of giving people a small dose of what they wanted, to cement them behind what they needed, was alive and well, and the BBC carried on recruiting – as it still does – largely from the top universities. But Broadcasting House could no longer continue on Reithian lines. In came such ostensibly 'subversive' programmes as *That Was The Week That Was*, which was in reality a modern-day variety programme – sketches, monologues and singing – performed by a far more upmarket and educated band of artists than would have been the case ten years earlier. For the first time it became fashionable to be young, provincial and working class. Popularity was the cue: hence the establishment of Radio 1, designed to 'nationalize' the trendsetting pirate pop radio stations such as Caroline and Luxembourg and ensure that, however much the nation was changing, Auntie would not be left behind. *Dixon of Dock Green* made way for *Z Cars*, set in Kirby New Town, while *Life With the Lyons* stepped aside for *Cathy Come Home*.

So successful was this renovation that today we look back on the 1960s and 1970s as halcyon days in the life of the BBC as the cultural embodiment of the nation. *Morecambe and Wise* were not just a Christmas comedy duo but an institution, as much a part of the festivities as turkey and the Queen's Christmas Broadcast (which was until 1996 exclusively produced by the BBC). *The Likely Lads*, *Porridge*, *Dad's Army*, *The Good Life*, *The Two Ronnies*: those were the days, we sigh, when the BBC was at its best. Thanks to satellite and cable, we moan, gone is the time when the whole nation could talk about last night's television in the office or the canteen. Just as in the 1960s we bemoaned the loss of *ITMA*, in the 1970s the loss of *Hancock*, and in the 1980s the loss of *Dad's Army*, so today we mourn for *Fawlty Towers*: a BBC class act which the nation shared each week.

To the new BBC, it is ratings that count above all else. A modern-day Muggeridge – Princess Di herself – is only the start. So radically changed is BBC culture that a new body – the Broadcasting Standards Council – was set up under a former deputy chairman of the BBC, Lord Rees-Mogg, to act as an outside monitor of traditional BBC standards. Where the old BBC existed to try to change class tastes, and so to change the classes, the new BBC competes to offer classes what they want and thus to cater for both élite and mass tastes, using mass programming to subsidize the production of the programmes that the commercial broadcasting market will not fund.

As brilliantly as any institution in this book, the BBC has adapted to survive. Take its traditional role as a standard bearer for the nation. This amounts to far more than Radio 4 playing the national anthem on the occasion of the birthday of members of the royal family. It is particularly true in matters of accent, with the BBC policing sloppy vowels and consonants, especially on Radio 4, the Establishment's very own bulletin board. As recently as 1981 an internal BBC booklet recommended the accent 'of the person born and brought up in one of the Home Counties, educated at one of the Southern Universities'.[9] And yet until the 1950s there was no such thing as received pronunciation.[10]

In the 1950s the sociologist William Walton distinguished between 'spiralists' (career professionals, who moved around to wherever their job took them) and 'burgesses' (traditional local businessmen and professionals, such as solicitors and doctors, who stayed in the same place all their life). This old, traditional middle class had been educated at the local grammar school and had moved on from there to the local Rotary Club and Freemasons lodge. It looked with some contempt at the new mobile breed who stood apart from the community, eyeing its next step up the career ladder. Distinction was exacerbated by speech. Where the burgesses' accent, for all that it was educated, revealed its regional origin, the spiralists – even if they had had no 'better' upbringing – had altered theirs at university to blend seamlessly with the 'received standard English' heard on the BBC, and especially the Home Service. A version, of course: John Snagge's or other still haughtier voices were always deliberately affected, but no one who wanted to be taken seriously attempted to copy every inflection. Received standard English was certainly not the accent of the aristocracy, which spoke with a far more clipped and gruffer, less pretentious voice. Rather, the aim was to lose a regional voice. This might loosely be termed the 'classless' accent. And yet, of course, it was not classless. It was created in the reformed public schools and southern grammar schools and was then made national by the BBC. The only people who adopted it were the aspiring middle classes, who used it as a barrier against the masses.

The introduction into the BBC of regional accents in the 1980s and 1990s has been a limited exercise, reflecting continuing class distinctions. Television continuity announcers and newsreaders – a very different species from presenters – have remained firmly Home Counties. And, with the exception of Radios 1 and 2 (which were always a breed apart, ushered in as the new, commercially sensitive BBC took shape), whenever the attempt has been made on the traditional channels – the old Third Programme and Home Service, now Radios 3 and 4 – there has been a tremendous outcry.

In the early 1980s a new newsreader was introduced to Radio 4. Susan Rae possesses one of the most correct, articulate and clear English-speaking voices one could wish to hear. She speaks with a refined Edinburgh accent. Within a day of her first broadcast, the BBC was flooded with angry calls and letters claiming that her accent was indecipherable and impenetrable. She was quietly transferred to BBC 1, where she has since gone on to a flourishing and well understood career as a presenter. A similar, if still more vitriolic, campaign was engendered by the beginning of *Anderson Country* on Radio 4. Gerry Anderson, an extremely popular broad-caster in his native Londonderry, was lured across the sea to anchor the network's flagship afternoon programme. Again, no sooner had he said hello on Radio 4 than the floodgates opened. Questions were asked in Parliament, the newspapers printed a series of 'why oh why' pieces and the nation – or rather, again, that tiny part of the nation that makes its views felt and has the power to be taken seriously – was up in arms. Forget that the content of the programme was dire. What mattered was Gerry Anderson's accent.

The spirit which led to the introduction of regional accents was essentially the same as that which rejected them in the 1950s: the BBC wishing to be seen as the voice of the nation. The question is: what nation? In the 1930s, 1940s and 1950s the BBC built itself on the national characteristics, embodied in the archetypal BBC programme, *Dixon of Dock Green*. George Dixon – everything we aspired to be, everything we saw as being best about Britain, and everything we valued: decent, hardworking, sensible, friendly and down to earth. Nowadays it is a fruitless task trying to pinpoint the archetypal BBC programme.

Consider this. The BBC does not simply produce soap operas. It produces different soaps for each class, for each lifestyle: *East-Enders* for the masses, *The Archers* for the refined, *Neighbours* for the young, *This Life* for middle-class professionals. You watch your soap according to your class – or, if you are especially keen to mark yourself out as different, you buck the system and express a love for the wrong soap. Similarly, each group has its own cookery programme. We all love Delia, or so we are led to believe. But the 'we' who loves Delia is the suburban middle class, as her viewing figures – on the minority channel, BBC2 – show. The reason we read about Delia this and Delia that is because the people who write the articles and produce the programmes are the very people who love Delia themselves, just as they are the people who watch and write about *Masterchef* – a show which almost parodies itself as a competition to see who can cook the most fancy dinner party food. We rarely read about the nation's obsession with *Ready, Steady, Cook*, *The Good Food Programme* or *Food and Drink* because they are designed for the masses: not the group who wants to spend £9 a pound on a Delia monkfish recipe, but the one who wants to see Michael Barry demonstrate how to make a fish pie in ten minutes with three haddock fillets.

Again, where in the past 'the news was the news was the news' (apart from days when, as the Home Service would sometimes begin its bulletins in the 1930s, 'there was no news today') and was read by identikit newsreaders from Richard Baker to Kenneth

Kendall, the new BBC now provides bulletins to suit a variety of different audiences. The morning starts with *Today* for the politics junkies. Then comes the lunchtime news, designed to capture the housewife. In the early evening there is the *Six O'Clock News* for the *Daily Mail* or *Express* reader who has finished work and is at home for his 'tea' in front of the TV news (which, legend has it, has to include a different animal story every day). The more heavyweight *Nine O'Clock News* follows. Finally at 10.30 p.m. there is *Newsnight*, designed to capture the following morning's *Today* listeners before they go to bed. Each programme has its own team of newsreaders and presenters, specially chosen to generate the desired image, from the pugnacious John Humphrys on *Today* to the comforting, winsome presence of Juliet Morris on breakfast TV, the unthreatening authority of Peter Sissons at six o'clock, the hail-fellow-well-met, all-round charm of Michael Buerk at nine and the indescribable Jeremy Paxman on *Newsnight*.

The picture is not one dimensional, however, for the BBC – reflecting the élite of which it is part – has always had difficulty with truly highbrow culture. As one commentator has put it of the 1930s:

> Highbrow-baiting was a favourite sport in the millionaire press, and it was taken up with enthusiasm on the golf links and in the smokerooms of the commercial and country hotels . . . Anti-intellectualism was also a matter of pride in the upper middle class. In the public schools, notwithstanding a certain weakening in the cult of athleticism, the tyranny of the 'bloods' was unimpaired, and the budding of the artist or poet was liable to be treated with sniggering contempt.[11]

The British aristocracy is famously philistine as a class, lacking most of the taste for original patronage that has characterized European aristocrats and their moneyed equivalents in the US. Twentieth-century Britain boasts no Fricks, Carnegies or Guggenheims. Where the Italians supported Verdi and Puccini, the British aristocracy supported Gilbert and Sullivan; where they had

opera, we had operetta. The Tate Gallery reports that its typical
visitor spends as much time in the shop and café – forty-five
minutes – as looking at the exhibits.[12] It should come as no
surprise that a Val Doonican CD is as likely to be found at
Highclere as Highbury. *Heartbeat* – village life in yesteryear – the
perfect middlebrow TV programme with nice, clean-cut Nick
Berry, attracts 18 million viewers, from the unemployed single
mother on benefit through, no doubt, to Tara Palmer-Tomkinson.
And the unenterprising middlebrow is becoming stronger still.
Contrast *Heartbeat* with a similarly popular programme in its time,
Dad's Army. *Heartbeat's* popularity rests on its utter predictability:
its safety first approach to plot, character and depiction of the
past. Yet *Dad's Army*, ostensibly no less nostalgic for the long
gone past, worked precisely for the way it inverted it. Sir Huw
Wheldon, the controller of BBC Television responsible for com-
missioning the programme, is recalled by Richard Hoggart as
offering an unexpected reason for its success:

> The expectation, this being Britain, would be that the really
> posh character would be the officer, and the lower-middle-
> class one the NCO. That expectation was turned upside
> down; the lower-middle-class bank manager was the com-
> manding officer of the Home Guard company, and the
> public-school product (his chief cashier) the NCO. That
> made all the difference, took the programme's very basis out
> of stereotyping and introduced all sorts of unexpected social
> and cultural reverberations.[13]

Middlebrow tastes accompany middlebrow lives. As Harold
Perkin puts it:

> With the spread of affluence (from the 1950s), the decline
> of domestic service and deference and, to a lesser extent,
> the growth of educational opportunity, the classes were
> becoming more alike in dress, in expectations of material
> comfort and personal services, in leisure and holidays, and

in lifestyle generally ... There came into being a kind of average lifestyle, home-centred, family-oriented, servantless, with leisure time devoted to home-based activities, television-watching, gardening, do-it-yourself decorating and home improvement, with weekend car trips to the country or seaside, and annual holidays in Britain or abroad.[14]

By 1971 more than 95 per cent of every class spent a large part of their leisure time watching TV, two-thirds spent some time gardening (except for the less skilled working class, only half of whom were gardeners), and more than half spent time on DIY, car cleaning and playing with children. Taking a drive, visiting the pub and walking were activities pursued by more than half of every class.[15]

Just as the plot of the Stephen King horror fantasy, *The Stand* (a perfect middlebrow book by a perfect middlebrow author), concerns a virus that subsumes almost everything it touches, so the middlebrow itself can turn the most anarchic of artforms into respectability, from the Mike Flowers Pops reworking of Oasis's 'Wonderwall' into perfect middle-of-the-road entertainment, through the 1990s revival of the punk Sex Pistols as a quaint diversion, to the entire genre's sublimation of the 1960s, a decade of angst and liberation, into a nostalgic beacon of excellence, with the Beatles – a source of horror to parents of teenagers at the time – now revered as showing current pop groups 'a thing or two'. But the most complete triumph of the middlebrow surely has to be the marriage of Gazza and Sheryl in July 1996. After selling the rights to the wedding to *Hello!* – *the* middlebrow magazine – the bride wore a dress designed by Isabell Kristensen, fashion designer by appointment to Princess Di and Fergie – who was captured modelling in *Hello!* the very next week. Seamlessly, we have moved from the union of Charles and Di, through the Andrew and Fergie wedding, to the Gazza and Shazza nuptials.

The pinnacle of the BBC pyramid remains Radio 4, the house station for the professional classes. While the rest of the BBC has attempted to secure its position by 'dumbing down', as the Americans put it (or 'responding to social and cultural change' as an internal BBC document has it), Radio 4 – with the exception of never-to-be-repeated flops such as *Anderson Country* – has remained a beacon of upmarket exclusivity. Its newsreaders are announcers, whom one still imagines wearing black tie as they speak. It still carries a daily religious service, as well as the national institution, 'Thought for the Day'. Every suggestion for reform is greeted with a barrage of élite protest, whether it be plans to cease transmission on long wave or – horror of horrors – a shake up in the roster of its thinkers of the day. Furthermore, Radio 4 is deliberately middle-aged. Where other stations – notably Radio 1 – seem to announce every week a new policy for making themselves 'relevant' to young people (and in the case of Radio 1 promptly losing their existing listeners), Radio 4 coasts along with its ever present supply of middle-aged programmes. Literally so, in fact, as many are in their forties, such as *The Archers, Desert Island Discs, Woman's Hour, The World at One, Any Questions, Start the Week, Saturday Night Theatre* and *Just a Minute*: all the channel's best loved and most admired programmes.

Yet the programme that best exemplifies Radio 4's role as a professionals' club is *Today*. This was not always so. When it started over thirty years ago, with Jack De Manio and John Timpson, it was rather light-hearted. Indeed one of the other founding presenters, Nigel Rees, has gone on to a second career as the nation's leading supplier of humorous quotations through his many books, and yet another Radio 4 programme, *Quote Unquote*. The rise of *Today* to its current exalted height is a relatively recent phenomenon. In the early 1980s the programme was regarded by the powers that be as tired, and was deemed fit for 'relevance'. It was split into two: *Up to the Hour*, which lasted from half past the hour and contained the jokey elements, and *Today*, which started on the hour. Within a day the heavens opened and the might of the Radio 4 audience made itself felt. The power of this audience is all the greater for not being due to its numerical strength but rather its quality. In *Doctor Slaughter*, by Paul Theroux, a politician asks at a dinner party how many people there are in the world. In response to the guesses of billions and trillions, he replies that there are five thousand. Five thousand who matter.[16] This is the *Today* programme's Britain, a country of no more than a million or two.

This is the most striking feature of the BBC: it broadcasts to the nation, for the nation. But today it defines the nation as a series of separate groups. So where the old model of the BBC as a 'generalist' broadcaster would allow people to stumble across new experiences and widen their horizons, today's 'niche' BBC only intends that you watch your programme – the programme designed to cater for your group. In *The Way We Live Now*, Richard Hoggart describes the dangers of this approach:

> We are virtually all, from whatever part of society we come, caught within our bit of the culture – or, better, cultures. Broadcasting, so much freer than the printed word, is able to say: 'The world is wider than we think; listen and look.' So far as audiences are concerned, this is the heart of the public service notion. Other forms of broadcasting, other impulses behind other structures, are implicitly committed to the formulation: 'We know you like this. Here's more of it'; or, at the limit: 'We know you like this sort of thing. Here it is, hotter and stronger or with a new twist to it, you poor nits.'[17]

Ironically for the BBC – the butt of a thousand Conservative jibes that it is nothing more than a subsidized form of anti-government propaganda – it seems that, as Margaret Thatcher put it, there is 'no such thing as society', only a series of different classes, each of which has programmes designed to appeal to it, not least the class from which the BBC's élite is itself drawn.

As with other closely knit professions, the media is rife with intermarriage and dynasties. Start plotting the family tree and it begins to seem as if every newspaper or TV station is linked through marriage. Sir Nick Lloyd, until 1996 editor of the *Daily Express*, is married to Eve Pollard, editor of the *Sunday Express* at the same time. Conrad Black, owner of the *Daily Telegraph*, is married to Barbara Amiel, formerly of the *Sunday Times* and now of the *Daily Telegraph*. The *Observer*'s Melanie Phillips is married to Joshua Rozenberg of the BBC. Martin Ivens, deputy editor of the *Sunday Times*, is married to Anne McElvoy, deputy editor of the *Spectator*. Andrew Marr, editor of the *Independent*, is married to Jackie Ashley of ITN. As for the generations, there are the Grades (Michael, Lew and his brother, Bernard Delfont), the Dimblebys (Richard Dimbleby, doyen of the BBC; father of Jonathan, ITV's political interviewer and lead presenter of its general election coverage, presenter of *Any Questions*, married to journalist Bel Mooney; brother of David, presenter of the BBC's *Question Time* and of the BBC's general election coverage, owner of the Dimbleby Press, formerly married to Josceline Dimbleby of the *Sunday Telegraph*), the Milnes (Alasdair, formerly director-general of the BBC, father of Kirsty of the *New Statesman* and Seamus of the *Guardian*) and the Wintours (Charles, former editor of the *Evening Standard*, father of Patrick of the *Observer* and Anna of *Vogue*). Lord Thomson of Monifieth, a former Labour minister and chairman of the Independent Broadcasting Authority, is the father of Caroline Thomson, deputy director of the BBC World Service. Then there are the wider intra-élite connections: Jane Corbin, of the BBC's flagship, *Panorama*, is married to John Maples, the shadow Health Secretary; Sue Cameron, presenter of *Newsnight*, is married to Tory MP Keith Hampson; and Marmaduke Hussey, former chairman of the BBC, is married to Lady Susan Hussey, lady-in-waiting to the Queen. Some, such as Lord Rees-Mogg, seem not to need familial links since they move so effortlessly between institutions in their own person – in his case from editor of *The Times* to deputy chairman of the BBC, founder member of the Broadcasting Standards Council and, inevitably, the House of Lords.

Nor should one put too much store, in terms of class diversity, in the tabloids and popular TV. Even supposedly working-class papers, such as the *Sun* and the *Star*, are written by the same middle-class graduates whom one finds in the BBC, just as downmarket BBC programmes are produced by the very same people who script *Newsnight* and *The Archers*. The 'repositioning' of the BBC is part of a wider modern trend in the world of arts and élite culture. Under Mrs Thatcher, arts professionals, subsidized by the taxpayer and valued only by a tiny minority of the public, had a difficult time justifying their share of the public-spending cake. But they never for a moment let up, from the 'bang people's heads together' approach of Sir Peter Hall to the Fabian style gradualism of the National Campaign for the Arts under, fittingly, the later general secretary of the Fabians, Simon Crine. Although arts budgets in fact stood up rather well – public arts funding increased in real terms under Mrs Thatcher and was to rocket sky high in the 1990s, courtesy of the National Lottery – subsidized companies started to turn to business for sponsorship, and with this came a shift of emphasis. Little by little the subsidized arts – and of course the BBC – realized that if they were to continue to expect taxpayer finance, they had to make a start at marketing themselves properly and making themselves genuinely popular. At the very least they began to announce proudly that the past season had played to, for instance, 92 per cent capacity, a hitherto unheard of defence of subsidy. Where before subsidy was supposedly designed to fund art specifically because no one would otherwise pay for it, now the language shifted and subsidy was referred to as an investment in the future so that commercially popular artforms such as film would continue to have a supply of classically trained actors.

This was always going to be a difficult line of argument to maintain. If an opera was sufficiently popular to sell out, why should the taxpayer have to pay for it as well? Why couldn't the Royal Opera House, for instance, charge a market rate when Pavarotti or Domingo sang? Why should the taxpayer subsidize the ticket price of a wealthy merchant banker? Moreover, by the

1980s any notion that subsidy would make high culture open to all had become laughable. Although 80 per cent of the population participates in some cultural endeavour, with cinema-going (45 per cent) and stately home visiting (33 per cent) the most popular forms, subsidized high culture still has a very narrow class profile. A survey of high culture audiences in 1993 found that nearly half were senior managers, professionals or business owners, 28 per cent had a household income of more than £30,000, and only 8 per cent were in clerical or manual jobs. This pattern is reflected across the arts: 26 per cent of professionals say they go to classical music concerts, compared with 6 per cent of skilled workers and below; and a survey of London artgoers concluded that they are 'typically middle-aged (35–59), middle class (A B C 1) and white'.[18]

But the subsidized arts and BBC are on a hiding to nothing if they seek to justify themselves on the same basis as the commercial arts. When a classical composer such as John Harle or Alexander Goehr is commissioned by the Proms, as popular a concert series as any in the world, 5,000 people may hear his piece live, and 100,000 or so on Radio 3. It is unlikely that the piece will receive a second performance. And what is the *commercial* point of the taxpayer financing such a piece? The only justification is precisely that it is an *uncommercial* activity – that very few people will hear it but that it is good for society as a whole that it has an airing. When Blur or Oasis record a new song millions will hear it – commercially. Where in the 1940s and 1950s the sense of deference was strong enough to overcome the lack of any utilitarian benefit to the people who provide the subsidy – taxpayers – by the 1970s people questioned by what right their hard-earned income was taken by the state to finance the purchase of a pile of bricks in the Tate. And if the BBC has nothing more to offer than competition with Sky, why should logic not take its course and the BBC be funded as Sky – commercially?

For one thing, culture at all levels is more accessible than ever. In 1990 more than 26 million seats were sold for theatrical performances in the UK. In 1989 total sales of fiction amounted to £3 billion, with the number of books sold having risen by over a third in the 1980s. Annual cinema admissions in the UK now total 100 million, having doubled since 1984. Annual spending on amateur photography is over £1 billion. In 1990 £1.7 billion was spent on CDs, tapes and records. Each year there are more than 12 million visits made to museums and galleries in England.[19] At the same time taxpayer subsidies to the arts went sharply up, through the extraordinary saga of the National Lottery we shall encounter in the next chapter.

Holes and balls

The sociologist Clifford Geertz calls sport a 'deep play', in which the innermost values of a culture are expressed. More than a mere gratuitous expenditure of energy, sport is 'a story we tell ourselves about ourselves'.[20] Which is why the Botham–Khan libel case in the summer of 1996 said so much more about Britain than it did about cricket. Ian Botham, a 'lad' without any airs and graces, versus Imran Khan, Oxford-educated Pakistani aristocrat. Botham told the High Court, as part of his evidence against Imran, that his mother would be 'very upset' about any slur on his upbringing. 'I don't quite understand what class has to do with it.'[21] Class had everything to do with it.

Every sport has its class labels. Ascot is for toffs, the Grand National for 'the people' (Newcastle even stages what it calls the 'Pitmen's Derby' the month after the Epsom Derby); Cowes is for debs, rugby league for miners. There are three classes of sport. No one expects crowd trouble at the top of the scale, a real tennis match – or even a lawn tennis match, for that matter. Polo, three-day eventing and carriage driving are hardly mass participation sports. That is their point. They are designed only to appeal to a certain set of people and prohibitive expense will ensure they never become otherwise. Next are sports such as cricket and golf which attract 'all sorts'. Although the 'sorts' are segregated – between municipal golf courses and Wentworth Golf Club, for instance – when they do mix there can be trouble. In 1993 Lee

Janzen, the reigning US Open golf champion, appeared in the clubhouse at Royal St George's during the British Open for a drink – wearing a baseball cap. Club members averted their eyes at the sheer horror. The stewards not only refused to serve him, they told him brusquely that he must leave the premises. Meekly, he took his cap off.

Why are some sports in one category and some in another? Culture and history explain much. Cricket is still a mystery to the French and the intricacies of the Tour de France to the British. Why else, for instance, would rugby union be a mass spectator and participation sport in Wales but a relatively exclusive one in England? The social structure of Welsh and English rugby cannot be removed from the structure of Welsh and English society. The code of amateurism handed down by the English public schools, the home of English rugby, is a vital part of the story. But slowly, as English society changes, even as traditional a public school sport as rugby union is beginning to change, the advent of money and professionalism making it now financially attractive to those who might otherwise have had to bypass it. When in 1995 the England captain, Will Carling, an ex-public school boy, was sacked after calling his bosses 'fifty-seven old farts', the change was clear to all. The Wasps and England winger, Damian Hopley, says he can no longer think of a complete XV which, like him, went to public school.[22]

As for the bottom category, sports such as football, darts or boxing are traditional routes off the streets for working-class boys. The Professional Footballers Association cannot name a single public schoolboy playing in any of the football leagues.[23] Why did such sports develop their attraction? Working men, as E. P. Thompson has shown, made their own culture, even if they did not start with a blank canvas. They shaped the sports of the élite – football and rugby, for instance – in their own way. Football matches were no mere commercial events foisted on an otherwise bereft working class. The introduction of the Saturday half day for skilled workers in the 1860s and 1870s and for many of the rest in the 1880s explains the timing of 'the match'. Football had also to appeal as a spectator sport, which was partly due to its status as a participatory sport: by Edwardian times over 6 million people a year paid to watch professional First Division football alone, and half a million played in leagues.

Football soon developed another attraction to the working man: the football pools. Although there had long been betting on the results of individual matches, once a system was invented for gambling on an entire series of results, and thus came down to a choice of numbers, the deciding factor moved from skill to luck – and consequently became much more popular. (The success of the National Lottery shows how gambling on a series of numbers has a mystique absent from almost any other form.) As early as 1907, 80,000 coupons were collected in Liverpool in a single week.[24] So popular did the pools become that not filling in the weekly coupon was thought eccentric. During the depression this became even more the case: the dream of a windfall kept many people going, and expenditure on the pools rose from £10 million in 1934 to £40 million in 1938.

But just as rugby union in England has started to develop a wider following, so the traditional working-class sport of football has started to develop a more upmarket following. Indeed, it is reverting to its roots. Football originated as a serious competitive sport in the public schools, and the Football League was made up of amateur, élite teams nurtured in the public schools, such as the Corinthian Casuals. Arsenal, buried now in a working-class part of Islington, began as an Old Etonian club. But as football became more widely popular it rapidly lost its public school aura. The professional classes have always been anxious to distance their leisure pursuits from those of 'the rest', so the rapid growth of football – by 1890, for instance, there were 203 football clubs in Liverpool alone – spelt its apparent death knell as such a sport.[25] The cleaning up of football in the 1990s, after the hooligan-ridden 1970s and 1980s, combined with the influx of money from Sky and the consequent improvement in stadium facilities, prompted a virtuous circle. Professionals – and their money – readopted football, were willing to pay the higher prices the clubs now demanded to finance improvements and foreign players' wages, which made the game still more attractive, which tempted new viewers, who put more money into the game. And so on.

Where cricket has a fine library of literary reportage, exemplified by the writing of Neville Cardus and C. L. R. James, football had to make do with 'autobiographies' of players with little more interesting to say than 'Davy headed the ball over to me and I knocked it into the back of the net'. But since football became a sport followed by people who can read and write, the genre started by Hunter Davies' *The Glory Game* in the 1970s has culminated in Nick Hornby's superbly funny *Fever Pitch* (1992), the odyssey of a Cambridge graduate Arsenal fan. A parody of the genre (though intended seriously) was a piece by Karl Miller, then editor of the *London Review of Books*, in the issue after Italia 90, the World Cup to which many ascribe the rise of the middle-class footie fan:

> The tackled player rolled about in a piece of German theatre that might have earned him a place in Goethe's Walpurgis-nacht . . . He [Paul Gascoigne] was a highly charged spectacle on the field of play; fierce and comic, formidable and vulnerable, urchin-like and waif-like, a strong head and torso with comparatively frail-looking breakable legs, strange-eyed, pink-faced, fair-haired, tense and upright, a priapic monolith in the Mediterranean sun – a marvellous equivocal sight.[26]

There are still plenty of pure working-class sports left. Although greyhound-racing may have tried (with some success) to move upmarket in the 1980s and 1990s through the addition of sparkling new restaurant facilities and grandstands, it remains a predominantly class based activity, as do pigeon-racing and darts (which today has 6 million players, all centred on the pub).[27] Fishing and snooker have always been slightly more ambiguous. Fishing is often linked to betting in its heartlands, but remains popular with others who see in it the partial fulfilment of the nostalgia for the countryside that we described in Chapter 7. Snooker (along with billiards and pool), which revolves around betting in its pub form, h: s always had a second life as an aristocratic hobby. But in its new, post-1970s life as a colour TV sport, it has a strange mix of classes. Competitors are portrayed as coming from the wrong side of the tracks (one leading player visits his father, in prison for murder, between tournaments), live audiences are from a similar background, and yet on TV it is watched by all classes.

Being keen on sport today involves no more exercise than pressing the TV remote control: a 1990s poll found that, of those who declared themselves to be 'very interested in soccer', only 14 per cent actually played it, while 98 per cent watched it on TV.[28] The enormous expansion in golf, and the ever increasing drive for new courses to be built to cater for the demand, is a result of the exposure the sport receives on TV. In the past golf was a self-consciously exclusive sport, the golf club a haven from the ever declining standards of the rest of the world. At the nineteenth hole, at least, a chap could be sure that his fellow chaps would know how to dress appropriately, and would be the right sort: no Jews, for instance, to lower the tone. Although long-established clubs seek to maintain some of their exclusivity, municipal courses open to all have sprung up nationwide.

What lies behind the changes to the class profile of sport over the century? As in every other walk of life explored in this book, the role of schools is paramount. Just as the public schools modernized their approach to exams, so they did with sport. Where in the past they concentrated on minority sports such as rugby (or rugger as it was known by the pupils), hockey and lacrosse, the new service agenda of public schools led them to concentrate far more on sports such as football. And the decline of 'amateurism' within the élite, as described in Chapter 2, has had a fundamental effect on sporting mores. For alongside the forces of nationalism, the media and the market, middle-class manners have also changed, towards a more hedonistic, casual and private approach. By 1939 there were two million private cars and income tax stood at less than 10 per cent for a man earning £500 a year. 'You need money in this England, but you do not need much money,' as Priestley put it.[29] Suburbanites began to lose the amateur ethic as consumption patterns became the defining character of class. Wimbledon turned professional when the lure of other professional tournaments and the subsequent increase in the number of professional players threatened to deprive the tournament of the best. In cricket, the ending of the Gentleman (amateur) and Player (professional) distinction in 1963 had less to do with notions of democracy and community than the straightforward decline of the amateur — higher taxes and the more rigid imposition of academic standards at universities made it harder to be an amateur. Even Gentlemen had to worry about money and exams. Certainly things were different from 1920 when Lionel Hedges, an Oxford blue, had dismissed

> a rather seedy looking middle-aged gentleman who called on him on the morning of a match. Imagining him to be a reporter, Lionel said to him brusquely, 'I have nothing to say to you.' The man tried to expostulate but Lionel repeated, 'I have nothing to say to you.' It only afterwards transpired that the seedy man was not a reporter but his tutor, with whom he was not otherwise acquainted.[30]

The horror of professionalism that led Lord Hawke in 1924 to 'Pray God, that a professional should never captain England'[31] and which ensured that Gentlemen's initials were transcribed appropriately before the surname, Players' after, since they were fit only to be addressed by their surname, was still alive in 1961 when the following correction was announced over the tannoy at Lords: 'Your cards show, at No. 8 for Middlesex, F. J. Titmus; that should read, of course, Titmus, F. J.'[32] Such amazing snobbery, which led Wilfred Wooller, captain of Glamorgan, to beckon the young Tony Lewis into his own changing room rather than undress in front of the rest of the team 'because one day you may be captain', had its lighter moments. Percy Fender, renowned for his voracious sexual appetite, was yelled at by the Australian batsman he was about to catch out, 'Drop it and you can sleep with my sister.' He made the catch. 'You see,' he explained, 'we had not been properly introduced.'

One sport – horse-racing – has always straddled the classes, by dint of meaning radically different things to different classes. Although it is socially exclusive, it has a huge popular following. Owners are by definition wealthy (the only way to find a poor owner, it is said, is to find a rich one at the start of the season and hunt him out again at the end), and often aristocratic or even royal. Jockeys tend to be from poor backgrounds, although National Hunt jockeys are often from 'good country stock', while followers come from all walks of life. Laura Thompson captures the simultaneously class-ridden and class-less racing crowd:

In 1991, the fact that everyone present at Epsom was acting a part, as if in a Great Exhibition whose theme was The English Character, had seemed to me enchanting and humorous in the way that the English can be. I knew that the men in dogfish checks were not really devilishly shrewd gamblers with pockets full of unkoshered money. I knew that the men in grey toppers were not really Lord Snooty. I knew that the Lycra miniskirts were not really cocktail waitresses at The Happy Hour in Hainault – or, if they were, that was not all that they were . . . It was a joke, but it was also an affirmation. It was done with joy, and it was done with respect for Derby Day. Now, though [in 1995], there seemed to be something almost dangerous about the role-playing . . . It wasn't funny, it was meaningless. And, if it was meaningless, it was therefore extremely meaningful: if there was no reason at all for prancing around a course, dressed as something out of the Great Exhibition, the fact that it was still being done gave to those class-ridden stereotypes an embittered significance. The class structure that is implicit in the structure of the racecourse had become horribly significant. The crowd wasn't just dressed as class stereotypes; it was acting the parts for real. The non-members were swearing and shouting, wrenching the rings out of lager cans with vicious force, stripping off their shirts as if daring the sun to scorch them. One of their girls, who was so drunk that she had begun to unbutton her suit, stumbled across the invisible electric fence that separated the Grandstand from Members'. 'Rosie!' screamed her boyfriend. 'Fucking get back here! You can't get in there, you silly cow! You'll get banged up!' Meanwhile, the members were staring at Rosie as if she was a seaside donkey that had infiltrated the parade of Derby entrants in the paddock. Their eyes were cold, full of conscious superiority. They were in, she was not, and they were loving it.[33]

Cricket has also long managed an accommodation between the toffs that run it and the rest, both through the Gentleman/Player divide, which gave it explicit status, and through more subtle means. In theory, cricket is based on the county. In practice, however, county grounds tend to be not in the heart of the county set but, so as to make them accessible to the prosperous suburban middle classes, in the most populous parts. Thus the county ground of Surrey County Cricket Club is in the middle of London, at the Kennington Oval, and the county ground of Lancashire in the middle of Manchester, at Old Trafford. Football was the concern of the workers, rugby union of the ex-public schoolboy. Cricket was for everyone. From W. G. Grace, through Jack Hobbs and Denis Compton to Ian Botham, we could all appreciate and revel in our cricketing heroes' exploits. Even if, as we have seen above, we felt that Botham was not of our stock, he was still the nation's Botham, as the 1981 Ashes series showed. A combination of media hype, commercial nous and bred-from-schooldays obsession has given twentieth-century cricket the appearance of straddling the classes. But when one looks closer, one sees that, even though the labels Gentleman and Player may have disappeared, the spirit behind them lives on. After the disastrous tour of India in 1992−3, the chairman of the selectors, Ted Dexter (a Gentleman if ever there was one, who was known in his playing days as 'Lord Ted'), could only comment that: 'We have to look at the whole matter of facial hair.' And it was not just his obvious talent that led Michael Atherton's team-mates to inscribe the initials 'FEC' by his dressing-room hook. What did the initials stand for? One mild version has it as Future England Captain. The more likely version, however, is Fucking Educated Cunt. Manchester Grammar School and Cambridge had something to do with it − just as it was the lack of a university education and the feeling that it was time, after the NCO-style Graham Gooch regime, to move back to the officer class, that counted against Atherton's only real competitor for the post, Alec Stewart.

So cricket has managed the same Whig trick as many of the English institutions we have discussed: it has skilfully adapted to conserve. For cricket, more than any other game, fuses the rural idyll with the city reality. The village cricket match, with its afternoon tea and country setting, tends now to be played between teams that live in the city but drive out to the country for the match. More tellingly still, cricket has long had strong − if fitful − cross-class attractions. Witness Hugh de Selincourt's 1920s classic, *The Cricket Match*. From Horace Cairie, who prays 'Oh God, please make me a sportsman', to the raffish Teddy White's racing tips, and captain Paul Gauvinier's serious concern, the book ends with the team departing back to their own worlds: 'At length the band stopped playing and dispersed, the gossiping groups broke up and straggled away, some singing uproarious catches along the still lanes. Slowly the square emptied, the colours went out of the sky, the night descended peacefully on the village of Tillingfold. Rich and poor, young and old, were seeking sleep.'[34]

If cricket has managed to become a national sport through the trick of appearing at one and the same time to be both for all classes and class specific, what is it that football offers as a national game? As the Corinthian Casuals and Old Etonians gave way to the northern professional teams, football came to be seen as vulgar by the middle classes that had formerly supported it. The Pilgrim Trust, which examined the effects of long-term unemployment in the 1930s, reported the humiliating spectacle of men on the dole 'silently lining the streets and watching those in work make their way to the game'.[35] Football was so popular that people would congregate outside the stadium, even if they couldn't afford to go inside. Why? Because by following a team you became someone. Your otherwise dreary and predictable life gained a measure of excitement and unpredictability. How would your team do next Saturday? How was your city doing in the national league? 'The best you can say for football,' wrote a Glaswegian critic in the 1930s, 'is that it has given the working man a subject for conversation.'[36] As Priestley put it in *The Good Companions*:

> It turned you into a member of a new community, all brothers together for an hour and a half, for not only had you escaped from the clanking machinery of this lesser life, from work, wages, rent, doles, sick-pay, insurance-cards, nagging wives, ailing children, bad bosses, idle workmen, but you had escaped with most of your mates and your neighbours, with half the town, and there you were, cheering together, thumping one another on the shoulders, swapping judgements like lords of the earth, having pushed your way through a turnstile into another and altogether more splendid kind of life ... It offered you more than a shilling's worth of material for talk during the rest of the week.[37]

Update the language and not much has changed since.

Not *much*, mind. The attraction of losing oneself in the crowd once a fortnight remains. But if you are lucky enough to follow a Premiership team, the pretence that one and all have come together for the regular ritual is barely credible. Such has been the change since the combination of Taylor Report induced all-seater stadiums and the huge influx of Sky TV's money that Premiership football spectators are no longer classless but of one class – the comfortably off. The cheapest ticket at White Hart Lane is £18. Go with two children and, with a burger and travel, you have kissed goodbye to £100. And no true fan will miss a home match. Which, with the ever-increasing popularity of football, means a season ticket, the very cheapest of which for Spurs fans, as one of the authors knows to his cost, is nearly £400 per seat.

The lives we lead – food, holidays and style

Whatever arguments may rage over Britain's political future in Europe, its cultural future is already with us. The multi-million-pound sale of the Dôme brasserie chain in the summer of 1996 was about far more than the mushrooming of cappuccino bars and pavement cafés in a few sophisticated parts of London. Continental breakfasts are now the norm – one often searches in vain for an old-fashioned British fry-up. And while the change resulted from the 1980s yuppies yearning for a replica of the continental sophistication they admired on their travels, the exclusivity is greatly diminished. Motorway service stations now all serve cappuccinos alongside baked beans on toast, and Belgian beers are available on the Tyne alongside Newcastle Brown.

As a nation we have more money available to spend on consumer goods than ever before. Between 1980 and 1996 household expenditure rose by 162 per cent. Men's earnings rose by 214 per cent and women's by 259 per cent.[38] An average married man who is the sole wage-earner in a household has today to work five minutes to pay for a loaf of bread, compared with nine minutes in 1971.[39] But this rise in disposable income means not that class differences have disappeared so much as that they have reinvented themselves as extra consumer choices. In the early 1970s a colour TV was the ultimate middle-class status symbol. Today the person on benefit has a video. Indeed, some definitions of deprivation even include the lack of a VCR as proof of 'relative poverty'. Given the range of goods available, it is what you choose to buy – and what you shun – that says what class you are in. The wealthiest fifth of the population, for instance, spend a great deal more of their wealth on education, pensions and housing than the rest.

And when it comes to the weekly shop, the main supermarket chains are as class-divided as the housing estates they serve. Tesco, for instance, which was traditionally regarded as the working-class supermarket, has now the clearest professional customer profile of any of the major supermarkets. Sainsbury has for its 'classless middle class' customers the feel of a comfortable pair of slippers, while Asda trades on its reputation for no-nonsense northern value – a deliberate appeal to the frugal classes. Kwiksave takes this approach to its logical, no frills extreme, with food even displayed in its cardboard warehouse packaging. Even soap powders are sold by class – Daz for the working class, the ads featuring Danny Baker and his 'swaps' campaign, while middle-class Ariel is presented on the box by white-coated technicians with their laboratory tests.

Although the 'foodie' tends only to be found among identikit professionals living in the South, and certain foods such as tara-masalata and avocado tend to remain their preserve, concepts of exoticism have changed remarkably over the past few decades, prompted by the demand for flavours discovered abroad to be available in Tesco. Cod, for instance, used to be a cheap fish, but is now on a par with Dover sole. And coley, which was regarded even in the immediate post-war years of rationing as fit only for pets, is now similarly priced. Sometimes this can lead to hilarious changes in outlook, such as that engendered by Ernest Hemingway's posthumously published novel, *The Garden of Eden*. A review by Tom Stoppard quoted Hemingway's mouth-watering description of a mysterious Spanish dish: 'It came in a large bowl with ice floating with the slices of crisp cucumber, tomato, garlic bread and red peppers, and the coarsely peppered liquid that tasted lightly of oil and vinegar. "It's salad soup," Catherine said. "It's delicious." "Es gazpacho," the waiter said.' Stoppard continued: 'Well, it isn't Hemingway's fault that you can now get the stuff in cans at Safeway.'[40] Much the same happened to our very own James Bond in Ian Fleming's *From Russia With Love*. Taken to an incredibly exotic meal in the best restaurant in Turkey ('a little place in the Spice Bazaar'), Bond is led through 'a maze of small, colourfully tiled, vaulted rooms to where Kerim was sitting at a corner table over the entrance to the bazaar'. Kerim, the master spy, translates the waiter's suggestion: 'He says the Doner Kebab is very good today.' With one noun, the 1990s reader is shunted from the mysterious East to a greasy take-away in the East End.[41]

So if our identikit lifestyle man has left behind the doner kebab, what has replaced it? Holidays are foremost – and they are as class-segmented as every other mass activity in the country. For top professionals – our Super Class – a second home, perhaps in the Cotswolds, is an essential component of a decent life. But a second home is for weekends: not a holiday home, for the idea of a holiday in England is anathema to most of them, conjuring up Blackpool, guest-houses, rain, yobs, fish and chips, and warm beer. Rather, it should be skiing in winter and Italy or France, particularly Tuscany or Perpignan in summer, staying in an old but functional cottage with a swimming pool, colourful locals, local wine, local food – 'produce' – and other identikit Brits. The problem with a British holiday for our Super Class, and those of a similar mindset, is that the hoi polloi simply have no class. As the right-wing social commentator Digby Anderson puts it on their behalf:

> Watch English young people in the off-licence. Before they have so much as got out of the door, their itching, tattooed fingers are already hooked into the first ring pull can of lager. As soon as it's off, the can is up to the lips, the contents downed in the street. Remember a society when only 'common' children ate in the streets? Now being 'common' is common. And the lager-swilling teenagers do it alongside their elders and no betters. Their parents are busy scratching in the streets – their scratchcards, that is – up against the nearest wall.[42]

Where we choose to take our holiday is one of our great obsessions – we take over twenty-three million foreign holidays a year, after all.[43] We study brochures, talk about it, and chew over our friends' experiences all year round. Partly this is because we simply want the sort of break that we will enjoy. But partly too it is because we want to make sure that we take the right sort of holiday. The horror felt by many on arrival in the Caribbean is brought on by the sudden revelation that the oiks have landed, as the Caribbean now features in several package holiday brochures. Where families from Wigan once went to Rimini for their summer treat, today the ever increasing spread of the package has made available previously unthought-of destinations such as America and Thailand. But as the world opens up for the package holidaymaker, so it in consequence closes for the 'independent' holidaymaker.

Harold Perkin has stressed that one of the key factors underlying the new lifestyle was the liberation of teenagers from parental control in the 1960s. This was an economic as much as a cultural development, as wages for teenagers increased, and new educational opportunities came hand in hand with universal student grants. With money to spend on clothes, records, bikes and leisure, a teen culture rapidly developed, from Bill Haley in the 1950s, through the Beatles in the 1960s to David Bowie in the 1970s, expressed in particular fashions and exploited by big business. This new culture was not only classless – public school groups such as the Hollies adopted fake working-class accents – but even reversed sociologists' so-called 'theory of stratified diffusion' (that trends in dress, music, leisure and so on start from the top down).[44]

This new culture was most obvious in dress. Where the period before the Second World War saw the rise of skirts above the knee for women, the 1960s saw the introduction not only of the mini-skirt and 'hot pants', but more lastingly of unisex, classless jeans and T-shirts which rapidly took over the world, in another example of upward diffusion. Blue jeans had once been the dress of the working man, developed into the uniform of the student in the 1960s, and were transformed into smart evening wear with a blazer and tie by the 1980s. A similar phenomenon was at work in the early 1990s with the spread of trainers. From being a casual piece of footwear worn by those who didn't care how they looked, they quickly became a source of competitive pride, as schoolchildren begged their parents for the most expensive pair and professional adults wore them at weekend dinner parties. The newspapers even reported schoolboys being mugged for their footwear by rampaging teenage gangs.

Can dress tell us anything any more about class? The Ian Botham–Imran Khan libel case in the summer of 1996 brought forth a river of comment about sport and class as we have seen, but some commentators preferred to concentrate on their wives' dress sense:

Kathy Botham, whose middle name should be Dutiful, played her part as always as Beefy's ever-faithful support. Dressed head to toe in courtroom colours of black and white, she looked the ultimate professional wife. Her nipped-in, tailored, dog-tooth jacket, worn over a plain white crew-necked top and polka dot flowing knee-length skirt gave her an efficient and serious air. An inch higher and it would have distracted from the court proceedings. An inch lower and it would have been frumpy. On anyone else clashing checks and spots would be a fashion faux pas but Kathy carried it off. She proved she's not the kind of woman to kowtow to ridiculous rules. She's strong-minded and adopted a strong look to match. She dressed to win. Her hair, neatly cropped and professionally highlighted, her shoes, black and sensible, and the large, square, brown leather briefcase over her shoulder, all spoke of her acknowledgement that attending court is a serious business. A simple gold chain around her neck and tiny stud earrings, added a touch of femininity. Jemima, the Trophy Wife, in contrast, walking up the steps four paces behind her husband, came dressed for Imran, and maybe for herself, rather than for the sombre atmosphere of Court 13. She was all flowing. Long, flowing hair, long flowing dress, long flowing 'dupatta' printed scarf, fluttering down her back. Her silver-grey dress by the highly fashionable designer label Ghost echoed in Western style the traditional Pakistani shalwar kameez she often wears by her husband's side. Casual and garden-partyish, rather like an upper crust flower-child, she kept her abundant hair barely under control with a plastic butterfly clip and had her bare toes peeking out of strappy, high-heeled sandals. Jemima looked more like she was arriving for a summer lunch date al fresco than a high-profile court date. It was left to her mother, Lady Annabel Goldsmith, to look sensible if not exactly smart, carrying a big, two-handled bag, which could have contained their packed lunch.[45]

Where we buy our clothes says it all. Marks & Spencer, John Lewis and Laura Ashley are suppliers by appointment to the 'classless middle class'. No one would, on the other hand, dream of buying a dress for a society wedding in C&A or Littlewoods. And BHS would not even sell a Barbour, the winter uniform of the city-based professional classes who like to act as if they have a country home. The Barbour must, of course, look as if it is a hand down – there is no greater faux pas than a clean, new Barbour. For those who need to parade their success, an Armani or Paul Smith suit is sufficiently recognizable to carry the right message, but still sufficiently expensive to be exclusive. But no longer exclusive is the mobile phone. In the late 1980s, when they first took off, their size was huge, as if to shout out to passers-by 'look – I'm important, I need a mobile phone'; today everyone from call-girls to chiropodists has one. By the year 2000 5.6 million people are expected to have one.

So class is not only about what we have termed 'foundations'. Across almost every walk of British life one can detect clear class patterns, from the output and make-up of the BBC, to the shop at which we buy our groceries. Far from leisure being the vanguard for the classless society, the way we live our lives is a daily, hourly testament to our place in Britain's class structure.

9. RACE

Integrating into classes

It may be that the biggest influence on children's educational progress is not the colour of their skin but the social class that they are born into – in particular, the expectations attached to their social class . . . Such attitudes may have a disproportionate effect on black and brown children, since most of them go to inner-city schools.

Economist, 8 February 1997

When Nelson Mandela toured Brixton during his state visit to Britain in the summer of 1996, he could have been forgiven for thinking he was in an African city. The ecstatic crowd cheering every moment of his tour of the south London district featured faces of every hue, but the overwhelming majority was black.

It was a far cry from his royal reception at Horse Guards Parade three days earlier. Then most of the onlookers and virtually all the participants were white. The South African president's guard of honour, the Irish Guards, contained one solitary black face, the more conspicuous for being diplomatically placed in the front rank.

These two snapshots raise one of the most critical but least discussed questions about contemporary Britain. Thirty years after the great wave of post-war immigration, are we a melting pot or a segregated society, in fact if not in law?

Immigration and integration

This is not a marginal issue: the United Kingdom's ethnic minority population is large and growing. When governments sought in the 1950s to encourage immigration from the former Caribbean colonies to overcome manual labour shortages, major British employers, such as the NHS, British Rail and, especially, London Transport, staged employment fairs in the Caribbean. Enoch

Powell, as Minister of Health (1960–63), was ironically at the forefront of this push to recruit nurses and support staff for the NHS, which reached a peak in the early 1960s. It was only in the late 1960s and early 1970s that Indian and Pakistani immigration took off, but by the mid-1970s Caribbean immigration had been overtaken by that from South Asia. Now totalling over three million (nearly 6 per cent of the national population), the ethnic minority population is expected to double over the next thirty years. Since a high proportion in the ethnic minorities are young, they will by then constitute nearly a fifth of the workforce.[1]

Immigration to Britain has focused overwhelmingly on a few large cities. London is an immigrant city on a par with New York but for centuries longer. Ethnic minorities account for more than a quarter of inner London's population. Add in the Irish-born and other distinct white minorities, and its non-indigenous population rises towards a third. Since immigrants tend to cluster on arrival in already populous areas, and to follow each other, nearly six out of ten live in the South East, with Greater London alone accounting for 45 per cent of the total ethnic minority population of the UK. The other main concentrations are in the West Midlands, Yorkshire, Humberside and the North West. Black Caribbeans and Africans are mainly based in the South East and West Midlands, and Pakistanis in Yorkshire and Humberside. Within cities, the concentration is equally marked. Tower Hamlets, for instance, has a population that is nearly a quarter Bangladeshi (who comprise upwards of 35 per cent of the electoral roll). Although the preponderance of Bangladeshis in the East End is of recent provenance, the area has been a traditional home for immigrants since the early years of this century, when Jews escaping from Eastern European pogroms settled there. As these immigrants became more prosperous, moving out to suburbs such as Chingford and Bounds Green, they were replaced by another wave – the Bangladeshis. A potent sign of this transition was the closure in the spring of 1996, through lack of demand for kosher food, of Blooms in Whitechapel, a celebrated Jewish focal point. But this moving out is emphatically a suburban, not a provincial, phenomenon. A black face in Bournemouth is most probably a figment of the retired colonel's imagination.

The typical first-generation immigrant settlement was cramped and close-knit. Council housing was often not available to new arrivals because a period of residence was a prerequisite. Thus they searched for the cheapest lodgings going, often becoming the victim of Rachmanite landlords. By the 1970s, when primary immigration had largely ceased, clear patterns had emerged. South Asians had high levels of owner-occupation – even among the low paid. Their particularly strong familial ties meant that owner-occupation was often the only way they could live *en famille* as they wished. By the early 1980s the proportion of blacks in council housing was far higher than that of South Asians, but only at the same level as whites.[2] Today, Indians are far more likely than any other ethnic group to own their own homes, and are the least likely to be in social housing. High proportions of blacks and Bangladeshis are in social housing: almost half of all blacks and six in ten Bangladeshis, compared with fewer than one in ten Indians.[3]

What are these houses like? According to government figures, higher proportions of each ethnic minority live in overcrowded houses than do whites. Nearly half of all Bangladeshis, for example, live in accommodation below standard, compared with only 2 per cent of whites. Around 40 per cent of Bangladeshis and 20 per cent of blacks and Pakistanis say that they are dissatisfied with their accommodation, compared with only 7 per cent of whites.[4] And of those who are home-owners, a third of black, Indian and Pakistani/Bangladeshis report difficulty in keeping up their mortgage repayments, compared with only a quarter of other ethnic minorities – and an eighth of whites.[5] Already we see the difficulties in trying to treat ethnic minorities as a single bloc, and signs that different minorities are integrating into different classes.

Successful social integration bears a myriad of faces: education, embourgeoisement, tolerance, intermarriage and entry to the public services and élite professions being the obvious. Examine them with reference to today's new minorities and three themes stand out:

- Britain's élite remains virtually impregnable to non-whites, forty years after the first big post-war wave of immigration.
- Residential segregation – meaning segregation of whites from non-whites – is marked, but less so than for both African Americans in the United States, and for many previous – white – immigrant groups in Britain, notably the Irish. To a significant extent, this mitigates the 'ghetto' effect and promotes integration. According to one survey, if you create a segregation index where zero signifies that an ethnic minority is spread evenly across a city, and 100 per cent that they live entirely in ghettos, then American blacks are typically 80 per cent segregated; for their British counterparts the figure is about 40 per cent.[6] Even Brixton has a majority of white residents. Intermarriage and cohabitation are also far from rare. According to the 1991 census: four in ten Caribbean men aged between sixteen and thirty-four had a white partner. In the younger age group, among those who were married, 31 per cent of men and 21 per cent of women had a white partner; Asians marry into other ethnic groups less often, but more than they used to. In the US, by contrast, just 4 per cent of black men and 2 per cent of black women have a white spouse.[7]
- Yet, as every prison officer and city dweller knows, this relative lack of segregation has not led to social advancement across the board. The social and economic record of the different ethnic minority groups has been remarkably divergent; and the best way to make sense of this is to set Britain's ethnic minorities in the context of the entrenched 'white' class system into which they are integrating.

On the first theme – ethnic minorities and the British élite – virtually the only blacks and Asians in the Palace of Westminster are the catering and support staff. If anything, the political integration of the ethnic minorities is slowing down. The 1987 election saw the return of the first Asian MP since 1929 and the first Afro-Caribbean MP ever. In the ten years to the 1997 election, the number of black and Asian MPs rose by a mere two – taking it to six out of 651. The number of non-white candidates actually fell in the 1992 election, and improved only slightly in the 1997 election. Labour, the majority choice for blacks and Asians, has engaged in controversial positive discrimination to boost its number of women MPs, while pointedly refraining from doing the same to favour ethnic minorities. In local government, too, the number of non-white council leaders in areas with large ethnic minority populations has fallen in recent years.

Of the élite professions, none is more symbolic than the law, a pillar of social order and attitudes. Non-white minorities in the US have made big advances in the judiciary in recent decades, reaching even the Supreme Court. Yet in England in 1997, not a single non-white face is to be found in the nation's top three courts comprising 140 judges. Among trial judges the non-white representation is a pitiful five out of 548 circuit judges, and thirteen out of 897 recorders. As for the rising élite at the Bar, there are twelve non-white QCs out of about 1,000. Only 2.3 per cent of solicitors are from ethnic minorities.[8] The Bar Council claims that things are changing at the grass roots, with 6 per cent of the 9,000 barristers in private practice now drawn from ethnic minorities. But some leading barristers are privately sceptical. One in a prestigious London practice notes that most of the non-whites he knows 'are in what people around here call "ghetto chambers" doing mostly routine criminal work'.[9]

Equally revealing is the police force, whose poor relations with non-white minorities in urban trouble-spots have been a continuous problem since the Notting Hill riots of 1958. Here again, non-whites are making it in at the bottom – they now comprise 2.9 per cent of Metropolitan Police officers – but not beyond – 91 per cent are constables, the lowest rank, compared with only 76 per cent of white officers. Not one of the Met's 180 superintendents – the rank in charge of police stations – is non-white. Similarly, only 2.5 per cent of prison officers are from ethnic minorities, 1.4 per cent of army personnel (and only 1 per cent of officers), and 1 per cent of fire brigade staff.[10]

It is the same in the media. Trevor Phillips, head of Current Affairs at LWT (one of the few senior black TV executives, the number of which can be counted literally on the fingers of one hand), recalls:

> Three years ago I came to the BBC to meet a senior executive. I had been presenting a weekly show for five years, so I wasn't entirely unknown. It happened that I was driving a large luxury car. The man at the gate, clearly unused to this, asked me whom I'd come to see. I told him and he said: 'You can park inside.' Then he looked at me and said: 'By the way can you remind me who you've come to pick up?' A black man in a big car can only mean two things – a drug dealer or a chauffeur.[11]

One result of all this is a virtual void in mainstream élite role models for young blacks and Asians. Lee Parker, a youth worker in Brixton, says that one of the biggest problems he confronts is the pervasive belief among young blacks that they have little chance of a 'proper' career. 'There is a need for accessible role models who are not musicians or sports figures.'[12]

The facts speak for themselves. Ethnic minority employees tend to be concentrated in a limited range of jobs. Thirty-four per cent of Bangladeshis work in the distribution, hotel and restaurant industries, for instance, compared with only 18 per cent of black men and 17 per cent of white men. Nursing is a traditional ethnic minority profession. But within it, 36 per cent of Asians and 44 per cent of 'other' minorities are charge nurses, ward managers or senior nurses; only 29 per cent of black nurses are in these grades, and are twice as likely to be unqualified as any other ethnic group. Whites are twice as likely to be managers as any of the ethnic minorities.[13]

A clear pattern of employment has emerged. In general – and strikingly – African, Asian, Indian and Chinese male employees have job levels similar to or better than white males. There are, for instance, proportionately more Chinese in the top category (professional, managerial and employers) than whites. Looking just at professionals, more Chinese, African, Asian and Indian male employees are in professional jobs than whites. Chinese males are in fact twice as likely as whites to be in professional jobs. But on further examination of the statistics it becomes clear that the bulk of white employment in this category consists of men employed as managers in large concerns, who account for 13 per cent of all white male employees. Thus men from certain ethnic minorities have permeated to a large extent certain professions, but have hardly touched others (such as the law and many large organizations).[14]

But the reverse is equally clear. The proportion of Afro-Caribbean, Pakistani and Bangladeshi male employees in the top category is less than half that of whites (12 per cent for each minority and 27 per cent for whites). Afro-Caribbeans and Pakistanis are most likely to be found in skilled manual work, with 39 per cent and 34 per cent of males respectively in such jobs; 70 per cent of Bangladeshi men are employed in semi-skilled or unskilled jobs, compared with 19 per cent of whites.[15]

Further, there is a high degree of polarization within these groups: the Chinese, as we have seen, are overly represented as professionals. Equally, however, 28 per cent are in semi-skilled and 40 per cent in unskilled jobs.[16] Segregation by classes is happening even within some ethnic minority groups.

Two, three, or four nations?

Observers from the US, where the debate over affirmative action is one of the most contentious in politics, are often surprised that there is so little pressure in Britain for affirmative action to break open the impregnable parts of the élite. Sir Herman Ouseley, the mild-mannered chairman of the Commission for Racial Equality, a statutory body established twenty years ago to counter racial discrimination, stresses Britain's political culture: 'In England, unlike in the US, change requires consensus. But if you try to shift the consensus too much, you become a dangerous extremist. This sentiment has become stronger, not weaker, in the 1990s.'[17]

Certainly, some members of the ethnic minorities are beginning to emerge as major players in the British economy. In February 1997 *Eastern Eye*, a magazine for British Asians, staged a dinner for Asian millionaires. The top one hundred alone were worth well over £400 billion, employed 250,000 people, and owned many high street brands such as Joe Bloggs Clothing, Horne Brothers, Ciro Citterio and Colorama. A typical story was that of Anwar Parvez, worth £100 million from the Bestway cash-and-carry business. As a five-year-old in Pakistan he walked eight miles to school each day. Today he sends his sons to Eton.[18]

But such examples, heartening as they are, are rare. In some respects the political consensus is weakening for the worse. Part of the consensus in the 1970s and 1980s was a tacit ban, agreed between the party leaderships, against provocative race rhetoric. Conservative campaigns in the mid-1990s about the ravages being inflicted on the social security system by asylum seekers, most of whom are non-whites, entered territory formerly taboo. Prior to the 1979 election Margaret Thatcher talked of 'feeling swamped' by immigrants, but quickly backed away from developing policies to reduce the swamping. By then new immigration had largely been stopped by law, which reduced the social pressure.

At the local level, however, inhibitions have always been less pronounced. Although a one-off, the election of a British National Party councillor, Derek Beackon, in a 1993 by-election on the Isle of Dogs in the East End of London followed a campaign full of 'swamping' rhetoric. In an area where upwards of a quarter of the population is Bangladeshi, there was plenty of support behind the laced curtains. Local Liberal politicians had risen to power by feeding the latent anti-immigrant sentiments through a barely concealed anti-immigrant programme known as 'Sons and Daughters', designed to give housing priority to the children of 'locals' (i.e. whites). The programme was never more than a slogan –

local authorities have statutory obligations with regard to housing policy – but the emotions the Liberals had aroused were not easily containable. A vote for the BNP was, literally, a protest vote.

There can be no doubt that racism is hindering integration. Every year around 130,000 incidents of racial harassment or abuse are reported countrywide – one every four minutes (and these are Home Office figures, rather than the still larger numbers put out by many black groups) – and the Commission for Racial Equality documents thousands more cases of discrimination. The press abounds with headlines such as 'Black Crime – The Alarming Figures' (*Daily Telegraph*) and 'Black Crime Shock' (*Sun*). But for every attack on a white person, there are thirty-six on Afro-Caribbeans and fifty on Asians.[19] Blacks are more likely to be victims of both household and personal offences – 13 per cent of blacks have been burgled, twice the figure for whites.[20]

Property offences are most common, with 40 per cent of young black and white offenders, compared with 12 per cent of Bangladeshis; 25 per cent of young blacks have committed a violent crime, compared with 20 per cent of Pakistanis and whites, and 10 per cent of Bangladeshis. And Pakistani and white men are more likely to have committed an act of vandalism than those from any other group.[21]

Despite these figures, and the less alarming truth they reveal, blacks are three times more likely than whites to be stopped by the police in London. National figures show that ethnic minorities are five times more likely to be stopped and searched than whites: over 25 per cent of all those stopped in 1993–4 belonged to ethnic minorities, who comprise less than 6 per cent of the population.[22]

What of racial segregation? The concentration of ethnic minorities in urban neighbourhoods, particularly in London, is not in itself surprising. Immigrant groups have almost invariably lived together in poorer neighbourhoods on arrival – and then often moved *en bloc* as they ascend the social scale. Just as Jews inhabited the East End, so Cypriot immigrants congregated in Camden in the 1950s; they and their children have decamped to Palmers Green and suburban Enfield – where, until his defeat, they were constituents of Michael Portillo, the son of a Spanish civil war *émigré*.

There is nothing new about discrimination and harassment. Anti-Irish prejudice and anti-Semitism go back centuries, the former more pronounced in recent times than the latter. Cromwell admitted the Jews in 1654 but slaughtered the Irish at Wexford and Drogheda. 'No dogs, no Irish, no blacks, no coloureds' ran the adverts, in that order, until the 1960s. Yet while such streaks run deep, they should not be exaggerated. The essential issue in Britain is not *whether*, but *how*, today's minorities are integrating, beyond the closed élite.

It is increasingly meaningless in this context to talk about ethnic minorities as a coherent group. Rather, a hierarchy of social and economic achievement is emerging, strongly related to the class divisions which mark British society at large.

More than half of the UK's ethnic minority population is from the South Asian subcontinent – India, Pakistan and Bangladesh. A quarter are black, with the remainder predominantly of mixed race or Chinese. Within the two largest groups, Indians make up over half of the South Asians, while blacks from the Caribbean outnumber those from Africa by just over two to one.

Take the controversial issue of single parenting. One in five black households consists of a lone parent with dependent children – more than four times the proportion for Indian and white households. Half of all black children live in single mother families, compared with fewer than a tenth of South Asian children and a sixth of whites.[23]

Then there is education, the engine of social mobility. Black Africans are the most highly educated of all minority groups, a quarter boasting higher education qualifications. Asians are also in the vanguard. In 1994 87 per cent of Asians aged sixteen and 66 per cent of eighteen-year-olds were in full-time education, compared with 72 per cent and 40 per cent respectively of those age groups nationally. By contrast, black Caribbeans as a group are performing significantly worse in schools than the white average – but not so much worse than the white average in the inner-city neighbour-hoods where they are concentrated, a critical distinction. In 1993 blacks were the least successful ethnic minority, with only 21 per cent gaining five or more GCSEs. Indians, however, had a similar level of success to whites, with 45 per cent passing five or more.

A tour of London's schools makes this point starkly. On the one hand, there are inner London's poor performing local authority schools, heavily populated with the Caribbean and white working-class residents of municipal council estates which account for up to half the total housing in some boroughs. On the other, there is the academically powerful independent school sector, far larger in London than nationwide, dominated by the white professional classes and, increasingly, the upwardly mobile Asian community. The assisted places scheme, which subsidizes the private school fees of children from poor families, was a particular boon to Asian families. As the head teacher of one independent school put it: 'The assisted places scheme has become a kind of positive discrimination for Asians.'[24]

Although the governing élite remains virtually closed, Asians in particular are rapidly joining the managerial classes. It is already the case that a higher proportion of Indians than whites are in professional jobs. They are also more likely to invest in the stock market and have higher rates of both home and car ownership. The ennoblement in the summer of 1996 by Labour of Swraj Paul, founder of the steel company Caparo, and now one of the country's richest men, created the first significant recruit from the new Asian élite into the national political élite. By contrast, blacks and Bangladeshis, as groups, are behind Britain's whites on both scores.

As Sir Herman Ouseley, chairman of the Commission for Racial Equality, notes, such diversity makes even the terminology of 'minorities' more problematic. Some Asians class themselves as black; many more do not, and 'feel that there are all sorts of issues associated with the concept of "blackness" that they don't want to be associated with'.[25]

But it is none the less still often meaningful to consider ethnic minorities as a whole, whatever the differences between groups. For instance, both men and women of working age from ethnic minorities are less likely to be economically active than whites. In absolute terms the gap is smallest for black Caribbeans and largest among Bangladeshis: 82 per cent of black Caribbean men and 70 per cent of women are economically active compared with 66 per cent of Bangladeshi men and a mere 20 per cent of women. The figures for whites are almost 90 per cent for men and over 70 per cent for women.[26]

The figures for economic inactivity are more startling: 60 per cent of young black men in London, aged between sixteen and twenty-four, are unemployed, compared with a no less worrying figure for all black age groups of 33 per cent.[27] These in turn compare with a figure for young whites of 14 per cent.[28] Twenty-seven per cent of Pakistani/Bangladeshis are unemployed – double the rate of Indians at 12 per cent. And all these stand in contrast to the white rate of 8 per cent.[29] It is figures like these that give rise to the view that young black men are 'a problem', rather than the asset that they could otherwise be.

Where next? Ram Gidoomal, a businessman who chairs the South Asian Development Partnership, argues persuasively that, at all levels, effective integration requires 'push' and 'pull' – a willingness within minority groups to become part of the main-stream (push), and a readiness of the establishment to welcome them in (pull).

Much depends on the strength of the 'pull' forces. The increasing openness of the private school sector is a telling indicator. So too may be initiatives such as 'Race for Opportunity', a new Business in the Community scheme backed by the likes of British Airways and Midland Bank to persuade companies it is in their own interest to work more closely with minorities. On the 'push' side, there is no better way of minorities advancing themselves than by following President Mandela's exhortation to the youth of Brixton: 'Stay in school.' But that, given the class-bound education system, is as much an obstacle as a means of advancement.

10. THE NATIONAL LOTTERY

All in a class cause

One cannot expect the restoration of the Royal Opera House or the construction of a new opera house in Cardiff to take priority over the legitimate demands of the health service, and that is why the lottery was created.

David Mellor

The National Lottery is the kind of institution the Church of England always wanted to be, but never succeeded in becoming. It is wildly popular. It requires personal participation in a simple ritual, complete with a weekly celebration on prime-time television and mid-week events for ardent believers. It unites its followers in shared language, norms and excitement, demanding small sacrifices in the hope of large rewards hereafter. It cultivates the better instincts, raising large sums for 'good causes'. Even the lottery logo – a hand pointing heavenwards with crossed fingers – could suitably adorn an altar. Unsurprisingly, at its conception, the bishops were its fiercest critics. 'Obscene', declared the Bishop of Wakefield as the first double rollover mesmerized the nation in New Year 1996. 'Morally flawed', his brother from St Albans told the House of Lords when the lottery legislation was before Parliament, advising his flock 'not to be seduced by the siren voices who say it is all for a good cause'.[1]

The seduction is now complete. A year after the 1994 launch, Camelot's turnover reached £4.4 billion – seven times the annual income of the Church of England and far in excess of the most optimistic projections. 'It has been the most successful launch of any lottery in the world,' concluded a consultants' report entitled *How Far Can It Go?*[2] 'A lot further' was the answer, as queues for lottery tickets and scratch cards extended through supermarkets and newsagents, new games were devised, and a new genre of TV programmes – starting with *Raising the Roof* – sprouted around the jackpot theme.

In retrospect, the least surprising revelation of the lottery was that most people enjoy a flutter. In one guise or another, legal or illegal, gambling has flourished for centuries among the British. As early as 1851, £1 million changed hands on the Chester Cup, then the most important horse-racing handicap of the year. 'Betting is generally prevalent in the United Kingdom,' reported a parliamentary inquiry in 1902.[3] An estimated four-fifths of the working class gambled regularly before the First World War; and the regularity increased in the inter-war period, with the football pools attracting between 10 and 15 million regular punters by 1939. A leading social historian remarks that gambling has long been 'a recurrent but strictly controlled element in such disposable income as the working class had'.[4] The National Lottery has, in effect, spread the gambling habit across society as a whole, making betting an integral part of the lives of two-thirds of the population. For most of them it is also strictly controlled, with the average stake being about £2.30 in the weekly game.

A century ago Matthew Arnold divided the classes between the 'heirs of the Puritans' and the devotees of 'beer, gin, and fun'.[5] The lottery marks a decisive triumph of the fun-lovers over the puritans. With thirty million regular players, it is the most popular cross-class institution in contemporary Britain, vying only with the NHS in passionate commitment. Unlike racing, where the only thing the workers and aristocrats had in common was that they bet on the same horses, Camelot's players enjoy the same thrills, pleasures and rewards.

The success of the National Lottery therefore raises two intriguing questions. Are the classes gambling together for the first time in British history? And is the lottery a cultural manifestation of a new, classless society? Seductive at first sight, such impressions soon dissolve on investigation. Scratch the surface – no pun intended – and the lottery turns out to be a brilliant commentary on British society in the mid-1990s. All the elements are there. The passion for easy wealth and undemanding pleasure. Vicarious engagement in a national sport, mobilizing every dimension of the electronic media. Shiny, modern presentation, buttressed by classless rhetoric. Vociferous insistence by those in charge that all sections of society participate and benefit equally, packaged in soundbites ('it's all in a good cause', 'a harmless flutter', 'punters are enjoying themselves for the price of a pint of bitter a week') which disguise the reality. And behind it all the Super Class and the Great and the Good, those who set the lottery up in the first place, who pack the quangos which distribute its proceeds, and who steer the enterprise for the benefit of themselves and their cultural pastimes. Last but not least comes the tabloid press, reflecting and exacerbating the mood of the 'millions of proles for whom the lottery', in the graphic vision of George Orwell's *Nineteen Eighty-Four*, 'was the principal, if not the only, reason for remaining alive. It was their delight, their folly, their anodyne, their intellectual stimulant.'

Peers to proles: we will encounter them all in the story of the National Lottery. To tell it we must start by going back – back indeed to the French Revolution, where in a sense it all began.

The Rothschild lottery

In 1789, the year of the Estates General and the storming of the Bastille, Nathan Meyer de Rothschild, scion of the great banking dynasty, came from France to found the London branch of the family firm. As events in Paris moved on from domestic upheaval to a twenty-three-year European war, Nathan's services to the British government came into ever more lucrative demand. A mega fortune made, his offspring established themselves at the heart of the English aristocracy. One son entered the House of Commons (the first Jew to do so without converting), while the family took virtual possession of the Vale of Aylesbury in Buckinghamshire, buying or building the great houses – palaces on the scale and model of the grandest Loire *châteaux* – of

Mentmore, Aston Clinton, Halton, Tring and Waddesdon. The only daughter of the Mentmore Rothschild married one of Queen Victoria's prime ministers, Lord Rosebery, while a grandson of Nathan Meyer was elevated to the House of Lords in 1885 as Lord Rothschild of Tring. Tring House is now a ballet school, but the Rothschild family continues to flourish. Two of its peers and one of its palaces – Mentmore – played a critical part in the evolution of the National Lottery.

The eldest grand-nephew of the first Lord Rothschild was Victor Rothschild, who succeeded to the title in 1937 and lived an extraordinarily mercurial life until the age of seventy-nine in 1990. Cambridge friend of Anthony Blunt, wartime member of MI5, distinguished scientist, and founder-director of Edward Heath's 'think tank' in 1971, Victor was the very epitome of the Establishment. One of his last acts of public service was to chair a royal commission on gambling in the late 1970s. (His very last act was to help design the poll tax for Margaret Thatcher.) A key recommendation of the Rothschild Commission was 'a national lottery for good causes'.[6] This was Rothschild's personal initiative – 'the lottery was very much Victor's baby', recalls a fellow commissioner.[7] Rothschild's lottery was to have three principal characteristics. It was to be a national monopoly, able to offer unlimited prize money in order to maximize revenue. The non-prize proceeds were to go to the arts, sport and 'other deserving causes', which between them were to receive more than one-third of the total proceeds. And it was to operate autonomously of the government once set up, its revenues ring-fenced from the Treasury.

In all three respects – his selection of beneficiaries, and his insistence that a lottery should be a national monopoly, insulated from the Treasury – Rothschild invented today's National Lottery. He even invented the term 'good causes' for his élite beneficiaries, a label which stuck thereafter. The idea of a national lottery was not novel in itself, of course; but no historical or overseas lottery had Rothschild's ends in view. The two proposals for a national lottery debated by the House of Commons in the decade before the Rothschild Commission envisaged the non-prize proceeds going, respectively, to the Treasury and to medical research (the latter cause popular among overseas lotteries). Rothschild was anxious to scotch both suggestions. In a passage of his report franker than any subsequent justification offered for ring-fencing lottery revenue for the arts and culture, Rothschild declared:

> In practice, a government of any party, subject to day to day public and political pressures, finds it impossible to devote more than meagre resources to good causes of the kind which are desirable rather than essential . . . There is a crucial need in our society for a source of substantial funds to provide support of a kind with which any government experiences great difficulty. The objective should not be to replace the function of central government but rather to fill the gap created by the inevitable disappearance, in a society where the accumulation of private wealth has become much more difficult, of private support of worthy causes on a large scale. The proceeds of a national lottery should not only be allocated outside the normal government machinery: they should be immune, subject to annual scrutiny by Parliament, from government influence.[8]

It is important to grasp Rothschild's argument, for it underpins the whole philosophy of the National Lottery as established by the Major government. It amounts to this. Nowadays there are too few super-rich around to patronize high art and culture. Nor can a government, elected to do the bidding of ordinary voters, be expected to provide much money for such purposes within the annual budgetary scramble for public spending. Yet these *are* immensely vital and worthwhile activities – 'good causes' – and they can only flourish if the government heavily subsidizes them in some way or other. What better way of doing so than for the government to license a national lottery, enticing the punters through the prizes which such a lottery alone can offer (because it is a monopoly), and then devoting a large slice of the proceeds, by prior agreement, to the 'good causes'? To make doubly sure that the elected government does not siphon off the cash for, say, the National Health Service, ministers should sign a self-denying ordinance to ensure that, in Rothschild's words, lottery revenue 'escapes or by-passes the normal government decision making procedures for resource allocation'.[9]

In other words, the gambling public could have its one-in-a-million chance of riches beyond dreams, but only in return for the Great and the Good directing the whole operation. His point about the shortage of modern patrons with sufficient wealth to sustain high culture was a fair argument in the high-tax and low-salary 1970s; in the 1990s, however, after the rise of the Super Class, it is based on a false premise. Moreover, the idea that the punters themselves might have a say over the distribution of lottery money is not even considered – although in characteristic patrician fashion it was appreciated that a safety-valve might be necessary to make the process more acceptable, hence the deliberately vague nature of Rothschild's 'other deserving causes' which were to be eligible for grants. The question of the eligibility of football under the sports category was also left open. In these respects, too, the Rothschild report was a blueprint for the eventual National Lottery.

The Rothschild Commission reported in the summer of 1978. With the Callaghan government in its death throes, there was no question of legislation before the Tories came to power. Then the idea fell foul of Margaret Thatcher's puritan streak. Thatcher briefly considered a lottery as a way of funding the NHS (an idea starkly at odds with Rothschild's), but, she recalls, 'I did not like a national health lottery because I did not think that the government should encourage more gambling, let alone link it to people's health.'[10] The lottery had to wait for John Major's arrival in 1990.

Yet the 1980s was not a fallow period for the evolution of the Rothschild lottery. The decade saw advances for his proposed 'good causes', which were to have a significant bearing on the lottery when its time came. To understand this we must return briefly to the Vale of Aylesbury and its Rothschild palaces.

When Hannah de Rothschild married Lord Rosebery in 1878 she was the greatest heiress of her age, bringing to the future prime minister – a rich but not super-rich Scottish earl – the great house of Mentmore. Inspired by Joseph Paxton, the architect of Crystal Palace, with breathtaking views over the Chilterns, Mentmore was a palace-museum crammed with fabulous French collections painstakingly acquired by Baron Meyer de Rothschild. So it remained until the death, in 1976, of the sixth Earl of Rosebery, the former prime minister's son. Taxation beckoned. Immured in fiscal crisis, the Labour government refused to buy the house and contents for the £2 million asked by the new Lord Rosebery, so the contents were sold (mostly abroad) for £6.5 million, amid a deafening outcry from the heritage industry and the media. Mentmore became the heritage scandal of the century. The house itself, denuded of its contents, is now headquarters of the Maharishi University, the spiritual home of the Natural Law Party, which campaigns for an end to crime, illness and poverty by raising the nation's transcendental consciousness through yogic flying.

Mentmore's fate was a significant influence on the Rothschild Commission, deliberating on its 'national lottery for good causes' at the very time of the break-up. It is unclear how concerned Rothschild was about Mentmore itself,[11] but its fate – particularly the government's refusal to spend a mere £2 million to protect the national heritage – highlighted and typified the 'problem' of how to safeguard the arts and heritage in an age devoid of generous patrons, public or private. Mentmore had another highly significant repercussion: the Thatcher government's decision in 1980 to establish the National Heritage Memorial Fund, with a small budget (in heritage terms) for buying important artistic works for the nation, and a membership of the Great and the Good committed to the task. By the time the lottery was established in 1992, the Memorial Fund was the obvious vehicle through which to channel its heritage funding. For this enhanced role the fund acquired a new chairman in 1992: none other than Jacob Rothschild, son of Victor, who had recently succeeded to his father's peerage and £90 million fortune. Jacob had every conceivable qualification for the job: Eton; a first in history from Christ Church, Oxford; a highly successful City career on the back of the family businesses; chairmanship of the Board of Trustees of the National Gallery, to which he himself is a generous benefactor. To cap it all, along with the £90 million he inherited an interest in Waddesdon, the only one of the great Rothschild houses to survive with its contents intact; since 1990, in association with the National Trust, he has restored the house to its original splendour at huge personal expense.

Jacob came on the scene just as his small quango was about to be transformed by the National Lottery into one of the richest patrons in the world. For 1992 also saw the publication of the Major government's White Paper, *A National Lottery Raising Money for Good Causes*, proposing the Rothschild 'National Lottery for Good Causes'. The idea had been gathering pace since John Major took office in November 1990. Sensing the lottery's populist potential, and sharing none of Margaret Thatcher's Nonconformist scruples, Major and Kenneth Baker, his first Home Secretary, wanted a scheme worked up for the 1992 election. This was easily done, since Baker simply adopted the Rothschild proposals, although with one addition to the 'good causes' – charities, to benefit alongside the arts, heritage and sport. Without charities it was felt that the beneficiaries would appear too élitist – a theme to which we shall return. There was the inevitable battle with the Treasury, which first resisted the lottery and then sought to cream off as much of the proceeds as possible.[12] But the 'good causes' were promised a remarkable 28 per cent of the total proceeds – the lion's share of the income not distributed to winners.

The lottery received star billing in the 1992 Tory manifesto. 'We believe a well-run, carefully controlled form of National Lottery would be popular, while raising money for many good causes, ' it declared.[13] As for the identity of the 'good causes', the manifesto mentioned 'good causes in the artistic, sporting, heritage and charitable fields'. It also specified a fifth object: the Millennium Fund, an initiative to sponsor a festival and prestige projects to usher in the new century. But no idea of the distribution between the five was given; nor was it clear what the criterion would be for allocating cash within these fields. All the manifesto said on these subjects was the supremely bland: 'We believe that the funds generated by a national lottery should be used to enhance the life of our nation.'

The election won, the newly formed Department of National Heritage, with the ebullient opera, classical music and sports-loving David Mellor as its first ministerial head, set to work framing legislation for the lottery. The hapless Mellor, besieged by the media over the break-up of his marriage and various amorous liaisons, lasted only five months in office. Yet he survived long enough to take two key decisions which, remarkably, went almost unchallenged through all the subsequent parliamentary discussions. He defined five 'good causes' – the arts, national heritage, the Millennium Fund, sport and charities – and stipulated that they should receive *equal* shares of the lottery revenue available for good causes. Given his objectives, this was a master-stroke: it ensured that the arts and culture would get first call on about two-thirds of the 'good causes' funding, since three of the five (arts, heritage and the millennium) were geared largely to them. Yet by including sport and charities, particularly charities, it broadened the field of those gaining *something* to embrace every conceivable worthy activity supported by the public. Needless to say, when the lottery was launched charities were invariably listed first among the 'good causes' to benefit; and when the lottery was in operation most of the punters thought they received *most* of the non-prize money.

Then there was the mechanism proposed for distributing the 'good causes' cash once raised. For arts and the national heritage, the money was simply handed over to existing quangos of the

Great and the Good to spend as they saw fit. So heritage lottery funding went to Lord Rothschild's National Heritage Memorial Fund, while arts funding was given to the Arts Council chaired by Lord Gowrie – a former arts minister and chairman of Sotheby's.[14] The Millennium Fund was to be administered by another assemblage of the Great and the Good, chaired by the National Heritage Secretary himself. The sports and charities funding was also handed over to appointed quangos, although less grand in their membership.

Not given to dissembling, David Mellor never disguised his motives. When the National Lottery Bill was introduced by his successor, the urbane Peter Brooke, Mellor insisted that the project was only worthwhile if it produced a 'quantum leap' in funding for the arts, heritage and sport.[15] More revealing still was his speech in a Commons debate in October 1995, when criticism of the 'good causes' was mounting.[16] 'It was never part of the original thinking of the lottery that charities would be beneficiaries,' he told MPs. They had been included only to provide 'compensation for any losses' incurred through the diversion of charitable giving as a result of the lottery, and because it had been thought that 'nothing could be worse than debates in this place being disfigured by people saying that charities were going to lose out and so we could not have a national lottery'. In case he had been misunderstood, he added with characteristic frankness, recalling the French king Henri IV's decision to convert to Catholicism for the sake of his Crown: 'Paris was worth a mass and the mass was bringing in the charities.' For, as he put it, the lottery had to carry 'credibility with the public, most of whom would not put money into the collecting tins of the organizations that have benefited'. As to the prime object of the exercise: 'In public spending, one cannot expect the restoration of the Royal Opera House or the construction of a new opera house in Cardiff to take priority over the legitimate demands of the health service, and that is why the lottery was created.' (Recall in passing that the one object for which Lady Thatcher *had* considered a lottery was the NHS.) Mellor concluded his speech with this plea: 'I have only one concern and it is that the national lottery should survive for long enough, without the money being taken for all manner of other things, to make a fundamental difference to the sporting and artistic fabric of the nation.'

It is almost time to turn from the 'good causes' to the punters who were expected to finance them. But before joining Camelot, Anthea Turner and the lottery millionaires, there remains the question: how did the 'good causes' get through Parliament unscathed, and why was there virtually no public debate about them prior to the launch of the National Lottery?

The answer is that parliamentary debate on the lottery legislation was dominated by wholly different issues. In the first place, the principle of a lottery was hotly contested, particularly by the bishops in the Lords and by some Christian members of both Houses. For Labour MPs the impact of the lottery on the pools industry was a major bone of contention. There was also controversy about whether or not the lottery should be run by a private company for profit, spilling into the tabloids when Richard Branson put together a not-for-profit consortium to bid for the franchise, which it lost to Camelot, a consortium led by British Aerospace. This issue rumbled on and on: when the lottery became a rip-roaring success, Branson and the Labour party played hard on the national loathing of 'fat cats', calling for the franchise to be taken away from Camelot.

As for the 'good causes', the little attention paid to them was carefully steered by the government on to those likely to be most popular. Peter Brooke set the tone in his speech introducing the National Lottery Bill, citing Chris Eubank 'who by making Moss Side his training base, hopes to lead by example and persuade the young people there that the opportunity to participate in sport offers an alternative to the world of drugs and crime . . . That is precisely the sort of benefit that the lottery is intended to bring to the nation.'[17] Yet even references of this kind were incidental. In truth the 'good causes' attracted little parliamentary controversy because most MPs and peers thoroughly supported the ends in view. The arts and heritage lobbies were not short of friends in either House, or on either side of either House. The Commons National Heritage Committee was chaired by the senior Labour backbencher Gerald Kaufman, strong supporter of the 'good causes'; the Labour leader nominated a member of the Millennium Commission; the chairman of the governors of the Royal Opera House was Baroness Blackstone, a Labour frontbencher in the Lords and Master of Birkbeck College, London; and so the list went on. Only after grants to the 'good causes' became the target of tabloid hostility, particularly after the £13 million paid by Lord Rothschild's quango for the Churchill papers, did the issue surface in the Commons. The National Lottery Bill passed the Commons with only thirty-nine votes against.

Indeed, insofar as the 'good causes' featured much in parliamentary debates, it was on the perverse argument that they might actually *lose* from the lottery. Much hot air was – and still is – expended on the subject of 'additionality': that is, whether lottery cash for the arts, heritage and sport would be treated as additional to existing public spending, or as a replacement for it. There was particular concern that the budgets for the Arts Council and the National Heritage Memorial Fund should not be cut because of the lottery. Astonishingly, in all the discussion about additionality, even after the lottery's success was apparent, the relevant figures were almost never mentioned. Lord Rothschild's heritage fund had a Treasury grant of £9 million in 1995–6, a year in which it received about £280 million from the lottery. The Arts Council for England gained a similar sum, far exceeding its Treasury grant of £190 million. In both cases the lottery would have constituted an enormous boon had direct public subsidies been abolished in one fell swoop. The Millennium Fund, moreover, was additional to no prior Treasury grant. Taking arts, heritage and culture together, the lottery boosted public spending from about £200 million to more than £1 billion a year.

Indeed, the arts industry became a victim of its own lottery success. The original lottery rules stipulated that grants could be used only for capital, not for revenue spending. By late 1995 this was already a manifest absurdity. Hundreds of millions were available to build and refurbish theatres, opera houses and concert halls; yet nothing more could be spent on the performances, orchestras or theatre companies for whom they were provided. When the Treasury started using the lottery to cut back marginally on its own direct subsidies – the National Heritage Memorial Fund lost £0.8 million in 1996–7 – the absurdity appeared greater still. Inevitably the rules were progressively relaxed, and with each change the Rothschild lottery came to be more like a straightforward public subsidy for the arts and heritage industries. Which, of course, was the original intention.

Now to the punters.

A classless flutter?

The National Lottery was launched to loud fanfares on 14 November 1994. It was an instant, astounding success. Everyone underestimated its likely popularity. The Department of National Heritage's working assumption had been of annual revenue in the £1.5 to £2.5 billion range after two or three years. By the end of its first year lottery sales had topped £4.3 billion. John Major's populist instincts were sound: from the moment the first lottery millionaire was created on 26 November 1994, the nation was transfixed by the weekly draw each Saturday evening. Nearly thirty million people – two-thirds of the adult population – were soon regular players in the weekly game. Thanks to the lottery, gambling was soon the fastest area of growth in consumer spending, with gambling expenditure shooting up from £3.7 billion in 1994 to £5.3 billion the following year – an increase from 0.9 to 1.2 per cent of all household spending. The proportion of adults gambling rose from two-thirds in 1991 to 91 per cent in 1995.[18]

So, is everyone gambling together in the classless society? Prior to the launch, ministers were insistent that they would be, not least to avoid the obvious charges of handing money from the poor to the rich. Presenting the National Lottery to the Commons, Peter Brooke claimed that 'in countries with lotteries, the profile of those who play almost exactly matches the profile of the population overall'.[19] After the launch, Camelot was insistent that this was the case in Britain too. 'All sections of society are playing in more or less equal numbers,' the company insisted after the lottery had been going for nine months. 'There isn't one socio-economic group playing at the expense of any other.'[20]

These statements are a travesty of the truth. It is true that the lottery is the first authentically national, cross-class gambling institution in modern Britain. But that is radically different to saying that all classes are playing in 'more or less equal numbers' with one group not playing 'at the expense of any other'. Virtually all the data on lottery players reveals that, in terms of numbers gambling and amounts gambled, the lottery depends dispro-portionately on the poorer social classes.

Lottery fever is least pronounced among professionals. Camelot data published in December 1995 showed the proportion of the AB professional and managerial class taking part to be far lower than for other social groups; and those ABs who played spent a far smaller proportion of their income. The distinction was starker still if household income was used as the yardstick. The average weekly bet among players from households with income of between £6,500 and £15,599 a year was £2.49 – 14p *more* than the average bet of those from households with more than £15,600.

Research by National Opinion Polls in late 1995 found these trends to be still more pronounced. Nearly two-thirds of those surveyed said they had bought a ticket within the previous seven days. Divided into social classes, skilled manual workers (C2s) were most likely to have done so (73 per cent), while managers and professionals (classes A and B) were way down at 46 and 50 per cent respectively. As to amounts bet, the C2s and Ds both spent more on average than As and Bs (£3.08 and £2.59 against £2.29 and £2.52), with the lowest social class, E, spending more than the As. Adjust these figures for income, and the regressive impact of the lottery is fully apparent, with the Es betting several times as much of their weekly income as the As. Other NOP findings reinforce this picture. Council tenants bet a third as much again per week as owner-occupiers; families without a car only 15p less a week than those with two cars; those with no telephone – representing the bottom tenth or so of the income range – only 15p less than those with a phone. Government figures for the first quarter of 1996, in the Family Expenditure Survey, give a similar picture: the bottom third of households, by income, were found to be devoting around 1 per cent of their weekly spending to the lottery, while the top third were spending less than 0.7 per cent.[21]

What of the official reaction to this research? Commissioned as it was by Oflot, the government's lottery regulator, the NOP study could not be entirely dismissed by ministers. So they did the next best thing: they declared it interim, ignored most of the findings, and put a favourable gloss on a few selected statistics. Thus in a statement 'commenting' on the NOP research when it was published in February 1996, Virginia Bottomley, the then National Heritage Secretary, stated:

> Enthusiasm for the lottery crosses every social and economic group. Quite rightly, the director general of Oflot will con- tinue to monitor and refine his research. But all the evidence indicates that the lottery is being treated as an amusing and harmless entertainment by the overwhelming majority of people. Most importantly, the Good Causes Fund continues to invest ever greater sums in communities throughout the United Kingdom.[22]

Yet more statistics and 'refined' research were hardly necessary: a few minutes looking at the lottery queues in Tescos, Safeways and Kwik Saves would have sufficed. Or reading the lottery coverage in the daily press. While the broadsheets were mostly concerned with which of the 'good causes' was getting what, the tabloids embraced the plight of the punters on tenterhooks for each weekly draw, and the heavenly bliss of the jackpot winners. Within weeks of its launch, the lottery was second only to the royal family in the tabloids' staple diet. And not always second: in rollover weeks, with jackpots in tens of millions, the coverage was on a par with the royal separation. Indeed, the lottery and the royal family were often combined for extra effect. When the first double rollover reached its climax in January 1996, the *Sun* blazed with 'RICHER THAN ER' alongside a picture of the Queen as part of a three-page spread. 'Tonight's £42 million winner will be holding loads more folding than the Queen,' the *Sun* told its readers, quoting 'wealth watchdog Dr Philip Beresford' saying: 'It's astonishing but in terms of liquidity the lottery winner will be far, far richer than the Queen.'[23] The accompanying '*Sun* says' column wished its readers the best of luck. 'We'd love a *Sun* reader to scoop the lottery jackpot. But don't worry if you don't win. Money can't guarantee happiness. ONLY BUYING THE *SUN* EACH DAY CAN DO THAT.' Lest any readers felt left out of the national excitement, the *Sun* set up 40,000 lottery syndicates, giving every reader free membership through a card in the daily paper on the day of the £42 million draw.

What purported to enrage the tabloids more than anything was the thought that the jackpot might actually be scooped by . . . a foreigner. Tabloid front pages in the week before the first double rollover were given over to scare stories that foreign lottery-busters were preparing to swoop, cornering all available lottery tickets and applying their sophisticated computer brains to all eventualities. Questions were asked in the House of Commons. Camelot issued daily statements of reassurance that no swoop was in evidence. But the tabloids remained on red alert. When a man bearing a Chinese name claimed a third share of the £42 million, the *Sun* proclaimed the news on its front page under the banner headline: 'NATIONAL WOKKERY'. Elaborating on 'Chinaman Mr Choy's £14 million Lotto takeaway', the paper's 'excrusive' noted: 'He collected his money this week and immediately banked it before jetting out of Britain.'[24]

As for the more sober middle classes, they may be the least committed lottery players, but they are none the less gambling as never before. The standard dinner party line is that lottery tickets are bought 'for the children, of course', who are glued to the box with everyone else for the prime-time draw on Saturday evenings. Why is middle-class puritanism so little in evidence? Partly because of the social and legal rehabilitation of gambling, alongside the eroding influence of the churches and official morality. But it may also be a follow-on from twenty years of middle-class gambling on the property market and – to a lesser extent – the stock market. And for the salaried classes as for the rest, escapism is at a premium. A report on consumer lifestyles by Mintel, the market intelligence group, yoked this together with the state of the economy, arguing that the lottery 'reflects a need for increased excitement and the hope of winning a fortune as a release from current financial constraints and hardship imposed by a low inflation economy and high unemployment'.[25]

What of the popular view of the 'good causes'? Kenneth Baker's 1992 White Paper said lottery advertising should be permissible not just to tell people how to play, but also 'to provide information about the good causes which will benefit from the proceeds'.[26] In the event, Camelot did not see the need to broadcast too much information about the 'good causes': its media spokespeople – invariably bearing impeccable cut-glass accents – simply stated at every opportunity that lots of money was going to good causes, particularly charities. Yet even the 'good causes' were secondary to the central message – 'IT COULD BE YOU' – which dominated Camelot's advertising. Unsurprisingly, most people never realized quite where the 28p in their lottery pound earmarked for 'good causes' was going. Mostly they thought it was going to charity. A mid-1995 survey by the Charities Aid Foundation found that punters volunteered a figure of 20p as the average amount of each lottery pound going to charity, when the real figure was 5.6p.

David Mellor's Paris was well worth its mass . . .

All in a good cause

As the *Sun* and Anthea Turner urged their fans to ever higher pitches of excitement, Lord (Jacob) Rothschild and his fellow guardians of the 'good causes' could hardly believe their good fortune. Victor Rothschild's commission had projected annual funding for the 'good causes' of £45 million in the fifth year of the lottery: the real thing yielded £1.6 billion in the first sixteen months, which even allowing for inflation in the interim was the difference between the icing on the cake and the cake itself. Even the charities, which had been complaining loudly that they would be losers, had to change their tune to saying that *some* charities would be worse off. For the arts and heritage quangos designated as repositories of upwards of £5 million a week, there could be no pretence that Camelot was anything but the Holy Grail.

The challenge facing the heritage and arts quangos was to know who to give it all to. In this they were hindered by the exclusivity of their membership, itself a reflection of the choice of the 'good causes' in the first place. It was no accident that the quango putting its foot in it most spectacularly was Lord Rothschild's National Heritage Memorial Fund. Its membership of fourteen, comprising two peers, five knights or dames, a professor and a naval commander, was not well suited for gauging the public mood. Its first grant was £13 million to the family of Sir Winston Churchill for the papers of the statesman. What they considered to be a cornerstone of the national heritage looked to the ordinary punter like a large hand-out to Britain's top nobs – not helped by the fact that the best known member of the family, the Marquess of Blandford, heir to the Churchills' stately home of Blenheim Palace, was a drug addict in and out of the courts (and the tabloids) for his addiction. Sir Winston's son was a sitting Tory MP of portly disposition, which did not help either. 'It was a public relations disaster, just as we thought we had done what the public would want as a first gesture,' said one of Rothschild's colleagues.[27]

Stunned by the hostile reaction, Rothschild and his colleagues reviewed their grant-awarding policy. They commissioned research on popular attitudes to heritage, and determined to find a few popular causes to intersperse with grants to the wealthy for their historic artefacts. This led them to adopt programmes of support for Britain's much neglected city parks, among other causes. It also led to one or two dramatic artistic gestures to the provinces – notably a £64 million project for the building of a futuristic Lowry centre in Salford, Greater Manchester, to house the city's L. S. Lowry collection in an enormous dockside complex including a virtual reality centre. Even to some art critics this appeared an excessive response to Salford's requirement, which was for a gallery large enough to hang the city's collection of 500 Lowries. Lord Rothschild's staff also worked up a few diverting, if spurious, statistics for him to throw at his critics, such as that the National Heritage Memorial Fund's annual lottery income would run the civil service for three days, would pay for 942 yards of the Limehouse link in East London, and that more people visited art galleries each year than attended football matches. All of which just about quietened the tabloids and nervous MPs. Anyway, even the lottery could consume only so much media attention, and far more of it was lavished on the doings of the winners, the riches of Camelot itself, not to mention the peccadilloes of the non-arts bodies, such as the decision of the charities quango to fund a prostitute outreach group.

So Lord Rothschild and colleagues were able to get on with the serious business of saving historic houses and stocking up the national art collections with treasures on the art market. Inevitably this meant giving millions more to wealthy families. 'We could hardly do otherwise,' said the same quango member who be-moaned the Churchill decision. 'Picassos, Dalis and Magrittes do tend to belong to rich people.' Indeed so: once national heritage had been designated a 'good cause', and its cultivation given to a committee chaired by Lord Rothschild, the money was bound to be spent largely thus. The fund's appointed advisers included Dame Jennifer Jenkins and Sir Angus Stirling, both former chair-men of the National Trust. And in a neat coincidence completing the Rothschild story, Georgina Naylor, the salaried director of the National Heritage Memorial Fund appointed by Lord Rothschild and his colleagues shortly after the lottery's launch, was a trained art historian who told an interviewer that the seminal event in her life was picking up a newspaper in 1977 as an eighteen-year-old school girl and reading about the Mentmore sale. 'The teenager decided that she would see to it that such a catastrophe never happened again,' reported the interviewer.[28] And never was the climate so propitious for the task.

The other two cultural 'good causes' quangos – the Arts Council and the Millennium Fund – behaved similarly. One of the Arts Council's first grants was £55 million to the Royal Opera House. This produced the inevitable uproar, and was quickly followed by a raft of small grants to the provincial arts. Something of a monthly ritual developed, whereby one multi-million award to a prime London institution would be shrouded in a mass of smaller provincial awards. The Millennium Commission broke rank and made a few very large awards outside the London cultural world, notably a grant of £42 million for a national cycle network and £40 million for Portsmouth Marina. But even those grants – and which social classes make most use of marinas and cycle tracks? – were outclassed by a £50 million award to the Tate Gallery for its new Gallery of Modern Art at Bankside on the edge of the City of London and next door to the offices of the *Financial Times*.

Inevitably, after a year or so of grants awarded on this pattern, a few *causes célèbres* emerged. Two in particular. Was Cardiff to get a new opera house, built to a remarkable avant-garde design; or was Cardiff Arms Park, the rugby stadium, to be rebuilt? And was the Millennium Exhibition, the huge national extravaganza to herald the new century, to be located in Greenwich or in Birmingham? We need not detain ourselves with accounts of the protracted public battles which occurred in both cases: the outcomes were classic judgements by the Great and the Good charged with the decisions. Cardiff won its rugby stadium but lost its opera house, atoning for the largesse accorded Covent Garden without disturbing the recreation of the London-based Super Class; but Greenwich won the far more important Millennium Exhibition, even though Birmingham's bid was universally regarded as technically and financially superior. Birmingham could only be rejected after several deferrals of the decision while frantic efforts were made by Michael Heseltine and fellow ministers to beef up the Greenwich application. The killer line came from an adviser to National Heritage Secretary Virginia Bottomley: 'Come on, you don't *really* think we can celebrate the millennium in Solihull?'[29]

With the good causes, as with the punters, an elaborate exercise in official misinformation was launched to disguise the true state of affairs. Appearing before an inquiry into the state of the lottery by the Commons National Heritage Committee fifteen months after its launch,[30] Bottomley 'underlined the huge success of the National Lottery' with these figures. Two-thirds of lottery awards had been for less than £100,000; 92 per cent had been allocated to schemes outside London; and almost 80 per cent had gone to charitable or voluntary organizations. The committee, under Gerald Kaufman's chairmanship, took such statistics at their face value, and produced a report which gave the lottery a clean bill of health, derided 'kill joys' who attacked it, and concentrated instead on the subsidiary question, which Labour had taken up, of whether or not Camelot should be the operator.[31]

Yet a more creative use of statistics about the 'good causes' it would be hard to construct. Taking Virginia Bottomley's figures and statements one by one, as at February 1996:

'*Two-thirds of awards are for less than £100,000, reinforcing the community emphasis of lottery funds.*' In fact, barely one-seventh of the total sum of £1.07 billion distributed to 'good causes' by then went in grants of less than £100,000. Nearly half of the £1.07 billion was consumed by twenty-five grants of more than £5 million apiece.

'*Ninety-two per cent of awards are made to schemes outside London.*' Entirely spurious, for London had gained the lion's share of the 25 multi-million-pound awards just mentioned. London and the South East, with 21 per cent of the population, had received about

40 per cent of lottery awards by value, while the North East, North West and Midlands combined, with nearly one-third of the population, had gained just 15 per cent. Furthermore, 20 per cent of the £1.07 billion had gone to just seven London institutions: an opera house, a ballet company, two art galleries, two theatres and Kew Gardens. This 'reinforced the community emphasis of lottery funds' for those living in London and enjoying ballet, opera, modern art and rare plants.

'*Almost 80 per cent of awards are to charitable and voluntary organizations.*' This one took the biscuit. Almost every artistic, cultural and heritage organization in the land has charitable status. Yet charities as most people understand them – the Oxfam and RSPCA variety – were only one of five 'good causes', receiving little over 5p in each lottery pound.

Doubtless the Rothschild lottery, including its 'good causes', will be reformed in due course. By 1997 Labour had shifted to proposing that at least part of the proceeds be devoted to health and education projects.[32] But whatever its fate, its origins and evolution provide a fascinating commentary on Britain in the 1990s. Appropriately enough, when Lord Rothschild himself was interviewed in early 1996, he was unrepentant about the Great and the Good. 'I suppose I am one,' he remarked. 'But someone has got to do all this work: and we do it for nothing, you know.'[33]

Notes

Chapter 1: A Class Act

1. Brian Deer, 'Still struggling after all these years', *New Statesman*, 23 August 1996.
2. Mori survey, 22 August 1991.
3. Cited in Robin Marris, *How to Save the Underclass* (Macmillan, 1996), p. 8.
4. *Financial Times*, 29 December 1995.
5. *Sunday Times* interview, 1 September 1996.
6. Peter Saunders, *Unequal But Fair? A Study of Class Barriers in Britain* (Institute of Economic Affairs, 1996); Will Hutton, *The State We're In* (Jonathan Cape, 1995); Paul Johnson and Howard Reed, *Two Nations? The Inheritance of Poverty and Affluence* (Institute for Fiscal Studies, 1996); David J. Lee and Bryan S. Turner (eds), *Conflicts About Class* (Longman, 1996); Robert Frank and Philip Cook, *The Winner-Take-All Society* (Free Press, 1995, New York); Marris, *Underclass*.
7. Anthony Heath and Peter Clifford, 'Class Inequalities and educational reform in 20th century Britain', in Lee and Turner (eds), *Conflicts About Class*, p. 223.
8. Greg Hadfield and Mark Skipworth, *Class: Where do you stand?* (Bloomsbury, 1944), p. 8.
9. Ibid., p. 12.
10. *Financial Times*, 23 October 1996.
11. Andrew Neil, *Full Disclosure* (Macmillan, 1996), p. 421.
12. 'Class politics is below the salt', *The Times*, 14 October 1996.
13. *Daily Mail*, 18 April 1996.
14. *Observer*, 1 December 1996.
15. Richard Hoggart, *The Way We Live Now* (Pimlico, 1995), p. 6.
16. Cited in Harold Perkin, *The Third Revolution: Professional Elites in the Modern World* (Routledge, 1996), p. 63.

17. Social and Community Planning Research, *British Social Attitudes: 13th Report* (1996), pp. 9, 86–7.

18. Department of Social Security, *Households Below Average Income: Statistical Analysis 1979–1993/94* (1996); Nicholas Timmins, 'Crude arithmetic of inequality', *Financial Times*, 16 November 1996.

19. *Changing Places*, an analysis of the British Household Panel Study 1991–4 by the University of Essex (1996), demonstrates this conclusively.

20. Joseph Rowntree, *Income and Wealth*, vol. 1, p. 31.

21. *Social Attitudes, 13th Report*, pp. 83–4.

22. Timmins, 'Crude arithmetic'; Marris, *Underclass*, p. 48.

23. *Independent*, 18 April 1996.

24. See the 1991 Mori survey, in which respondents identified themselves as 'middle class' in the following proportions: AB 55 per cent; C1 41 per cent; C2 25 per cent; DE 16 per cent.

25. Nicholas Timmins, *The Five Giants: A Biography of the Welfare State* (Fontana, 1996), pp. 451–2.

26. *The Times*, 25 July 1996; press conference 20 November 1990.

27. *Prospect*, October 1996.

28. Joseph Schumpeter, *Social Classes in an Ethnically Homogeneous Environment* (Meridian Edition, 1955), p. 159.

29. Michael Young, *The Rise of the Meritocracy 1870–2033* (Penguin, 1958), pp. 15–16.

30. Marris, *Underclass*, pp. 141–4 and the references cited there.

31. Saunders, *Unequal But Fair?*.

32. Ibid., p. 35.

33. Ibid., Chapter 7.

34. Marris, *Underclass*, p. 146.

35. This is based on Andrew Adonis's observations when writing on education for the *Financial Times* (1991–3).

36. Private conversation between Andrew Adonis and an education minister in 1992.

37. From the 1993 guide, cited in Hadfield and Skipworth, *Class*, p. 60.

38. 1868 Schools Commission, cited in Brian Simon, *Education and the Social Order* (Lawrence & Wishart, 1991), p. 24.

39. Cited in Timmins, *Five Giants*, p. 92.

40. Heath and Clifford, 'Class Inequalities', pp. 212–16, 222.

41. Johnson and Reed, *Two Nations?*

42. David Willetts, *Blair's Gurus* (Centre for Policy Studies, 1996), p. 23.

43. *Financial Times*, 26 October 1996.

44. 1994 Mori survey of independent school parents.

45. Michael Beloff, 'Oxford selection: logic or lottery', *The Times*, 3 January 1997.

46. University of Oxford Careers Service, annual reports, and private information.

47. 1995 figures.

48. Private conversation.

49. A phrase coined by John Plender of the *Financial Times*.

50. Christopher Lasch, *The Revolt of the Elites and the Betrayal of Democracy* (W. W. Norton, New York, 1995), p. 41.

51. These remarks are based on many such conversations when Andrew Adonis wrote about education for the *Financial Times*.

52. Robert M. Blackburn and Jennifer Jarman, 'Changing Inequalities in Access to British Universities', *Oxford Review of Education* (1993), p. 200; Higher Education Statistics Agency for 1995 figures.

53. Figures (for England and Wales only) from Law Society: *Trends in the Solicitors' Profession: Annual Statistical Report 1995*.

54. Private information.

55. Anthony Seldon, in David Marquand and Anthony Seldon (eds), *The Ideas That Shaped Post-War Britain* (HarperCollins, 1996), p. 257.

56. *Hansard*, 25 October 1995, col. 1050.

57. Saunders, *Unequal But Fair?*, pp. 16–17.

58. Cited in 1995 Rowntree report, *Income and Wealth*, vol. II, pp. 8–9.

Chapter 2: Education

1. *Sunday Telegraph*, 2 December 1990.

2. Paul Johnson and Howard Reed, *Two Nations? The Inheritance of Poverty and Affluence* (Institute for Fiscal Studies, 1996).

3. See *We Should Know Better*, George Walden (Fourth Estate, 1996).

4. Attitudes towards independent schools, Mori survey, August 1996.

5. A point first made by Andrew Marr, *Independent*, 5 October 1995.

6. *The Times*, quoted in Jeremy Paxman, *Friends in High Places: Who Runs Britain?* (Michael Joseph, 1990), p. 158.

7. *Horizon*, March 1940.

8. Nicholas Timmins, *The Five Giants: A Biography of the Welfare State* (Fontana, 1996), p. 75.

9. Ibid., p. 76.

10. Michael Young, *The Rise of the Meritocracy, 1870–2033* (Penguin, 1958), p. 63.

11. Timmins, *Giants*, p. 86.

12. Ibid.

13. Young, *Meritocracy*, p. 63.

14. A. H. Halsey, in Brian Harrison (ed.), *The History of Oxford University*, (Oxford University Press, 1994), p. 53.

15. Private conversation.

16. Walden, *Know Better*, p. 36.

17. Figures supplied by Independent Schools Information Service.

18. Incorporated Association of Preparatory Schools survey, reported in *Sunday Times*, 18 February 1996.

19. Ibid.

20. Walden, *Know Better*, p. 40.

21. Private conversation.

22. *The Times*, 16 October 1989.

23. Quoted in Paxman, *Friends in High Places*, p. 171.

24. *Telegraph Magazine*, 17 February 1996.

25. *Guardian*, 10 October 1995.

26. *Independent*, 28 January 1989.

27. Chris Woodhead, 'Boys who learn to be losers', *The Times*, 6 February 1996.

28. Terence Kealey, 'High cost of a free education', *Sunday Times*, 10 March 1996.

29. Walden, *Know Better*, p. 31.

30. 'Good schools make for even better house prices', *Independent on Sunday*, 8 December 1996.

31. *Observer*, 3 March 1996.

32. Ibid.

33. Roy Hattersley, *Mail on Sunday*, 18 February 1996.

34. *Observer*, 3 March 1996.

35. Ibid.

36. Ibid.

37. Anne McElvoy, 'Blessed are the left-footers', *Spectator*, 30 March 1996.

38. Woodhead, 'Boys who learn'.

39. Halsey, *Oxford*, p. 585.

40. Ibid.

41. *Varsity*, 1 October 1993.
42. *Encounter*, 1955.
43. Halsey, *Oxford*, p. 577.
44. *Varsity*, 1 October 1993.
45. Report to Old Etonian Association, April 1992.
46. Halsey, *Oxford*, p. 599.
47. Ibid.
48. Ian McIntyre, *The Expense of Glory* (1993).
49. *Sunday Times*, 31 December 1995.
50. Robin Pedley, *The Comprehensive School* (Penguin, 1963).
51. *The Times*, leading article, 13 July 1961.
52. Tony Crosland, *The Future of Socialism* (Jonathan Cape, 1956).
53. *Educational Priority*, Department of Education and Science, vol. 1 (HMSO, 1972).
54. Adrian Wooldridge, *Meritocracy and the Classless Society* (Social Market Foundation, 1995).
55. *Sunday Telegraph*, 7 January 1996.
56. Ibid.

Chapter 3: The Super Class

1. John H. Goldthorpe *et al.*, *Social Mobility and Class Structure in Modern Britain* (Oxford University Press, 1980), pp. 60, 251.
2. See F. M. L. Thompson, *English Landed Society in the Nineteenth Century* (Longman, 1963); and David Cannadine, *The Decline and Fall of the British Aristocracy* (Yale University Press, 1990).
3. Harold Perkin, *The Rise of Professional Society: England since 1880* (Routledge, 1989), esp. pp. xii–xiv, 1–17.
4. A theme taken up in Perkin's later book *The Third Revolution: Professional Elites in the Modern World* (Routledge, 1996).
5. Robert Frank and Philip Cook, *The Winner-Take-All Society* (Free Press, New York, 1995).
6. *Daily Mirror*, 22 November 1994.
7. *Daily Mail*, 23 November 1994.
8. *Financial Times*, 1 December 1994.
9. *Today*, 16 December 1994.
10. *Financial Times*, 24 December 1994.
11. *Guardian*, 15 December 1994.
12. *Guardian*, 16 and 24 December 1994.

13. Sir Iain Vallance, 'Justice on executive pay', *Financial Times*, 25 January 1995.
14. Stephen Fay, *The Collapse of Barings* (Richard Cohen Books, 1996), p. 269.
15. *The Times*, 15 October 1996.
16. Nick Leeson's letter to the British media, 12 July 1995.
17. Fay, *Barings*, p. 33; *Daily Mirror*, 6 March 1995.
18. Fay, *Barings*, pp. 55, 218, 269.
19. This paragraph draws on Fay, *Barings*, pp. 17–20, 78, 137–8.
20. *Treasury guide to the UK privatisation programme* (1995), pp. 3–5.
21. Jasper Rose and John Ziman, *Camford Observed* (Collins, 1964), p. 240.
22. Brian Harrison, *The History of the University of Oxford: The Twentieth Century*, vol. VIII (Oxford University Press, 1994), pp. 72–3.
23. Report of the Royal Commission on Doctors' and Dentists' Remuneration (1960), Cmnd 939, p. 44.
24. Michael Zander, *The State of Knowledge about the English Legal Profession* (Macmillan, 1980), p. 37.
25. *The Times*, 19 August 1996.
26. Michael Yardley, *Sandhurst: A Documentary* (Harrap, 1987), p. 245.
27. *New Earnings Survey 1995*, Central Statistical Office. Figures from Table 8 of the streamlined analyses (figures for full-time males).
28. *Financial Times*, 25 February 1997.
29. Review Body on Doctors' and Dentists' Remuneration, 25th Report (1996), Cm 3090, para. 1.28, p. 12.
30. *Financial Times*, 1 February 1996.
31. *The Times*, 16 September 1996.
32. Ibid., 22 May 1996.
33. *Legal Business*, July/August 1996.
34. *Litigation*, July/August 1996.
35. *Board Earnings in FT-SE 100 Companies*, Monks Partnership, August 1996.
36. *United Kingdom Board Earnings*, Monks Partnership, October 1995.
37. *The Times*, 16 January 1997; *Daily Telegraph*, 18 January 1997.
38. The story is told in David Butler, Andrew Adonis and Tony Travers, *Failure in British Government: The Politics of the Poll Tax* (Oxford University Press, 1994).
39. Based on comparative boardroom pay figures for 1981 and 1995 kindly supplied by David Atkins of the Monks Partnership.

40. See, for instance, Sir Robin Butler, 'The New Public Management', Frank Stacey Memorial Lecture 1992, and Sir Peter Kemp, *Beyond Next Steps: A Civil Service for the 21st Century* (Social Market Foundation, 1993).

41. *Legal Business*, July/August 1996, p. 32; Cm 3090, para. 1.5, p. 7.

42. *Financial Times*, 25 January 1995.

43. Quoted in the *Independent*, 9 December 1995.

44. *University of Oxford Careers Service Report 1993–94*, pp. 15–22.

45. P. S. Atiyah, *Law and Modern Society* (Penguin, 2nd edn, 1995), p. 12; *Legal Business*, July/August 1996, p. 36.

46. P. A. Thomas, *Tomorrow's Lawyers* (Penguin, 1992), p. 5; *Guardian*, 17 February 1989.

47. Antony Beever, *Inside the British Army* (Chatto & Windus, 1990), p. 83.

48. Audit Commission, *A Doctors' Tale: the work of hospital doctors in England and Wales* (1995) and *The Doctors' Tale: the audits of medical staffing* (1996).

49. Private conversation, January 1997.

50. Christopher Lasch, *The Revolt of the Elites and the Betrayal of Democracy* (W. W. Norton, New York, 1995), p. 35.

51. Figures from Law Society's Trends in the Legal Profession (1995) and information from the Bar Council.

52. *The Lawyer*, 7 May 1996.

53. *The Times*, 16 January 1997.

54. Henry Porter, 'Are you being served?', *Guardian*, 30 May 1996.

55. *Financial Times*, 24 July 1996.

56. Ibid., 26 July 1996.

Chapter 4: Politics

1. Ben Pimlott, *Harold Wilson* (HarperCollins, 1993 edn), p. 307.

2. Hugo Young, *One of Us* (Pan, 1990 edn), p. 208.

3. Speech to the British-American Chamber of Commerce, 11 April 1996.

4. 'Simon Haxey', *Tory MP* (Collins, 1939), pp. 180, 190–91.

5. Andrew Adonis, 'The Transformation of the Conservative Party in the 1980s', in A. Adonis and T. Hames (eds), *A Conservative Revolution? The Thatcher–Reagan Decade in Perspective* (Manchester University Press, 1994), pp. 159–65.

6. David Butler and Dennis Kavanagh, *The British General Election of 1987* (Macmillan, 1988), p. 203.

7. Patrick Seyd *et al.*, *The Politics of Conservative Party Membership* (Oxford University Press, 1994), p. 46; Patrick Seyd and Paul Whiteley, *Labour's Grass Roots: The Politics of Party Membership* (Oxford University Press, 1992), p. 34.

8. Figures from Byron Criddle's analysis in Chapter 10 of David Butler and Dennis Kavanagh, *The British General Election of 1992* (Macmillan, 1992).

9. Figures are for MPs returned in the 1992 election, from Criddle's study in Chapter 10 of Butler and Kavanagh, *General Election of 1992* (esp. pp. 224–6).

10. John Rentoul, *Tony Blair* (Little, Brown, 1995), pp. 57–8.

11. Christopher Lasch, *The Revolt of the Elites and the Betrayal of Democracy* (W. W. Norton, New York, 1995), p. 43.

12. Roy Jenkins, *A Life at the Centre* (Macmillan, 1991), p. 170.

13. Press Association report and *Daily Mirror*, 8 May 1996.

14. *Financial Times*, 30 March 1996.

15. Review Body on Senior Salaries, Report 38: *Review of Parliamentary Pay and Allowances* (1996), vol. 1, para. 34, p. 10.

16. Ibid., vol. 2, pp. 10–11.

17. Ibid., paras. 47–9, p. 12.

18. *Hansard*, 10 July 1996, cols. 496–7. The following quotes are taken from subsequent columns.

19. Private conversation.

20. Seyd *et al.*, *Conservative Party Membership*, p. 46.

21. Seyd and Whiteley, *Labour's Grass Roots*, p. 34.

22. Ivor Crewe and Anthony King, *SDP: The Birth, Life and Death of the Social Democratic Party* (Oxford University Press, 1995), p. 501, Table 15.1.

23. Seyd does not include figures for chairmen: this information comes from conversations with Tory officials at Central Office.

24. E. S. Schattschneider, cited in Crewe and King, *SDP*, p. 280.

25. Anthony Heath, *Understanding Political Change: The British Voter 1964–1987* (Pergamon, 1991), p. 68.

26. Ibid., p 93.

27. Seyd and Whiteley, *Labour's Grass Roots*, p. 34.

28. Crewe and King, *SDP*, p. 273.

29. Ibid., pp. 274–9.

30. Ibid., pp. 281–2.

31. Peter Mandelson and Roger Liddle, *The Blair Revolution: Can New Labour Deliver?* (Faber, 1996).

32. *Financial Times*, 3 August 1995.

33. Bruce Anderson, *John Major: The Making of the Prime Minister* (Fourth Estate, 1991), p. 212. The following details are from Chapters 8 and 9.

34. *First Report of the Committee on Standards in Public Life*, chaired by Lord Nolan, May 1995.

35. Peter Riddell, *Honest Opportunism: The Rise of the Career Politician* (Indigo, 2nd edn, 1996), p. 289.

36. Ibid., pp. 296–9.

37. A concept developed by Pippa Norris and Joni Luvenduski in *Political Recruitment, Gender, Race and Class in the British Parliament* (Cambridge University Press, 1995).

Chapter 5: Crown and Lords

1. *Economist*, 5 September 1992.

2. Sarah Bradford, *Elizabeth: A Biography of Her Majesty the Queen* (Heinemann, 1996), p. 123.

3. Walter Bagehot, *The English Constitution* (Fontana Collins, 1963 edn), pp. 82, 85, 111, 139.

4. This paragraph draws on a revealing series on Europe's royal houses by Christian Tyler in the *Financial Times*, 27 April, 4 May, 11 May, 18 May, 25 May, 1 June 1996.

5. David Cannadine, 'The Context, Performance and Meaning of Ritual: The British Monarchy and the "Invention of Tradition", *c.*1820–1977', in Eric Hobsbawm and Terence Ranger (eds), *The Invention of Tradition* (Cambridge University Press, 1984).

6. See Frank Prochaska, *Royal Bounty: The Making of a Welfare Monarchy* (Yale University Press, 1995), especially Chapter 4 on the late Victorian Royal Family and 'the cult of benevolence'.

7. Bradford, *Elizabeth*, p. 303. By 1963 the Queen was the only head of a major state not to have visited the Federal Republic. She remains head of state of fifteen Commonwealth countries.

8. David Cannadine, *The Decline and Fall of the British Aristocracy* (Yale University Press, 1990), p. 301.

9. Jeremy Paxman, *Friends in High Places: Who Runs Britain?* (Michael Joseph, 1990), p. 65.

10. Bradford, *Elizabeth*, p. 367.

11. Ibid., p. 240.

12. Ibid., p. 253.

13. Peter Hennessy, *The Hidden Wiring: Unearthing the British Constitution* (Victor Gollancz, 1995), pp. 56–7, 62, 66–7.

14. Bradford, *Elizabeth*, p. 156.

15. John Grigg, *The Monarchy Revisited*, W. H. Smith Contemporary Papers No. 9 (1992), p. 4.

16. Jonathan Dimbleby, *The Prince of Wales* (Little, Brown, 1995), p. 508.

17. Stephen Haseler, *The End of the House of Windsor: Birth of a British Republic* (I. B. Tauris, 1993), p. 3.

18. Brian Harrison, *The Transformation of British Politics 1860–1995* (Oxford University Press, 1996), pp. 334–47.

19. Ibid., pp. 337–8.

20. David Cannadine, *Aspects of Aristocracy: Grandeur and Decline in Modern Britain* (Yale University Press, 1994), p. 234.

21. Andrew Adonis, *Making Aristocracy Work: The Peerage and the Political System in Britain 1884–1914* (Oxford University Press, 1993), pp. 267–9.

22. Alistair Horne, *Macmillan 1957–1986* (Macmillan, 1989), p. 83.

23. N. D. J. Baldwin, *The Contemporary House of Lords* (University of Essex PhD thesis, 1985). The figures are for 1981, but the proportions have not changed markedly since.

24. Tim Hilton, 'A Colourful Life of Grey', *Guardian*, 8 August 1991.

25. Richard Norton-Taylor and Kevin Cahill, 'Who Owns Britain?', *Guardian*, 13 August 1994.

26. Cannadine, *Decline and Fall*, p. 121.

27. Ibid., p. 646.

28. Dr Brian Mawhinney, speech to the Conservative Political Centre, 7 February 1996.

29. The Earl of Carnarvon, Lord Bancroft, the Earl of Selborne, Viscount Tenby and Douglas Slater, *Second Chamber: some remarks on reforming the House of Lords* (privately printed, 1995).

Chapter 6: Health

1. Annual Abstract of Statistics, Table 3.30 (HMSO, 1996).

2. The total number of those economically active in the UK was 28,701,000 (1996). Labour Force Survey (HMSO, January 1997).

3. David Owen, *Our NHS* (Pan, 1988), p. 13.

4. Ibid., p. 14.

5. Vicente Navarro, *Class Struggle, the State, and Medicine* (Martin Robertson, 1978).

6. Owen, *Our NHS*, p. 15.

7. Cited in Nicholas Timmins, *The Five Giants: A Biography of the Welfare State* (Fontana, 1996), p. 112.

8. Cited in Michael Rawcliffe, *The Welfare State* (Dryad Press, 1990).

9. Cited in A. Lindsey, *Socialised Medicine in England and Wales* (University of North Carolina Press, 1967).

10. Quoted in Navarro, *Class Struggle*.

11. Ibid.

12. Rawcliffe, *Welfare State*.

13. Cited in Timmins, *Giants*, p. 130.

14. Timmins, *Giants*, p. 163.

15. UCAS Department of Research and Statistics Bulletin, July 1995.

16. BMA Cohort Study, *Background and Initial Career Aspirations of Medical Graduates*, December 1995.

17. Ibid.

18. Julian Ashley, *The Anatomy of a Hospital*.

19. *The Times*, 10 January 1996.

20. Ibid.

21. Ibid.

22. *Health Service Journal*, 15 September 1994.

23. *Hospital Doctor*, 28 March 1996.

24. Ibid.

25. *Appointing NHS Consultants and Senior Registrars: Report of a Formal Investigation* (Commission for Racial Equality, April 1996).

26. Review Body on Doctors' and Dentists' Remuneration, 25th Report, 1996, p. 39.

27. *Independent*, 8 September 1995.

28. John Duckworth, *The Official Doctor/Patient Handbook* (Harriman House, 1994), p. 58.

29. *Independent*, 8 September 1995.

30. Ibid.

31. Fabian Pamphlet 542, *A Public Services Pay Policy*.

32. Incomes Data Services Ltd Report, 1 February 1996.

33. Ibid.

34. *Doctor/Patient Handbook*, p. 142.

35. *Creative Career Paths in the NHS – the Agenda for Action*, NHS Executive, January 1996.

36. Ibid.

37. NHS Statistical Bulletin, 18 August 1995.

38. Ibid., p. 265.

39. Michael Benzeval, Ken Judge and Margaret Whitehead, *Tackling Inequalities in Health* (King's Fund, 1995), p. 10.

40. Margaret Whitehead, *The Health Divide* (Penguin, 1992), p. 263.

41. Figures taken from Benzeval *et al.*, *Tackling Inequalities*, p. 12.

42. Rudolph Virchow, *Living Longer* (publisher not known), p. 108.

43. Variations in Health, Department of Health, 1995.

44. Benzeval *et al.*, *Tackling Inequalities*, p. 12.

45. Sara Arber, 'Class, paid employment and family roles', *Social Science and Medicine*, vol. 32, no. 4 (1991), pp. 425–36.

46. Whitehead, *Health Divide*, p. 331.

47. Ibid.

48. Ibid.

49. Virchow, *Living Longer*.

50. *Economist*, 17 September 1994.

51. David Blane, 'An assessment of the Black Report', *Sociology of Health and Illness*, November 1985, p. 426.

52. *Black Report* (Penguin, 1992), p. 43.

53. Ibid.

54. Ibid.

55. Ibid.

56. Francis Drever and Margaret Whitehead, 'Mortality in regions and local authority districts in the 1990s', *Population Trends*, Winter 1995.

57. Raymond Illsley and Julian Le Grand, 'Regional inequalities in mortality', *Journal of Epidemiology and Community Health*, 1993, p. 444.

58. Peter Townsend, 'Widening inequality of health in northern England', *British Medical Journal*, 30 April 1994.

59. Drever, Whitehead, *Mortality*.

60. Whitehead, *Health Divide*, p. 248.

61. Ibid., p. 249.

62. Ibid., p. 327.

63. Blane, 'Assessment of Black Report', p. 435.

64. Ibid.

65. R. Balarajan, 'Inequalities in health within the health sector', *British Medical Journal*, 1989.

66. Benzeval *et al.*, *Tackling Inequalities*, p. 133.

67. Ibid.

68. Ibid.

69. Whitehead, *Health Divide*, p. 254.

70. Ibid.

71. *Social Trends*, 26 (HMSO, 1996).

72. Ibid.

73. Benzeval *et al.*, *Tackling Inequalities*, p. xxii.

74. Ibid.

75. Ibid.

76. Ibid.

77. Whitehead, *Health Divide*, p. 318.

78. Ibid.

79. Ibid., p. 278.

80. Ibid.

81. Benzeval *et al.*, *Tackling Inequalities*, p. 104.

82. Ibid.

83. Ibid., p. 99.

84. Ibid., p. 102.

85. Ibid.

86. Ibid.

87. Ibid.

88. Whitehead, *Health Divide*, p. 278.

Chapter 7: Housing

1. *Scotsman*, September 1993.

2. Priestley and Perkin citations from Harold Perkin, *The Rise of Professional Society: England since 1880* (Routledge, 1989), p. 268.

3. Cited in David Smith, *North and South* (Penguin, 1994), p. 37.

4. George Orwell, *The Road to Wigan Pier* (Secker and Warburg, 1937).

5. Smith, *North and South*, p. 43.

6. Ibid., p. 44.

7. Research for *Southern Discomfort*, by Stephen Pollard and Giles Radice (Fabian Society, 1993).

8. Greg Hadfield and Mark Skipworth, *Class: Where do you stand?* (Bloomsbury, 1994), p. 124.

9. Figures supplied by Department of the Environment.

10. 'When Surrey takes over the country', *Sunday Times*, 2 July 1995.

11. Ibid.

12. Housing and Planning White Paper, 1996.

13. *Sunday Times*, 2 July 1995.

14. *Observer*, 26 June 1996.

15. *Sunday Times*, 2 July 1995.

16. Smith, *North and South*, p. 272.

17. *Observer*, 26 June 1996.

18. Charles Landray, *The Creative City* (Demos, 1995).

19. *The Times*, 27 April 1995.

20. Department of the Environment, 1996. The precise figure is 50.3 per cent. Figure calculated for this book.

21. Jenny Morris and Martin Winn, *Housing and Social Inequality* (Hilary Shipman, 1990), p. 36.

22. Martin Pawley, 'A prefab future', *Roof*, July 1989.

23. Study by South Bank Polytechnic, cited in *Housing*, February 1994.

24. *Daily Mail*, 19 June 1996.

25. Alan Clark, *Diaries* (Weidenfeld & Nicolson, 1993), p. 350.

26. *Sunday Telegraph*, 14 April 1996.

27. This paragraph draws on Hadfield and Skipworth, *Where do you stand?*

28. *Black Report* (Penguin, 1992), p. 52.

29. Robin Haynes, 'Inequalities in health', *Social Science and Medicine*, vol. 33, no. 4.

30. Margaret Whitehead, *The Health Divide* (Penguin, 1992), p. 327.

31. Ibid.

32. David Blane, 'An assessment of the Black Report', *Sociology of Health and Illness*, November 1985.

33. Whitehead, *Health Divide*, p. 328.

34. Michael Benzeval, Ken Judge and Margaret Whitehead, *Tackling Inequalities in Health* (King's Fund, 1995), p. 53.

35. *Observer*, 2 May 1996.

36. 'Housing and Homelessness – a Public Health Perspective', Faculty of Public Health, 1992.

37. *Housing, Homelessness and Health*, Standing Conference on Public Health Working Group Report, Nuffield Provincial Hospitals Trust, 1994.

38. Cited in Morris and Winn, *Housing and Social Inequality*, p. 52.

39. English House Condition Survey 1991, Department of the Environment, 1993.

40. Ibid.

41. John Short, *Housing in Britain* (Methuen, 1995), p. 23.

42. Ibid.

43. Ibid.

44. Ibid.

45. Speech to the Social Market Foundation, 26 April 1995.

46. *Living with the State*, Institute for Fiscal Studies, 1996, p. 2.

47. Revival of Private Renting Housing, *Housing Studies*, 1996.

48. The prime source for the next two paragraphs is *Living with the state*.

49. Paul Harrison, *Inside the Inner City* (Pelican, 1985), p. 225.

50. Ibid., p. 227.

51. Peter Malpass, Matthew Warburton, Glen Bramley and Gavin Smart, *Housing Policy in Action*, Bristol University Press, 1993.

52. *Guardian*, 9 August 1995.

53. Quoted in *Safe As Houses*, Hamnett, Harmer and Williams (PCP, 1991), p. 2.

54. *Financial Times*, 10 May 1996.

55. Cited in *Safe As Houses*, p. 3.

56. Smith, *North and South*, p. 205.

57. Ibid., p. 201.

58. *Observer*, 30 July 1995.

Chapter 8: Lifestyle

1. Cited in 'A Miracle of the Air', *Spectator*, 21 October 1996.

2. Cited in David Marquand and Anthony Seldon (eds), *The Ideas That Shaped Post-War Britain* (Fontana, 1996), p. 201.

3. Ibid.

4. Cited in 'A Miracle', *Spectator*, 21 October 1996.

5. Cited in Ben Pimlott, *The Queen* (HarperCollins, 1996), p. 285.

6. Ibid.

7. Edith and Tom Kelly, *Books for the People* (Penguin, 1977).

8. Cited in Richard Hoggart, *The Way We Live Now* (Pimlico, 1996), p. 102.

9. Ibid., p. 205.

10. The next few paragraphs draw heavily on Harold Perkin's *The Rise*

of Professional Society: England since 1880 (Routledge, 1989), pp. 266–88.

11. Raphael Samuel, cited in *Property, Democracy and Culture*, Savage, Barlow, Dickens and Fielding (Routledge, 1992), p. 113.

12. *Sunday Times*, 25 August 1996.

13. Hoggart, *Way We Live*, p. 124.

14. Perkin, *Professional Society*, p. 420.

15. Ibid.

16. This is taken from a piece by Mark Lawson in the *Guardian*, 26 June 1996.

17. Hoggart, *Way We Live*, p. 123.

18. *Sunday Times*, 25 August 1996.

19. National Arts and Media Strategy Monitoring Group, 1992 report, cited in Jordan and Weedon, *Culture and Politics* (Blackwell, 1995), p. 43.

20. Cited in Richard Holt, *A History of British Sport* (OUP, 1989), p. 3.

21. *Sunday Express*, 22 July 1996.

22. Ibid.

23. Ibid.

24. Holt, *Sport*, p. 183.

25. Ibid., p. 151.

26. *London Review of Books*, August 1990.

27. Holt, *Sport*, p. 192.

28. Ibid., p. 318.

29. Cited in Holt, *Sport*, p. 350, from which much of this paragraph draws.

30. Ibid., p. 291.

31. Ibid., p. 107.

32. Ibid.

33. Laura Thompson, *Quest for Greatness* (Michael Joseph, 1996), p. 101.

34. Cited in Holt, *Sport*, p. 265.

35. Ibid., p. 160.

36. Ibid., p. 168.

37. Ibid., p. 169.

38. Information from House of Lords Library. Figures are based on current prices.

39. Figures taken from Greg Hadfield and Mark Skipworth, *Class: Where do you stand?* (Bloomsbury, 1994), p. 87.

40. Cited by Sean French, *New Statesman*, 14 April 1995.

41. Ibid.

42. *Spectator*, 2 December 1995.

43. Hadfield and Skipworth, *Where do you stand?*, p. 146.

44. The next paragraphs draw on Perkin, *Professional Society*.

45. Gill Swain in *Daily Mirror*, 16 July 1996.

Chapter 9: Race

1. *Social Focus on Ethnic Minorities* (HMSO, 1996), p. 10.

2. Ibid., p. 24.

3. Ibid., p. 25.

4. Ibid., p. 26.

5. Ibid., p. 27.

6. *Economist*, 8 February 1997.

7. Ibid.

8. Ibid., p. 43, Lord Chancellor's Department statistics.

9. Private conversation.

10. Metropolitan Police statistics.

11. *Guardian*, 10 June 1996.

12. *Financial Times*, 22 June 1996.

13. *Focus on Ethnic Minorities*, p. 42.

14. Trevor Jones, *Britain's Ethnic Minorities* (Policy Studies Institute, 1993), p. 69.

15. Ibid.

16. Ibid., p. 70.

17. *Financial Times*, 22 June 1996.

18. *The Times*, 19 February 1997.

19. *New Statesman*, 15 April 1994.

20. *Focus on Ethnic Minorities*, p. 29.

21. Ibid., p. 30.

22. *The Runnymede Bulletin*, March 1995.

23. *Focus on Ethnic Minorities*, p. 20.

24. Private conversation.

25. *Financial Times*, 22 June 1996.

26. *Focus on Ethnic Minorities*, p. 39.

27. *Runnymede*, March 1995.

28. *Focus on Ethnic Minorities*, p. 46.

29. Ibid., p. 346.

Chapter 10: The National Lottery

1. *Hansard*, HL Debs., 22 May 1993, cols. 400–488.

2. *How Far Can It Go?*, Henley Centre, December 1995.

3. Ross McKibbin, *Ideologies of Class* (Oxford University Press, 1990), p. 102.

4. Ibid., pp. 101–38.

5. J. Harris, *Private Lives, Public Spirit: A Social History of Britain, 1870–1914* (Oxford University Press, 1993), p. 8.

6. Royal Commission on Gambling, Final Report, Cmnd 7200 (1978), vol. 1, chapter 13. For Rothschild and the poll tax see David Butler, Andrew Adonis and Tony Travers, *Failure in British Government: The Politics of the Poll Tax* (Oxford University Press, 1993), pp. 48–50.

7. Private discussion.

8. Gambling, Final Report, I, p. 226.

9. Ibid.

10. Margaret Thatcher, *The Downing Street Years* (HarperCollins, 1993), p. 610.

11. Conversations with surviving members of the royal commission.

12. Kenneth Baker, *The Turbulent Years* (Faber, 1993), pp. 462–5.

13. Conservative Manifesto 1992, printed in *The Times Guide to the House of Commons 1992*, p. 324.

14. In both cases formally separated lottery boards were set up, but sharing the same membership and staffing as the original quango.

15. *Hansard*, HC Debs., 25 January 1993, col. 744.

16. Ibid., 25 October 1995, col. 1050.

17. Ibid., 25 January 1993, col. 716.

18. Household gambling figures from Mintel consumer spending report, January 1996.

19. *Hansard*, HC Debs., 25 January 1993, cols. 719–20.

20. Press Association report, 26 August 1995.

21. Ben Laurence, 'Lottery's one-way ticket for the poor', *Observer*, 13 October 1996.

22. Department of National Heritage press release, 20 February 1996.

23. *Sun*, 6 January 1996.

24. Ibid., 12 January 1996.

25. Mintel, *British Lifestyles*, January 1996.

26. 1992 White Paper, p. 5.

27. Private conversation.

28. *Independent*, 10 May 1995.
29. Private conversation.
30. Department of National Heritage report of Secretary of State's presentation to the Commons committee, February 1996.
31. National Heritage Committee Report, *The National Lottery* (1996).
32. *The Times*, 2 December 1996.
33. Interview with Andrew Adonis, March 1996 (partly published in the *Financial Times*, 23 March 1996).

Index

Note: Page numbers in **bold** indicate Tables